T0385364

of related interest

The Trans Partner Handbook
A Guide for When Your Partner Transitions
Jo Green
ISBN 978 1 78592 227 5
eISBN 978 1 78450 503 5

Transitioning Together
One Couple's Journey of Gender and Identity Discovery
Wenn B. Lawson and Beatrice M. Lawson
ISBN 978 1 78592 103 2
eISBN 978 1 78450 365 9

THE REFLECTIVE WORKBOOK FOR PARTNERS OF TRANSGENDER PEOPLE

Your Transition as
Your Partner Transitions

D. M. Maynard

Jessica Kingsley *Publishers*
London and Philadelphia

First published in 2019
by Jessica Kingsley Publishers
73 Collier Street
London N1 9BE, UK
and
400 Market Street, Suite 400
Philadelphia, PA 19106, USA

www.jkp.com

Copyright © D. M. Maynard 2019

Library of Congress Cataloging in Publication Data
A CIP catalog record for this book is available from the Library of Congress

British Library Cataloguing in Publication Data
A CIP catalogue record for this book is available from the British Library

ISBN 978 1 78592 772 0
eISBN 978 1 78450 672 8

Printed and bound in Great Britain

The accompanying PDF can be downloaded from
www.jkp.com/voucher using the code SUEXYXA

To my husband, Simon, the bravest man I know!
Your journey has been a gift to witness, an honor to share, and an inspiration
that has taught me
the importance of being true to yourself!!
I love you more than words could ever express!!!

CONTENTS

ACKNOWLEDGMENTS

First and foremost, I want to thank all of those who have honestly voiced their thoughts and experiences in my workshops, with an especially heartfelt appreciation to those who have entrusted me to share personal pieces of their own stories.

To the Faculty and Administrators I have worked with in the HWJM Schools: thank you for your open-mindedness, embracing my journey, and for being willing to learn that which was not part of your experience, but what is now yours to lovingly bring into the classroom.

To my L&M "Reading is Optional Book Club Members": thank you for your thoughtful questions and respectful inclusiveness!

To my OHP Group: thank you for all the hugs, for not giving up on me, and for constantly reminding me that the promises are there for me, too.

To my supportive cheerleaders—Ashley Barros, Christie Block, Maureen Bodson, Yolana Cumsky Winick, Nancy Ekloff, Genesis Fisher, Michael George, Jacqueline Juliano, Lisa Krawciw, Denise Lasiuk, Mary Marino, Jay Minsky, Martha Murphy-George, Maureen O'Brien, Luc Olivier Charlap, Patty Pearsall, Mei Pike, Roneldy Pingitore, Esther Pollack, Donna Restivo, Mark Rosenstein, Chris Straayer, Jonathan Sutton, Florence Tannen, and Gary Wellbrock: thank you for your encouragement and for being in my corner.

To my Mom, Dad, Aunt Sue, Uncle Steve, and sister Stacy: I write with all of you, as the Angels on my shoulders.

To Mia and Andreia: thank you for being pioneers, wise beyond your years, and my courageous teachers.

To the Jessica Kingsley Publishers Team: thank you for this glorious opportunity, for all of your creative talents, and for making this lifelong dream of mine come true.

To Andrew James, my incredible Senior Editor: thank you for your polite patience, wise advice, gentle guidance, and for giving me the chance of a lifetime.

To Emma Holak, Alexandra Holmes, Simeon Hance, and Yojaira Cordero, my Bonus Team at JKP: thank you for your incredible expertise, professional assistance, and wise suggestions.

To Tina Andreadis, Andrew V. Cheu, Jonathan Lyons, Judith Moman, Marie Spohn, and Barbara Warren: thank you for kindly extending your specialized knowledge to me and treasured time to enable this workbook to succeed.

To Darby Maloney, Gale Schneider, Steven Terzuoli, and Wendy Yalowitz: thank you for always listening with your heart and for being a major part of my support team.

To my 2MaPaSis—Barbara Baughan and Maria Riccardi: thank you for wiping my tears, holding my hand, bringing laughter when I craved it the most, and for being in my life!

To my chapter readers—Cathleen Benites, Juliet Brown, Rosemary Capelle, Stephanie Cosola, Teresa Dawber, Jodi DeSantis-Helming, Robbie DiBella, James Dougherty, Patricia A. Gormley, Judie Halpern, Mary LoCascio, Cheryl Minsky, Benay Shear, and Dee Wojis: thank you for caring enough to offer your editing skills (even when you were exhausted), believing in me, loving me unconditionally, and your very precious friendships!

To my brilliant therapist readers—S. J. Langer, Kit Rachlin, and Karalyn Violeta: I thank you all, beyond words, for sharing your extensive expertise, no-nonsense honesty, intellectual insight, and abundance of assistance throughout the entire process of writing this workbook!

Chapter 1

YOUR PRIVATE SPACE: AN INTRODUCTION

IN 2010, my partner of more than 17 years told me he was transgender. I had no idea what this meant or how it would affect my relationship and my life. That being said, no one is more surprised than I that one day I would have both the clarity and opportunity to share what I have learned from the experience of loving a person who transitioned while we were together. My greatest hope is that my journey, and the journeys of those who have so bravely shared their stories with me, will bring you, the partner, a sense of comfort and the knowledge that you are not alone. I want to emphasize that anything I voice is simply my path combined with the stories of others and is not intended to suggest that your path will necessarily be the same as mine or anyone else's.

I never want to pretend that moving through the transition was easy or painless for me. Nor do I ever mean to imply that I am proud of the way I handled myself on many an occasion. When I think back now, there were moments when I am embarrassed by my thoughts, actions, or words, but there were far more times I was courageous, loving, caring, protective, and supportive. In time, many days were filled with pure joy and celebrations. There is no script or perfect way to travel this road as the passenger while someone you love deeply finds their destiny during the transition process.

As I was looking for support during this time, I desperately tried to sort out all the changes that were occurring. I had wished for a workbook that offered me a private place to express my thoughts yet afforded me some type of structure as a partner of someone in transition. Everything I found focused on the person who was transitioning or transitioned. The only resources I found that included information for partners always placed emphasis on how the partner could help or support the person who was trans-identified. Rarely, if ever, was there space or room for the needs and feelings of the partner.

Then I thought, "How could the experiences that partners have had and are living through be teachable moments to anyone else?" First and foremost, I am a teacher! For more than 30 years I was a classroom teacher, guiding young minds and encouraging them to become lifelong learners. Implicit in the title of educator is a need to protect and nurture those who were under my care. Ensuring a space that fostered tolerance and was free of judgment afforded my students an opportunity to grow from every situation they encountered. As a classroom teacher, my mission was less about teaching and more about questioning, so that those learning, in essence, were their own teachers through exploration. Knowing this, whenever something occurs in my life, I ask myself: What are the lessons embedded within the moment? This is always followed by self-reflection, which has enabled me to draw my own conclusions. Instinctually, I had to become the student, so that I could navigate where I was going and the path I would follow to get there.

This self-reflective workbook is born of my personal desire to offer what I learned from my experience as a partner and is based on a multitude of requests of the people who have taken my workshops at conferences throughout the world. I have compiled and incorporated all the questions, exercises, and tools that were used during these workshops, which partners expressed were helpful. This resource has something for everyone, but not every part will be necessary for every person. Take what you want and leave the rest behind. There are no rules or absolutes in reference to which exercises, tools, or questions to reply to now or if ever. Respond to those that speak to you and your needs.

The chapters are presented in the workbook in a specific sequence, which made sense for what I would have preferred in a resource to guide my journey as my partner transitioned. It should be stressed that you may choose to use this workbook out of order, for each chapter stands independent of the others. As part of your process, it does not matter the order in which you journal the questions you opt to answer from each chapter. You may not be ready for some portions, you may be past others, or you may be right on time for exactly what is being offered. Skip those that do not apply to you at this time. Some questions may become more relevant later on during the transition, while others may never be necessary for you to answer. The choice is always there to add to your responses or reply in a completely different way as time goes on. If you find a later chapter discusses a topic that addresses your needs, move on to that chapter.

Remember to take breaks when you feel it is necessary and know that it is possible to return to any question when you feel refreshed. Make time to go for walks, watch television, or do other things that comfort you. Keep in mind that journaling can be very helpful, provide clarity, and be extremely cathartic; it can also be exhausting, foster ambivalence, and be extremely emotional. Knowing this, I included a Deserving De-Stress Delights section in each chapter, offering specific ways to refocus your energy from the transition and channel it towards finding a place of inner peace and calmness.

Do what feels right and helpful to you. You cannot make a mistake and your thoughts can remain private. No one ever needs to know your entries; however, if, at some point, it feels comfortable to share your journaling with either your significant other or a trusted individual, the option is available to you. This decision is solely yours to make. The routes I took and even the wrong turns I made were all part of the journey that has led me to the privilege of writing this workbook. The life lessons I developed over time can now be shared with others. The intent of this journal is simple: to create a space that feels safe, right, and honorable for all partners, as they map out their own path. The questions posed and the exercises and tools provided within this workbook are those I asked of others and used myself. I realized the answers were always inside of me, as they already are inside of you, waiting to be written down.

AUTHOR'S DISCLAIMER NOTES

- These terms will be used to refer to the non-transitioning partner: the trans partner and partner.

- These terms will be used for the person in transition: trans-identified partner, transgender individual, and significant other. There will be times when the partner not in transition will refer to the person in transition as: partner. Please note that these terms also include those who identify as: crossdressers, gender nonconforming, gender nonbinary, gender fluid, intersex, transsexual, and questioning people.

- For some people, the transition process continues throughout their lifetime; for others, they consider the transition over once all the social and/or medical interventions they desired are in place. For the partner, the duration of the transition process of their significant other can be connected to one of these two circumstances or based on the period when the major focus of the relationship is on the transition. Many partners I know or who have attended my workshops refer to their relationship in terms of before, during, and after the transition, referring to "after" as the period when the topic of the transition is no longer front and center on a daily basis. Therefore, many of the questions that include periods of time may use the phrase "before, during, and after." You may choose to respond in terms of this sequencing or elect to answer only in terms of "before and during." I include this disclaimer to acknowledge and honor those for whom the transitioning period is never over; for whom the term "after" may never apply.

- It is recognized that more than one person in the relationship can be transgender and gender nonconforming (TGNC) or in transition. This workbook is offered from the perspective of the partner who is in a relationship with someone who is now trans-identified. The workbook is intended to help anyone who is searching for a reflective resource in respect to their partner's transition.

- In reference to polyamorous relationships, monogamous couples, or the primary partner/s in the relationship: the vignettes, questions, tools, and exercises contained within this workbook can be used by anyone, whether you are the primary partner or not. Although the word "couple" is the main word used in reference to the relationship, these practices can be used for whatever configuration your relationship takes. The word "couple" refers to two individuals in relation to each other, but I acknowledge that those two people can be in multiple and/or open relationships throughout, before, during, and after the transition.

- In reference to the stage you entered the relationship: this workbook is intended to be useful for those partners who were in the relationship before the transition was known, for those who were present during the transition, and/or for those who were in the relationship after the transitioning was completed. The focus of most of the vignettes, questions, tools, and exercises contained within this workbook is for those partners who were in the relationship before and during the transition. However, several of my workshop attendees have expressed that they have been useful for those who have entered the relationship post any medical and/or social aspects of the transition and for family members or friends.

- LGBTQ and LGBTQQIA+, or other variations, will be used as inclusive terms for anyone who identifies on the continuum; the term used is never meant to exclude or offend any person or group that prefers one variation of this umbrella term over another. Its usage will reflect the details of the story or something specific to the passage it is contained within. The key is that the partner's needs, best interest, and/or perspective will be the focus in each and every instance.

- Length of relationship: this workbook is intended to be used by partners irrespective of the duration of the relationship, whether it is long-term or short-term.

- *This book does not provide medical or legal advice.* The information contained in this book is for informational purposes only. The opinions expressed in this book are those of the author, and any ideas or suggestions contained in the book are based solely on the author's experiences. This book is not intended to be a substitute for professional medical or legal advice. Always seek the advice of your physician or other qualified healthcare provider with any questions you may have regarding a medical condition or treatment and before undertaking a new healthcare regimen, and never disregard professional medical advice or delay seeking it because of something you have read in this book. In addition, you should seek the advice of legal counsel familiar with the subject matter and authorized to practice in your jurisdiction before acting or relying upon the opinions and information presented in this book.

CONTENTS OF THE CHAPTERS

1. Your Private Space: An Introduction

This chapter serves as an introduction that will explain the structure and purpose of the book. The workbook will serve as a place free of judgment for you, the partner, to journal your own journey and support your process throughout the transition. It is a self-reflective, private space where you can voice any of your thoughts, feelings, fears, concerns, worries, confusions, joys, and celebrations in writing. Each of the following chapters will focus on one or two critical aspects of the transition that may affect the life of the partner.

2. Unexpected and Confused

These partner-specific questions, exercises, and vignettes will focus on the possible initial fears, thoughts, worries, and concerns that partners may experience once they learn their partner will transition. The tools will be based on such topics as safety issues, the validity of the relationship, self-doubts, and the unknowns of the relationship now.

3. Who Are You?

This chapter will confront the challenges some partners experience when asked to address the transitioning person in a different way. These questions, exercises, tools, and vignettes will refer to the possible need to use a different pronoun or name, and are intended to help navigate when photos and memories of the past may no longer be celebrated or visible. This chapter will help partners learn how to incorporate the new pronoun and/or name in intimate moments, during arguments, and at social events.

4. Grief May Apply

This chapter will examine the reality that many partners express an experience of loss and find that a mourning period applies as they process the transition. This section will focus on the five stages of grief: denial, anger, bargaining, depression, and acceptance (Kübler-Ross & Kessler, 2005). Through reflective inquiry, partners will explore how this might pertain to their relationship during the transition. As grieving can be a non-linear process, so the path may be for the partner throughout the transition.

5. It Can Be a Foreign Language

This part of the workbook will tackle the often overwhelming world of new vocabulary. Partners will respond to questions and exercises that will assist them in unraveling various label options and their own comfort level of implementation. Exercises will be included to help partners understand appropriate ways and times to incorporate the nuances and culture of this new language.

6. Medical and Social Options: Sorting It Out!

This chapter explores some of the challenges of medical choices facing the partner with respect to the surgeries and hormones that the person in transition may need to access and the side effects that may occur as a result of these interventions. This chapter will offer the trans partner specific questions, exercises, tools, and vignettes to help them discover how to talk about these decisions as a couple and determine what areas of the medical and/or social transition, if any, they can comfortably participate in. For example, partners will need to determine to what extent they will be involved with the medical options, such as attending doctor appointments or assisting with post-surgical recovery.

7. Friends and Family: Will They Stay, or Will They Go?

This chapter will assist the partner in dealing with the possible reactions of friends and family members to the transition. Trying to understand what, when, why, and how to engage with others before or during the time when partners are themselves adjusting can be extremely overwhelming and isolating. In addition, specific tools will assist partners to gauge their comfort or ability to discuss the transition with children or young relatives. Lastly, partners will explore the possibility of joining new social circles or creating a family of choice.

8. Work: In or Out?

This chapter will explore the importance of when, why, or, indeed, if one will share the transition with employers, employees, clients, and/or co-workers. It will provide a reflective space to discover whether the partner will elect to work with human resources personnel at the workplace and to gain an understanding of what legal rights they have at work. Financial security and medical insurance policies at work can become compromised when partners or those transitioning out themselves.

9. Insurances, Gender Markers, and Documents... Oh My!

The partners will be alerted to options that some trans-identified people investigate with respect to legally changing their gender marker and/or legal name. Altering the transitioning person's name and/or gender on birth certificates, passports, financial and/or health insurance policies, bank accounts, social security card, marriage certificates, college diplomas, and transcripts can be an exhausting job. These suggestions for the trans partner will offer a way to cope with the overwhelming reality of all these changes. Each jurisdiction and/or country have its own laws and policies; therefore, the partner's understanding of how they may want to assist their trans-identified partner approach these time-consuming choices must be carefully thought through.

10. Privilege: Loss or Gain?

This chapter explores how one's privilege is or has been affected through the intersections of patriarchy, misogyny, racism, homophobia, feminism, and male privilege. Will the partner feel a loss of equality, such as being overlooked when making a purchase as a couple? In contrast, will the partner experience positive gains such as an increase of physical safety due to the transition? Learning how to accept these potential changes can positively affect the partner's self-worth and confidence on many levels.

11. Let's Talk About Finding a Therapist

Many times, concerns can be alleviated if the partner connects with a knowledgeable and experienced therapist. For some, the search for an appropriate therapist can be time-consuming and/or critical. Through journaling their needs and the guided support provided by the tools offered in this workbook, partners can learn how to find the path that is best for them.

12. Partners in Sex

This chapter views the sexual intimacy of the relationship through the eyes of the partner. The partner will determine what is sexually acceptable for themselves throughout the transition. By journaling, the partner will identify what turns them on or off, measure the level of their attraction to the person transitioning, and learn how to communicate their personal preferences. With the use of questions and exercises, the partner will also be asked to investigate their own gender and sexual identities, as the transition progresses.

13. Celebrations Come in Different Sizes

This chapter assists partners in understanding whether they can move forward in the relationship. The answer to this inquiry can be fluid and vary from day to day, month to month, and year to year. Whether the partner remains in the relationship or not, the journey deserves to be acknowledged and celebrated by those who have experienced any portion of this transition as a couple.

14. Where Are You Now?

This chapter will reflect on the pulse of the partner's journey by asking them to re-evaluate, honestly and continuously, their thoughts, feelings, concerns, worries, and confusions. The partner will be asked to focus on their future and examine how they have transitioned due to the other person's transition. Additional questions, exercises, and vignettes will be included for both partners to communicate openly as a couple and live a life that embraces the transition as a journey!

15. You Are Not Alone (Resources)

The last chapter will offer articles, books, websites, support groups, and more that focus on the needs of the partner.

SET-UP

Each chapter will contain most, if not all, of these sections.

1. Affirmative Anecdotes

The poetic anecdotes were created for partners and appear throughout each chapter. They are meant to inspire, comfort, and empower you when you need them most. Their presence is intended to set the tone and intention before you begin the chapter. They are meant to embrace you in any way that soothes your heart. The affirmations may be used as a springboard for writing or as a conversation starter with someone else.

2. Vital Vignettes

These vital vignettes serve as an introduction to the questions. They represent parts of my own journey intertwined with the experiences of others. The vignettes are included to help you to gain some insight from the unknowns that I navigated as my partner's transition unfolded. Providing these passages as a precursor to the questions is meant to offer reflective thoughts based on my own experience and of those who freely, but anonymously, shared their stories during the workshops that I have led and/or attended.

3. Graphics Galore

Most chapters in this book will contain graphic organizers, which can be used to assist you in visually expressing your thoughts without having to write them in a narrative format. In order to serve you best, they may be placed in a different order within each chapter. Every graphic organizer can be used for various purposes, but if you find one type works best for you, use it as often as you like. Remember, this entire workbook is for and about you and your process.

Bar Graph is an image that can be viewed to observe the ranking of data, which is translated into bar-like structures to display findings on a topic or question. Through the illustrations of the gathered information, the user can evaluate the comparison of the bars to reach their own conclusions in reference to a single topic or question. This graphic organizer encourages you to assess the importance or value of these topics, independently of the other topics, based on a personal rating system of 1–10. In contrast to the Pie Graph graphic organizer, though both organizers enable the user to view the topics in comparison with the others, the bars of the Bar Graph do not need to add up to 100 or 100%.

Box is a format for notes or can be used as a place to store information connected to one topic or subject, which compartmentalizes or assesses a situation. It is visually comprised of multiple boxes to create a framework.

Pie Graph is a visual representation of percentage showing the comparison of various categories based on a single subject, question, or circumstance in the shape of a pie. Some think of it as a pizza pie with each slice standing for a different component of the topic. The total composition of all the parts is summed to 100 or 100%. Each part or section is assigned a percentage based on its user's point of view. The goal is to exhibit a quick way to prioritize or place a value on every critical factor that affects the outcome of the subject, question, or circumstance in relation to the other topics.

Splash should be imagined as if you took a liquid, such as water or paint, and splattered it on a blank canvas. It is intended to let your juices flow as you brainstorm with no judgment or organizational care. Respond to the statement or inquiry with a word or short phrase and quickly splatter your reply. By creatively splashing words and/or short phrases, attempt to express your responses randomly by scattering them on paper. When you have completed the graphic organizer, it should almost look as if you have created a canvas of words by squirting them on the page. It encourages you to elicit a reaction that is guttural and has a desire to be released on paper.

T-Chart can be used to show different perspectives in relation to the same topic or question. There are many versions of this graphic organizer that can host two, three, or more columns. The two-column graphic usually lists or states two aspects of a problem, unknown, or dilemma. A three-column T-Chart format can assist the user in making a decision by comparing and contrasting the positive, negative, and equal/neutral (+/–/=) options in response to an inquiry, conflict, or situation. Another variation is KWL, which houses what a person "Knows," "Wants to know or learn," and then does "Learn."

Timeline is sequential and helps record the order or timing of a situation or event that has occurred. It assists in creating a tentative time frame to complete a future or current task that may be time sensitive with numerous factors or parts.

Venn Diagram is a comparison graphic organizer that aids in comparing and contrasting a situation or an inquiry. Once a question is posed, one side of the connecting circles is filled in with one point of view. Then the other side of the diagram is completed with the other response in relation to the same question, showing the reply to the inquiry from a different point of view. The last step is to notice if any of the replies from the two sides overlap. If any are the same or very similar, that response is removed from both sides and placed in the center interlocking portion of the graphic organizer. The outcome is visually seeing where the two responses are in agreement and where they differ.

Webs are often described as visually presenting a topic and its subtopics in the way that a spider's web scatters branch-like patterns, which generate from a central source. Every part of the growing web is connected to an initial word or phrase. Once the beginning word or phrase is placed in the center position, the user's associated words or phrases are placed in the outer connecting circles in response to the central statement. This pattern continues until the web is completed or the response to the question or statement is personally finished.

4. Reflective Responses

There are several ways you can partake in the questions posed in this workbook, but ultimately the hope is for you to use them in the manner that works best for your needs. Some individuals may only choose to write their responses to a select group of questions in each chapter, whereas others may reply to each and every question. You may even elect to repeat this process more than once throughout the transition process. Each chapter poses questions that are intended to help and assist you discover where you stand with regard to processing the transition and what is comfortable for you. Your responses may remain the same for a long period of time or they may evolve as you explore your options and have time to digest all that you are experiencing and feeling. Each and every path has its own value and purpose. I suggest that you are gentle with yourself as you journal and process all aspects of this part of the journey.

5. Deserving De-Stress Delights

Each chapter offers structured ways to release any stress from the transition and direct your energy towards de-stressing and rewarding yourself in a loving and tender manner. Intentionally allowing time to simply stop, breathe, and rest from journaling and processing is essential for your wellbeing. This section reminds you to carve out space to engage in activities that rejuvenate and honor you through self-care, which will help you feel pampered and nurtured.

6. Empathy-Embracing Exercise

This exercise is meant to help you gain an awareness of the importance of speaking your truth, regardless of the consequences. It is intended to aid in diminishing your own possible pain, confusion, or acceptance level, as your trans-identified partner transitions. Perhaps thinking of a private and difficult experience from your past or in the present will create a deeper understanding of the emotional journey your trans-identified partner may experience. Its presence in the workbook is purposed to evoke empathy for the journey your partner is on, by honoring your needs, and to better prepare you for the transition process.

7. Sampler Share

These samplers create a space where some partners shared their own response to questions posed in this workbook. All of the partners' names have been changed to respect the privacy of both the trans partners and their transgender partners. The responses are included simply to open your mind to a variety of ways others have approached the writing based on their situation. Their replies are placed towards the end of the chapter, but please keep in mind that if these testimonials become intrusive or prevent your own process from evolving, feel free to refer to them at a later time or not at all. However, some partners have found the guidance of these "Sampler Shares" especially helpful when they had a block when journaling or were unsure that the question was one they wanted to answer. There are no absolutes when using this workbook, only offerings to help you gain a greater understanding of your own needs and wishes.

8. Couple Communication Corner

This exercise offers a list of questions trans partners will be given as a tool that supports communication with their trans-identified partner. You may even elect to create your own questions. It is suggested that you and/or your partner journal your individual responses prior to discussing it with each other as a tool to process your own thoughts. Partners are invited to initiate a discussion in relation to the transition, when they are comfortable, by sharing their thoughts and concerns with the person in transition through an open dialogue. The questions posed or produced by you for use in this section are intended to help start the conversation. Many couples find comfort in doing this exercise in a cozy corner of their home to engage in these private and personal talks.

QUESTION #1

Before you proceed to Chapter 2, I invite you to respond to the following question:

What do you hope or expect to learn or gain from reading and journaling in this workbook?

....

....

....

....

....

....

....

....

....

....

....

....

....

....

Chapter 2

UNEXPECTED AND CONFUSED

VITAL VIGNETTE

For some partners, finding out that your partner is now trans-identified can be a time celebrated with prideful excitement and a welcome relief. The news can create a special closeness in the relationship and an opportunity to embrace all that is to come in the future. For others, however, being told that your significant other is transgender, especially when you were unaware of this fact and never expected this possibility, can be initially confusing, induce worry, trigger concerns, and prompt an array of fears. Sometimes, a partner can experience a combination of all of these emotions. It is critical that you do not judge your response to the information you have been told, but rather honor all of the thoughts that are in your mind and heart. Every partner brings their own history to this disclosure and can react and internalize this knowledge in a way that is unique to their own circumstance. There is space enough for everyone's journey and for every emotion that arises! Some partners need time to process this news in solitude, while others may have a desire to research and gather as much information as possible. Some may want to discuss all the details with the partner who now identifies as transgender, whereas others may find it more suitable to process this new reality with a close friend, family member, spiritual mentor, or therapist. Each preference must be honored and respected. The challenge in this situation is deciding which choice works best for you and when. Although controversial, your need to process this news may not be aligned with the wishes of the person who is transgender. As a result, this can cause a great deal of conflict within the relationship. Each person's needs must be considered, communicated, and valued. Sometimes outside professionals can play a critical role in the next steps to assist each person to find their own voice. Ideally, those involved in the transition will be in sync and have enough clarity to reach a consensus that is acceptable to both of them.

However, the reality is that, in some cases, the process can be extremely painful

> AFFIRMATIVE ANECDOTE
> *I don't understand,*
> *How did I*
> *Not know?*

for both or one person in the relationship. If this happens, and it sometimes does, the partner may need to make a decision as to whether they will choose to honor their own needs above those of their partner in transition, or whether they are able to place the trans-identified person's needs and wants above their own. It can be a time of great struggle for some and a very natural flow for others. For some partners, this exploration will be an easy passage, obvious and painless; for others, it may be an overwhelming journey, filled with much internal conflict. Knowing and accepting that you have the right to travel the path that brings you the most comfort and peace will ease the pressure and will allow you to understand what is best for you, while searching for your own voice and needs in the relationship.

For those partners who clearly identify themselves as being at ease with learning that their significant other is transitioning, you may find it more helpful to jump around and not answer or complete every option offered in this workbook. You may be able to process the transition in a way that is not confusing, concerning, worrisome, or scary. Perhaps your mindset is due to the geographic area you live in, the history you have experienced within the LGBTQQIA+ community, or the time period in which you have grown up. Maybe your experiences have made the transitioning process of your partner's transgender awareness one that is not filled with questions or opposition. If this is the case, simply use this journal as a tool to assist you in housing your written thoughts and respond to whichever questions and exercises that best serve your needs.

For the portion of those partners who identify themselves as possibly overwhelmed, concerned, fearful, and/or worried with learning of the transition, this workbook can be a major form of support at a time when you can no longer recognize yourself and/or your relationship, your own needs, and what your next steps may be in the near future. Discovering anything unexpected can be difficult to grasp, especially when you have been in a relationship or an environment where the word "transgender" was not a part of your vocabulary. Trying to sort out all the unknowns and hundreds of questions that may be racing in your mind can baffle and numb the thought processes of even the most articulate and verbal individual within a very short span of time. Challenging as life may be, once you are told this information, it can be extremely empowering and helpful to write down everything that is happening. Simply documenting the when, how, and what of a situation enables you to process all you are experiencing and feeling. Later, when you are able to think more clearly and express your feelings in words, having a detailed diary of your thoughts, fears, or questions may foster the clarity, that in time, will return once again. The guttural racing of thoughts can be never ending. Documenting when and how you found out your partner is transgender or may be considering transitioning helps to recall the words and thoughts that were going through your mind as you received the information.

Journaling the specifics of it all can even help with clarity when you may choose to relay your process to a therapist or confidant in the future. Some people are unsure of how they feel when learning their significant other is transitioning. My recommendation is to answer what you can, but to pace yourself. It is not a test and there is no right or wrong answer. Feel free to peruse other sections or chapters in this workbook at any time.

You are in charge of how to navigate this journey of exploration in the hope of discovering how to fulfill your needs. Those needs and wants are an entire layer in and of themselves. In truth, as you may be figuring this all out, your previous life commitments and the transition are occurring simultaneously. This fact may compound the reality of your daily life. Carve out time and a place to journal about your uncertainties, fears, worries, and concerns in a safe space. The tools are for all those who have learned their significant other is now questioning their gender or identifying as transgender. Some questions may hold more significance or feel more relevant than others. Make this work for you and create your own course of understanding yourself. All the questions, exercises, and additional tools were included in this workbook for you!

GRAPHICS GALORE

Splash

Can you free-flowingly jot down all the emotions you feel or felt when you learned about the transition? By creatively splashing words and/or short phrases, quickly attempt to express your answers randomly with as many responses as possible scattered on the paper. (Examples: angry, very content, scared.)

GRAPHICS GALORE

Web

Although the transition may be unexpected and confusing, now that you know, this is a space for you to share the range of emotions you are experiencing. Exploring positive and exciting thoughts, as well as those that are baffling, can be extremely cathartic. Select one concerning thought or celebratory feeling and write it down in the center of the web. Then branch out and write other specific detail subtopics in the outer circles. This graphic exercise can help you organize and understand the topic in depth with fewer words, yet still enable you to express yourself.

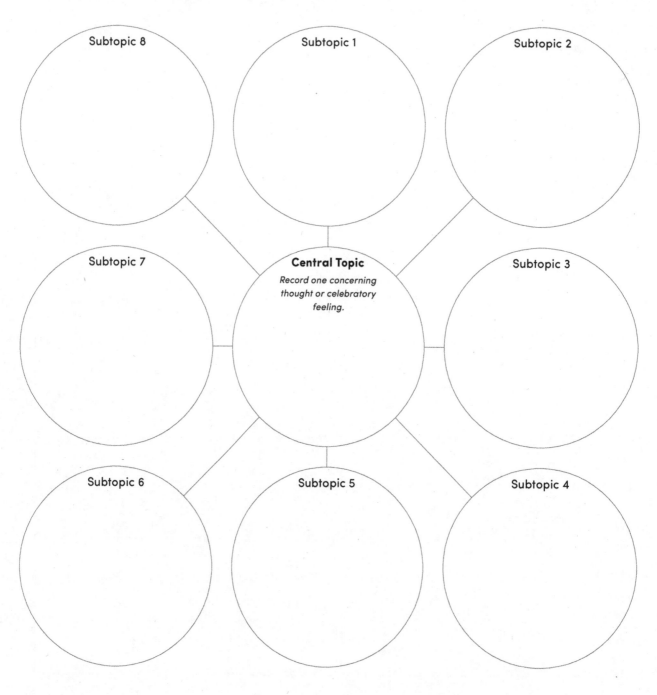

REFLECTIVE RESPONSES

1. How and when did you find out your partner was thinking about transitioning or has decided to transition?

....

....

....

2. What do you think it meant when your partner told you they need to transition?

....

....

....

3. How do you feel about the possibility or reality of your partner transitioning?

....

....

....

4. Now that you think about it, can you recall any situation, event, activity, or moment that might have indicated to you that your partner was considering transitioning?

....

....

....

5. Do you believe your life will remain the same or be different after the transition?

....

....

....

6. Now that you know, are there any fears, worries, and concerns going through your mind about the transition?

....

....

....

AFFIRMATIVE ANECDOTE

Being scared
Is not knowing
The answers
To all of my questions.

7. Do you fear you will not be allowed around children now that your partner is trans-identified?

....

....

....

8. Do you fear that you or your partner could be fired if it became known that your partner is transgender?

....

....

....

9. How will you cope or adjust if family or friends reject either one of you?

....

....

....

10. Is there an appropriate way to ask your partner if it is necessary for them to transition now, or if it is possible for them never to transition?

....

....

....

11. What thoughts, feelings, fears, concerns, or worries can you share with your partner?

....

....

....

12. What thoughts, feelings, fears, concerns, or worries can you share with others?

....

....

....

13. What thoughts, feelings, fears, concerns, or worries can you not share with your partner?

....

....

....

14. What thoughts, feelings, fears, concerns, or worries can you not share with others?

....

....

....

15. What can or should you do if you resent your partner about the transition?

....

....

....

16. How can you help and show support for your trans-identified partner?

. . . .

. . . .

. . . .

17. What safety issues do you envision for your trans-identified partner and yourself before, during, and after the transition?

. . . .

. . . .

. . . .

18. Is there a way you can ensure both of you are safe at your home, work, on the street, and especially in public bathrooms throughout the transition?

. . . .

. . . .

. . . .

19. How do you feel about your partner dressing in their gender-affirming clothing?

. . . .

. . . .

. . . .

20. How do you think the transition will affect or change your relationship with each other?

. . . .

. . . .

. . . .

21. How do you think the transition will affect or change your relationship with others?

....

....

....

22. How do you think your partner thinks the transition will affect your relationship?

....

....

....

23. What are your choices, options, and desires for remaining in this relationship throughout the transition process?

....

....

....

24. What are your choices, options, and desires for leaving this relationship throughout the transition process?

....

....

....

25. How much are you willing to, wanting to, or able to be a part of this transition?

....

....

....

26. Do you think you will still be a couple during and after the transition?

. . . .

. . . .

. . . .

27. Do you think people will be able to tell that your partner is transgender?

. . . .

. . . .

. . . .

28. Do you think the focus will ever not be on the transition?

. . . .

. . . .

. . . .

29. Do you believe your trans-identified partner will still use the same name and/or pronoun they were assigned at birth?

. . . .

. . . .

. . . .

30. Do you think there are other people going through this type of transition? If so, will you try to find them? How?

. . . .

. . . .

. . . .

GRAPHICS GALORE

Venn Diagram

What are the five greatest concerns, fears, or worries for each of you in regard to your relationship now that the transition is part of your future? It is helpful to explore whether you both share any of the same concerns, fears, and worries in order to address them. It is equally important to understand which concerns the other needs to discuss or is thinking about at this present time.

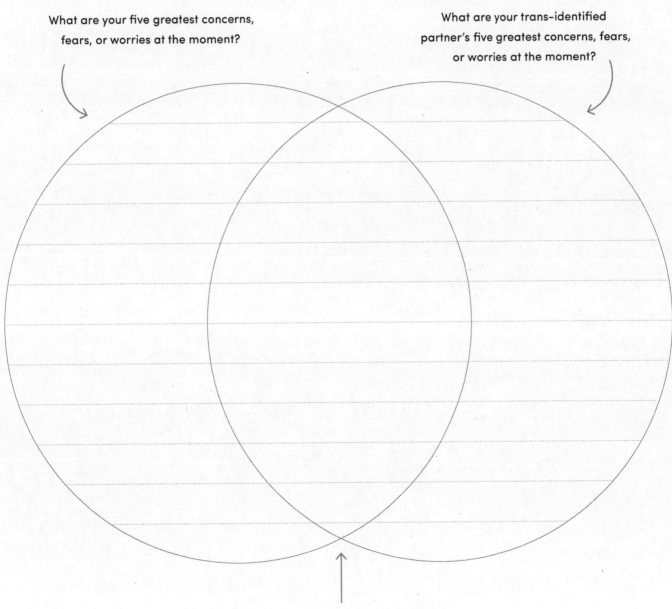

What are your five greatest concerns, fears, or worries at the moment?

What are your trans-identified partner's five greatest concerns, fears, or worries at the moment?

Do any of your and your partner's five greatest concerns, fears, or worries overlap at the moment?

GRAPHICS GALORE

T-Chart

Write down what you now **know** about the transitioning process, then list what you **want** to know about the transition process. Continue filling in the chart as you **learn** the answers to the wants in relation to the transition process.

Know	Want	Learn

DESERVING DE-STRESS DELIGHTS

Meditation

Relaxing your mind and body at a time of stress can be very helpful in providing clarity and calmness. I found meditation in any form to be extremely comforting and it helped me to quiet many of my worries and fears in relation to the transition. These are ways others and I meditated, which helped us find solace and tranquility. As unusual as this may seem, some days I went for a walk in an active or loud area for a period of time. I found the sensory sights and sounds around me blocked out all the noise in my head, and I could just be an observer of my environment. Horns beeping, doors slamming, and people talking became music to my ears and surprisingly soothed me. In contrast, other days I needed the beauty and solitude of the beach. I would hear the ocean and look at the sunset, feeling at peace as I sorted things out. Sometimes I needed to cry alone. I did not even realize how cathartic it was to listen to the water and appreciate nature. For some people, hiking and walking in the woods or taking a stroll on the first snow day brought them much tranquility. Still others have shared that they found peace attending support groups, religious services, or speaking with a spiritual mentor quite comforting. If I wanted a more structured approach to practice stillness, I attended a meditation class.

> AFFIRMATIVE ANECDOTE
>
> *What scares me most?*
> *What worries me most?*
> *How can I take care of me?*
> *How can I take care of we?*

Listening to a guided audiotape of peaceful music or participating in a gentle yoga class were also relaxing. These experiences enabled me to be passive as I received the directed suggestions. It was soothing to close my eyes and embrace the gentleness of the harmonious sounds. If walking or being guided by an outside entity did not seem to be what I needed, I sought out an activity that was both repetitive and mindless, such as doing a jigsaw puzzle, a word search, or simply coloring or sketching. Most de-stressing for me was a mini-nap. I would set an alarm for 5–10 minutes and close my eyes as I sat in a chair or lay on a bed. Often, I repeated a mantra or imagined myself in a specific place that I loved and just let myself breathe. When the time was up, I felt renewed and ready to face the world of the unfamiliar!

Journal your reaction to this Deserving De-Stress Delight.

....

....

....

....

....

....

....

....

....

....

....

....

....

....

....

....

....

....

....

....

....

....

GRAPHICS GALORE

Timeline

I wish I had kept a log of all the critical happenings that occurred throughout the transition process, but I did not. This tool can help you keep a record of these moments as time goes by.

Complete the timeline as you find out different, relevant pieces of information about the transition. You may need or choose to use this information to discuss these events with a therapist, for medical needs, or for your own point of reference. Examples to record: when you may have realized that transitioning was possibly necessary; when you might have been told of the need for social or medical changes; when your partner began using a different bathroom; when your partner began to wear clothing of their affirmed gender; when you chose to discuss the transition with a specific person.

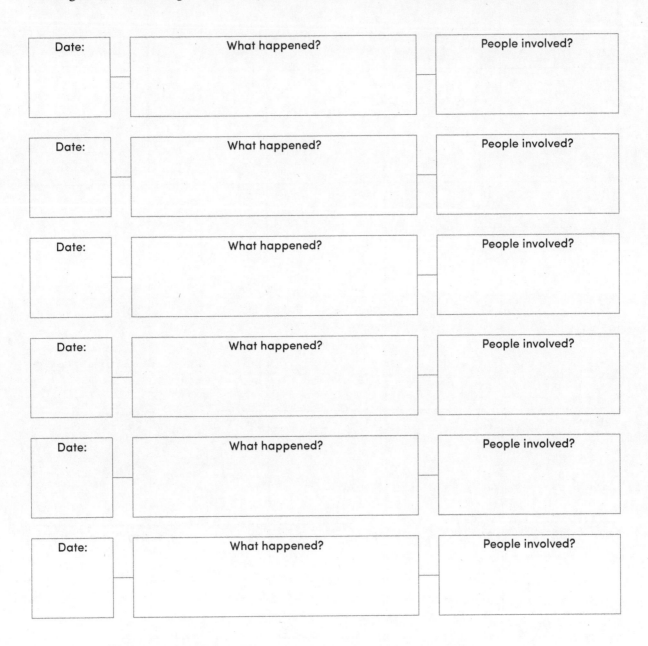

Date:	What happened?	People involved?
Date:	What happened?	People involved?
Date:	What happened?	People involved?
Date:	What happened?	People involved?
Date:	What happened?	People involved?
Date:	What happened?	People involved?

GRAPHICS GALORE

Box

The uncertainties of what it means to be in a transgender relationship can be abundant and endless for some partners, especially when it is all so new. List any uncertainties that are overwhelming your mind. Writing them down can help release some anxiety and gain some power over your life. Some partners may choose to share these thoughts with their trans-identified partner or someone else. That choice is yours! (You may prefer to focus more on celebratory thoughts and/or feelings.)

1	2	3	4	5
6	7	8	9	10
11	12	13	14	15
16	17	18	19	20
21	22	23	24	25
26	27	28	29	30

EMPATHY-EMBRACING EXERCISE

Realizing that every experience you have in life has the potential to prepare you for the next challenge or venture that presents itself to you is empowering. Knowing you have survived and made it through a difficult or overwhelming situation fosters positive hope.

Have you experienced anything else in your life, other than the transition, that has been unexpected and confusing in any way? If so, what has it been and how did you cope, address, or handle this information?

> AFFIRMATIVE ANECDOTE
> *We may not*
> *Know why,*
> *But we know*
> *Change is*
> *Going to happen!*

GRAPHICS GALORE

Bar Graph

To what degree do these concerns and related topics matter to you? Based on a scale from 1 to 10, with 1 being the lowest and 10 being the highest, color or shade in your response. This visual will help you see where your greatest concerns lie and can help you to communicate this to your trans-identified partner, therapist, spiritual mentor, or for your own personal understanding. The bar graph results may vary as the transition progresses and your thoughts may shift.

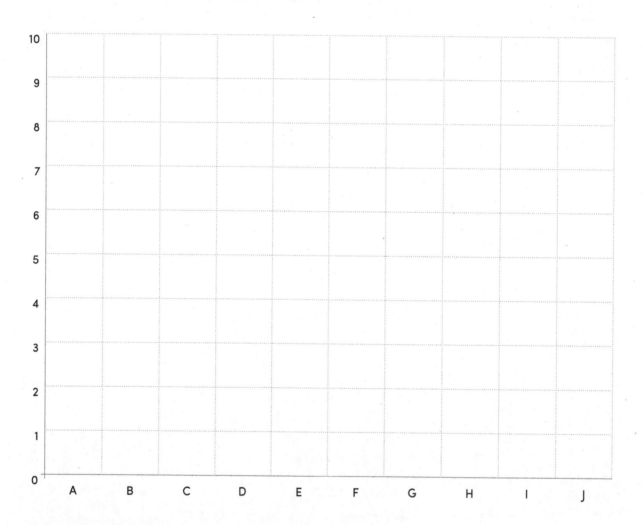

Use these ideas to fill in the bar graph or feel free to create your own!

A. Your attraction to your partner.

B. Your partner's attraction to you.

C. Your sex life.

D. Your own finances or employment.

E. Your partner's finances or employment.

F. Your relationship with each other.

G. Your relationship with family/children.

H. Your relationship with friends.

I. Your trans-identified partner's social/medical changes.

J. Your partner's safety and yours.

GRAPHICS GALORE

Pie Graph

To what degree do these concerns and related topics matter to you? Decide how important are these topics to you in relation to each other? Place the number that corresponds with a suggested topic within as many slices of the pie that conveys how each one matters to you. Only one number should be placed in each slice. You do not need to use all the topics but do fill in all the slices. Feel free to create your own topics and assign them their own number.

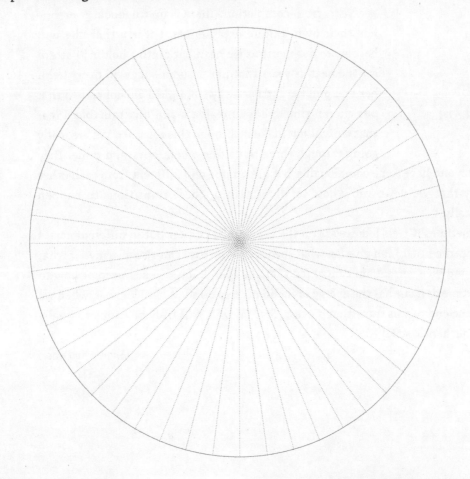

1. Your attraction to your partner.

2. Your partner's attraction to you.

3. Your sex life.

4. Your own finances or employment.

5. Your partner's finances or employment.

6. Your relationship with each other.

7. Your relationship with family/children.

8. Your relationship with friends.

9. Your trans-identified partner's social/medical changes.

10. Your partner's safety and yours.

SAMPLER SHARE

Now that I know, are there any fears, worries, and concerns going through my mind about the transition?

Transition is the Leviathan of emotional roller coasters. I now know how deeply I love my wife and how committed we are to continuing to live our lives together. But we are still a long way from riding off into the sunset. I fear what is yet to come on a journey that is still at least another 3–4 years from completion. There is no rulebook. Everyone has their own unique experiences. I worry that she will become so dysphoric as we head back into a holding pattern for the next 25 years that her despondency will overwhelm her and pull her farther away from me. I am concerned that our chosen timeline is unrealistic and unattainable. I fear that we will not make it through this together. We are really going through three transitions: hers, ours, and mine. They intersect and have some commonality but are unique and different from each other. I worry that we don't know how to allow each of these transitions to happen organically.

> AFFIRMATIVE ANECDOTE
>
> *Ask questions,*
> *Get answers,*
> *Keep asking*
> *More questions.*

Sometimes it feels like we are on the same roller coaster but in different cars! I am concerned that I can give her what she needs but that I can also give myself what I need and vice versa. I am concerned that she even knows what I need or how to support me or if she has the energy or inclination to do so. What I know is, when we get to the end of this transition process, that my wife will truly be happy to finally be her authentic self.

(Shared by Grace)

COUPLE COMMUNICATION CORNER

When partners or couples speak spontaneously out of anger or fear about the unknown, without thinking it through, they can sometimes regret the way they phrased it. Rehearsing what and how partners may want to ask or discuss with their trans-identified partner, and/or others, can help partners and couples before they actually communicate their thoughts. This gives the non-transitioning partner a moment to reflect and pause before they converse about emotional topics. Partners may choose to practice asking these questions with a trusted friend, family member, spiritual mentor, or therapist first.

Explain your thoughts and feelings about these statements to each other. Do you and your trans-identified partner answer these questions in the same way or differently? Discuss your responses to understand how you view them and make time to celebrate all you learn from being willing to communicate with each other.

1. Do you think you will still be attracted to your trans-identified partner during and after the transition?

   The partner's thoughts: The trans persons's thoughts:

   ....

   ....

   ....

> AFFIRMATIVE ANECDOTE
> *I am important!*
> *I am visible!*
> *My needs matter!*

2. Do you think your trans-identified partner will still be attracted to you during and after the transition?

   The partner's thoughts: The trans persons's thoughts:

   ....

   ....

3. How do you think the transition will affect your sex life?

   The partner's thoughts: The trans persons's thoughts:

   ....

   ....

   ....

4. How do you think the transition will affect your finances or employment?

The partner's thoughts: The trans persons's thoughts:

. . . .

. . . .

. . . .

5. How do you think the transition will affect your partner's finances or employment?

The partner's thoughts: The trans persons's thoughts:

. . . .

. . . .

. . . .

6. How do you think the transition will affect your relationship with each other?

The partner's thoughts: The trans persons's thoughts:

. . . .

. . . .

. . . .

7. How do you think the transition will affect your relationship with your family/children?

The partner's thoughts: The trans persons's thoughts:

. . . .

. . . .

. . . .

8. How do you think the transition will affect your relationship with your friends?

The partner's thoughts: The trans persons's thoughts:

. . . .

. . . .

. . . .

9. What social or medical changes do you think your trans-identified partner will need to undertake to feel whole?

The partner's thoughts: The trans persons's thoughts:

. . . .

. . . .

. . . .

10. Do you think your trans-identified partner will be safe in public throughout and after the transition?

The partner's thoughts: The trans persons's thoughts:

. . . .

. . . .

. . . .

Chapter 3

WHO ARE YOU?

VITAL VIGNETTE

It may seem insignificant to some, but a person's name is extremely intertwined with their identity. Perhaps this is why a large majority of transgender persons change or adjust the name they were assigned at birth. Each individual has their personal reasons and usually selects the name change, when desired, with extreme care. This name change is not necessarily done as part of a team, and many times the non-transitioning partner can be unaware that the name will or has evolved. The surprise and unexpectedness of the name change can be deeply saddening and very confusing for the partner. As with the rest of the process, whenever possible, this too could be something that the transitioning partner may consider including the partner in. Even when the partner is included, much needs to be ironed out involving the name change, especially the specifics of timing in relation to who is told, when, and how. To add further adjustments, the partner may be faced with the reality that the transgender partner desires to be addressed by a pronoun never used before. Again, to some this may seem like an extremely reasonable request, but to the partner this desire may be overwhelming, confusing, and destabilizing. It may be understandable that the person transitioning wants their pronoun to match their affirmed gender; however, the acceptance and learning curve for this may be quite difficult for partners and could take a while to grasp. Even the most embracing partner may require time to adjust to the request of referring to the trans-identified partner using the new personal pronoun and/or a new name.

Many family members, friends, and employers may also require a period of time to adjust to using the name and pronoun changes that the transitioning partner desires. Some people will even consciously or unconsciously rebel against the name or pronoun changes. Any errors, whether intentional or accidental, can cause much public embarrassment and confusion to everyone involved. This adjustment is something that

> AFFIRMATIVE ANECDOTE
>
> *He, she,*
> *They, sie,*
> *Ze, ve,*
> *What about*
> *Me?*

partners and/or others may need to figure out for themselves, and if time is necessary to process these changes, it must be granted. Although the person transitioning is usually and understandably elated about the name or pronoun change, there can be some sense of loss felt by the partner, family members, or friends. This grief needs to be acknowledged and spoken about, for it should not be overlooked. For some, it is an erasing of something that has been a major part of the transitioning person's history, and although that reality may not be extremely painful for those in transition, there can simultaneously be a strong feeling of mourning for others. Both sides have a right to be recognized, without judgment or criticism of any party involved.

In addition to no longer using the transitioning person's name or pronoun, partners are often asked to remove any photos and/or memorabilia connected to the life the transitioning person lived prior to the transition. These requests, though critical to those in transition, can cause major sadness, loss, anger, and resentment for the partners who treasure the past history and memories of their life together.

Where is the space, time, and place for the partner who is in desperate need for catch-up time? The pain the partner and others can experience is real and it must be discussed, valued, honored, and respected. The focus of this chapter creates that space and place for partners to process and acknowledge this possible loss and pain through writing and sharing their feelings, thoughts, and, for some, real grief.

Negotiating when, with whom, and under what circumstances the past history can be discussed is both extremely time-consuming and exhausting. These very sensitive conversations may require an enormous amount of patience and compromise throughout the entire transition. These dialogues may even continue long after the transition is no longer a major focus of the relationship. Unanticipated circumstances involving reunions with old acquaintances or relatives may require a rehashing of history or past memories, which may once again require an explanation of the changing of pronouns or name. The loss can be relived during very subtle or matter-of-fact tasks such as seeing the old name when opening daily mail, sorting through legal documents, looking through photo albums, or simply viewing the name on your door or buzzer to your apartment. It is recommended that each one of these possible scenarios be addressed and thought through as much as possible. If the partner is requested to use new pronouns and a new name or to eliminate artifacts that make the transgender person feel very uncomfortable, it must be understood that it can all feel too much at first. To have these changes become automatic for the partner, time and communication can be the best healers and the kindest methods for the desired outcome sought by the person in transition. Above all else, having patience and understanding can be key for this part of the transition process!

GRAPHICS GALORE

Splash

What are the pronouns or possible names your partner is considering using now that they are contemplating or are transitioning? By creatively splashing words and/or short phrases, quickly attempt to express your answers randomly with as many responses as possible scattered on the paper.

GRAPHICS GALORE

Venn Diagram
What artifacts are displayed in your living environment that may need to be taken out of view in order to move forward with the transition?

What artifacts and/or photos are you willing to remove?

What artifacts and/or photos is your transgender partner willing to remove?

What artifacts and/or photos are you both agreeing to remove?

REFLECTIVE RESPONSES

1. What is your partner's preferred identity now? (Name, pronoun, and gender.)

    . . . .

    . . . .

    . . . .

2. Will you play a role when your trans-identified partner selects their name and/or pronoun?

    . . . .

    . . . .

    . . . .

3. How will you prefer to be introduced individually and as a couple? When will this begin?

    . . . .

    . . . .

    . . . .

4. Will there be different criteria for different people, for each one of you?

    . . . .

    . . . .

    . . . .

5. What names and pronouns will be used for each of you during intimate moments?

    . . . .

    . . . .

    . . . .

6. Did any person's reaction to the transition in relation to pronoun use or name change surprise you? If yes, who and how did they surprise you?

....

....

....

AFFIRMATIVE ANECDOTE

Why are you smiling?
My life is erupting.
How can you be happy?
Our life is being erased.

7. As you look around your home, what are you willing to remove?

....

....

....

8. Which of these removals or decisions will be made by you, your partner, and together?

....

....

....

9. What will be the time frame for each one of these decisions/removals?

....

....

....

10. How will you refer to, state, or use the new name, pronoun, or gender when you discuss memories and/or the past with each other or other people?

....

....

....

GRAPHICS GALORE

Web

What artifact does your trans-identified partner want removed that you do not want taken down or put out of view?

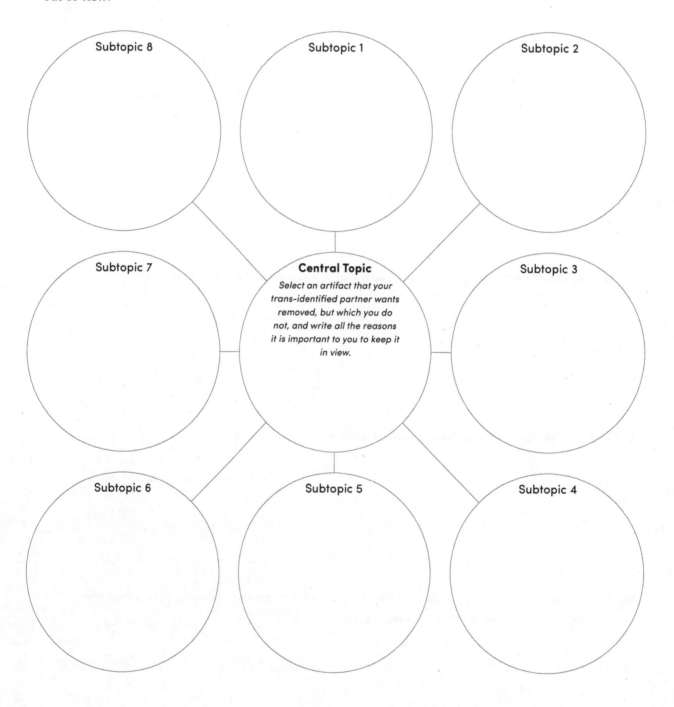

Subtopic 8

Subtopic 1

Subtopic 2

Subtopic 7

Central Topic
Select an artifact that your trans-identified partner wants removed, but which you do not, and write all the reasons it is important to you to keep it in view.

Subtopic 3

Subtopic 6

Subtopic 5

Subtopic 4

GRAPHICS GALORE

T-Chart

What do you view as positives, negatives, or neutral about your partner changing the name and/or pronoun they were assigned at birth?

+ (Positives)	– (Negatives)	= (Neutral)

DESERVING DE-STRESS DELIGHTS

Creating

When things around me were feeling as if they were falling apart, I built or made something that gave me a sense of strength and purpose. Nothing I created was earth-shattering, but each endeavor helped remind me that I had value and importance. Since I love craft activities, I created collages of words and pictures to express how I was feeling, knitted or crocheted scarves and hats, embroidered or needlepointed images, and even painted, simply to express myself. Others have shared that they took photographs of anything that appealed to them or scrapbooked old photos as a tool to cope with their grief and as a way to record their past. Some partners physically built pieces of furniture, made a dog/bird house, or designed shelving for their home. One person planted a garden of their favorite vegetables and flowers. Find whatever it is that feels creative to you and provides an outlet that validates your worthiness. Creating is something I would encourage as a means of honoring your talents and increasing self-esteem.

> AFFIRMATIVE ANECDOTE
>
> *Picking a pronoun,*
> *Choosing a name,*
> *Redesigning our home,*
> *No one is to blame!*

Journal your reaction to this Deserving De-Stress Delight.

··

··

··

··

··

··

··

··

··

··

··

··

··

··

··

··

··

GRAPHICS GALORE

Timeline

When and with whom will you or your partner begin using their new pronoun/name?

With whom?	Anticipated date to discuss it with the person:	Their reaction:
With whom?	Anticipated date to discuss it with the person:	Their reaction:
With whom?	Anticipated date to discuss it with the person:	Their reaction:
With whom?	Anticipated date to discuss it with the person:	Their reaction:
With whom?	Anticipated date to discuss it with the person:	Their reaction:
With whom?	Anticipated date to discuss it with the person:	Their reaction:
With whom?	Anticipated date to discuss it with the person:	Their reaction:

GRAPHICS GALORE

Box

List all of the artifacts requested to be removed from view and check off if and when each one is taken away or down. Just because an artifact is listed, it does not mean it must be removed. This is simply a place to record those artifacts in question and their location.

1	2	3
4	5	6
7	8	9
10	11	12
13	14	15
16	17	18

EMPATHY-EMBRACING EXERCISE

AFFIRMATIVE ANECDOTE

*Calling on
Crystal balls,
Fortune tellers,
Soothsayers,
Can our history
Be part of our
Future?*

Part of a partner's journey may involve adjusting to using a new name or pronoun. This exercise question shows a partner that this is part of what many people have done in other instances. The greatest learning tools for grasping the change in name and pronoun are patience with yourself, willingness, time, and much practice.

Do you know anyone from your past who has asked you to call them by a different name, pronoun, or honorific, perhaps due to marriage or for other reasons? How long did it take you to adjust to this new name, pronoun, or honorific, and how did you learn to adjust to the change?

....

....

....

....

....

....

....

....

....

....

....

....

GRAPHICS GALORE

Bar Graph

To what degree does/did it feel sad or upsetting to you to remove artifacts, photographs, or to use the name/pronoun requested by your partner? Based on a scale from 1 to 10, with 1 being the lowest and 10 being the highest, color or shade in your response. This visual will help you see where your greatest concerns lie and can help you to communicate this to your trans-identified partner, therapist, spiritual mentor, or for your own personal understanding. The bar graph results may vary as the transition progresses and your thoughts may shift.

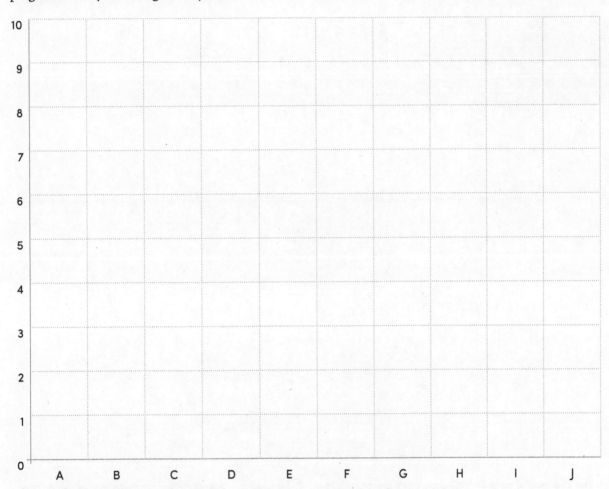

Use these ideas to fill in the bar graph or feel free to create your own!

A. The changing of trans-identified partner's pre-transition name/pronoun assigned at birth.

B. People misgendering your trans-identified partner.

C. Removal of trans-identified partner's pre-transition photos.

D. Removal of the couple's pre-transition photos.

E. Removal of trans-identified partner's pre-transition photos with family.

F. Removal of trans-identified partner's pre-transition photos with friends.

G. Removal of trans-identified partner's special events pre-transition photos.

H. Not saying name/pronoun assigned at birth in public.

I. Not saying name/pronoun assigned at birth during sex/intimacy.

J. Not posting documents, awards, or licenses that contain the written name/pronoun assigned at birth anywhere.

GRAPHICS GALORE

Pie Graph

To what degree does/did it feel sad or upsetting to you to remove artifacts, photographs, or to use the name/pronoun requested by your partner? Decide how important these statements are to you in relation to each other. Place the number that corresponds with a suggested topic within as many slices of the pie that conveys how each one matters to you. Only one number should be placed in each slice. You do not need to use all the topics but do fill in all the slices. Feel free to create your own topics and assign them their own number.

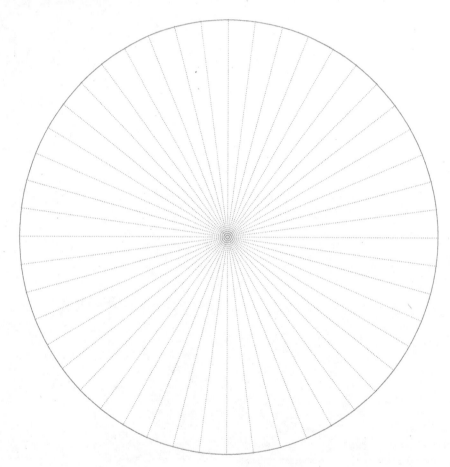

1. The changing of trans-identified partner's pre-transition name/pronoun assigned at birth.

2. People misgendering your trans-identified partner.

3. Removal of trans-identified partner's pre-transition photos.

4. Removal of the couple's pre-transition photos.

5. Removal of trans-identified partner's pre-transition photos with family

6. Removal of trans-identified partner's pre-transition photos with friends.

7. Removal of trans-identified partner's special events pre-transition photos.

8. Not saying name/pronoun assigned at birth in public.

9. Not saying name/pronoun assigned at birth during sex/intimacy.

10. Not posting documents, awards, or licenses that contain the written name/pronoun assigned at birth anywhere.

SAMPLER SHARE

Did any person's reaction to the transition in relation to pronoun use or name change surprise you? If yes, who? Explain how they surprised you.

AFFIRMATIVE ANECDOTE

How can we Remain a couple When you are not Remaining?

I met my boyfriend's parents for the first time about seven months into dating. I was genuinely shocked that after coming out to them over ten years ago, his mother was still misgendering him. Continually. She even used his birth name a few times, despite him having legally changed his name. I was caught off-guard. I froze. I looked to my boyfriend for a sympathetic eye-roll or some sign of him being shocked and appalled as well. Nothing. He seemed completely unfazed. I was uncomfortably preoccupied. Would she think I was crazy for using male pronouns? Would she dislike me? It made *me* feel like I was doing something wrong. I feared and avoided pronouns for our entire first night out: Through drinks. Through dinner. Through a comedy show and through a train ride home. I just smiled politely and pretended nothing was going on. I asked my boyfriend about it after dropping them off at the hotel. He dejectedly told me that they had "backslid a little." It felt like a lot to me! It made me sad that he didn't correct them. Why wouldn't he stand up for himself? Could I stand up for him? He has said he doesn't want me correcting strangers, so I knew I definitely shouldn't correct his parents.

Our relationship was becoming serious and it felt pretty important that these people liked me. Fighting back the fact that blood rushes to my ears and I lose hearing for a second when he is addressed with female pronouns made it difficult to even keep up with conversation. It was exhausting. The rest of the trip I bucked up and used his correct pronouns. Continually! It was easier the more I did it. Turns out they were willing to ignore my pronouns and I was willing to ignore theirs. Not the most socially aware unspoken agreement I've ever been part of, but we really got along splendidly for the rest of the visit. Me with my pronouns and them with theirs.

I'm still with my boyfriend and I will definitely be seeing his parents again. In general, they are ridiculously kind, generous people that I enjoyed spending time with and even look forward to spending time with in the future. I will just know to give myself a little pronoun pep-talk before their next visit. If my boyfriend can handle the feelings that bubble up every time his family misgenders him, then so can I.

(Shared by Lucy)

COUPLE COMMUNICATION CORNER

When partners or couples speak spontaneously out of anger or fear about the unknown, without thinking it through, they can sometimes regret the way they phrased it. Rehearsing what and how partners may want to ask or discuss with their trans-identified partner, and/or others, can help partners and couples before they actually communicate their thoughts. This gives the non-transitioning partner a moment to reflect and pause before they converse about emotional topics. Partners may choose to practice asking these questions with a trusted friend, family member, spiritual mentor, or therapist first.

Explain your thoughts and feelings about these questions to each other. Do you and your trans-identified partner answer these questions in the same way or differently? Discuss your responses to understand how you view them and make time to celebrate all you learn from being willing to communicate with each other.

1. When do you prefer a particular artifact and/or photo be removed and why?

    The partner's thoughts: The trans persons's thoughts:

    . . . .

    . . . .

    . . . .

2. Why are you requesting for a particular artifact and/or photo not to be removed?

    The partner's thoughts: The trans persons's thoughts:

    . . . .

    . . . .

    . . . .

3. Where will you store your artificats and/or photos that are removed?

    The partner's thoughts: The trans persons's thoughts:

    . . . .

    . . . .

    . . . .

4. Which artifacts and/or photos, if any, will be thrown away or gotten rid of some way?

The partner's thoughts: The trans persons's thoughts:

. . . .

. . . .

. . . .

5. Will certain artifacts and/or photos that are removed, be replaced?

The partner's thoughts: The trans persons's thoughts:

. . . .

. . . .

. . . .

AFFIRMATIVE ANECDOTE

Loss of Pronouns, Names, Pictures, Memories. Loss of...

6. How will the artifacts and/or photos that are removed be replaced?

The partner's thoughts: The trans persons's thoughts:

. . . .

. . . .

. . . .

7. How would you like to handle misgendered moments?

The partner's thoughts: The trans persons's thoughts:

. . . .

. . . .

. . . .

8. What full name or names would you like to be addressed with now?

The partner's thoughts: The trans persons's thoughts:

. . . .

. . . .

. . . .

9. How will you decide how you will explain the changing of pronoun/name to others?

The partner's thoughts: The trans persons's thoughts:

. . . .

. . . .

. . . .

10. What will you say when the changing of pronoun/name will be explained to others?

The partner's thoughts: The trans persons's thoughts:

. . . .

. . . .

. . . .

Chapter 4

GRIEF MAY APPLY

VITAL VIGNETTE

It is extremely difficult to explain how grief and loss may play a major role for some partners who are told the person they are in a relationship with is planning or has begun to transition. The reverse also holds true. For some partners, learning this information can be a time of celebration with few or no feelings of loss or grief.

AFFIRMATIVE ANECDOTE

Grief,
So many stages,
All at once!

This chapter will focus on those who have experienced or are experiencing any sense of loss, pain, or grief once they have understood that the person they are in a relationship with is planning to or has begun transitioning. From the outside looking in, this pain, loss, and grief may seem unjustified or baffling because the person in transition is still alive and can often be in their life on a daily basis. It is true that the non-transitioning partner can still talk to the trans-identified partner, eat with them, and do many or most of the things together that they did prior to knowing about the transition. Yet in reality, so much is changing. Your daily life may never be the same again and will continue to change for a length of time, even though it might not appear so different to others. It can be a seemingly invisible loss and source of pain or grief for those who are in the relationship.

Many partners have shared that the transition feels like an erasing, fading, or passing of the relationship they are or were in. Some partners have expressed that they felt lost and unsure of what to do to feel secure. Who can a partner turn to if they need to discuss this hurt and feeling of betrayal? Where is the space to share the loss of a person when the person is still there? How does a partner convey what it is like to not recognize almost anything about the relationship they knew and/or the person they originally met and hoped to create a specific future with, without sounding harsh or unsupportive?

The partner in transition may be considering or may be in the process of changing their name, pronoun, gender expression, and/or gender marker. Their gender can be affirmed through medical, social, and/or legal means. As part of their journey, body parts of the person in transition may be altered, removed, or added. In addition, if hormones are part of the medical transition, hair and scent can be affected, their voice might change, and the visual shape of the person's body could be different. The trans-identified partner may elect to begin to dress in a way that is unfamiliar to their partner, as well as make a myriad of other choices that may help the partner in transition feel at peace with themselves but leave the non-transitioning partner feeling disoriented.

It needs to be acknowledged that the person who is transitioning deserves and has every right to embrace any and every aspect of the transition in order to be true to themselves. The challenge comes into play when these critical necessities for the person who is transitioning affect the social, emotional, personal, and intimate life of the partner. For some partners, there can be a painful and deep mourning period filled with all or some of the stages that Kübler-Ross and Kessler explain in their book *On Grief and Grieving* (2005). Some partners speak of experiencing grief similar to these five stages: denial, anger, bargaining, depression, and acceptance, as described by Kübler-Ross and Kessler (2005).

Denial can be explained as a stage of disbelief, shock, or feeling that the situation is temporary and that perhaps you misunderstood. For example, you know your partner in transition has had surgery but somehow you think it will all be undone the next time you see them. Although you do realize they had surgery, part of you denies this is the reality.

Anger can be directed towards the partner in transition for changing your world. It can be focused on those who are celebrating or questioning any aspects of the transition, especially friends and/or family. It can be expressed as anger towards yourself, as you take blame or responsibility for causing the transition to happen. In addition, you may feel anger at yourself for not being able to be as supportive as you wish you could be at this time in the transition process.

Bargaining is a type of mental or even verbal deal making. Perhaps you think you can propose that your trans-identified partner only dresses as their affirmed gender at home. Maybe you can offer to welcome a social transition, but only if they promise not to make any medical changes. This stage is filled with the "what ifs" or "if onlys" where agreements are conditional—thoughts or requests such as "What if I use your chosen name in public, but when we are intimate, I use your name assigned at birth?"

Depression can be the stage of much sadness, isolation, exhaustion, and an abundance of tears. It may feel as if this stage will never end! Kübler-Ross and Kessler clarify that it does end for most people, but if depression is part of your journey, it can be viewed as part of the grieving process. It should be recognized that situational depression, not clinical depression, could be an appropriate and necessary response to grief.

Acceptance does not mean that you need to be happy or joyful about the outcome of the transition. It simply means that you know the transition has happened or is going to happen. Then you react or respond by realizing that your partner is transgender and that the transition may include aspects that you cannot alter. This stage can also incorporate a heartfelt and celebratory experience filled with elation and happiness.

These stages do not necessarily occur in the same order for all people and they may not all be part of the partner's mourning process. Some of these stages can be felt simultaneously or be present in waves or cycles. The thoughts a partner may experience can become something they never expected, and this could feel shameful. The things a partner may say out of anger or denial to the trans-identified person may feel embarrassing or surprising. Some non-transitioning partners have shared that they do not even recognize themselves during this time of mourning or grieving. The pain and loss expressed by many partners during this grieving period needs to be validated, honored, and allowed without judgment from the transitioning partner, family members, friends, or others who may truly have no idea how the partner feels.

Most importantly, the partner must respect their own feelings and consider seeking professional help or assistance from others, especially if they feel they are unable to function or keep the transition to themselves, even if they have agreed to honor the trans-identified person's request to live stealth. Some trans-identified partners ask their partner to keep the knowledge of the transition to themselves and not share this information with others until the person in transition is comfortable enough or to tell others. It should be acknowledged that some trans-identified partners may elect to always live stealth and never disclose that they have transitioned. This desire of the transgender partner must be weighed against the needs of the partner not in transition. This critical aspect of the transition can demand much discussion. The needs of both must be conveyed to each other and respected with a healthy compromise for the sake of both the individuals involved and the relationship. If you are unsure whether what you are experiencing is appropriate and part of the grieving process, a trained therapist may be your greatest resource.

It cannot be stressed enough how therapy, in both a couple's setting and individual setting, can be of major assistance throughout the entire process of the transition. In addition, forming a support team of people who will be available 24/7 could bring much comfort and relief to partners when they need to talk, grieve, or sort things out with others. Attending conferences that address the needs and questions partners may internalize can also prove to be an outstanding resource that will offer another level of support for partners. For some partners, speaking with a spiritual mentor has been an option that helped bring them comfort. If a partner is experiencing emotional pain or grief, there are ways to assist in easing these feelings. The partner does not need to suffer alone. The loneliness, fears, confusions, and isolating mindset can be devastating for those partners who may be overwhelmed and confused.

The choice and decisions a partner seeks during this time can be quite personal and private, and should be on a timeline that suits their needs. My perception of what seemed like positive aspects versus negative aspects of the transition evolved over time. At first I viewed the various changes as either good or bad, but as I began to accept the transition, I was able to think of the changes as what has remained and what has changed as a result of the transition. This shift in thinking helped me embrace the transition and arrive at a place of peace within myself, but this took me a great deal of time. I offer this reality because I felt it was necessary for me to acknowledge the transition as positive versus negative during my stages of anger; however, in acceptance,

I no longer saw the transition as such a polarizing experience. What matters most is that partners understand that they are safe to express all they are feeling, that space is created for varying perspectives throughout the transition, and that there are professional ways to get the help they deserve.

Time can serve as a factor that may help with the adjustment period as partners become used to so much newness. Communication and support may also be used as tools to assist in easing the grief for some partners. Discussing issues, concerns, worries, and fears with each other, exploring what the process could entail in the future, and including the partner through patient conversations of the next steps could possibly alleviate some level of the loss, pain, and grief. Accepting that these five stages may be rather insignificant to some and yet crucial to the health of other partners provides space for all those who love someone who is now trans-identified.

GRAPHICS GALORE

Splash

Can you express all the words associated with loss or grief? By creatively splashing words and/or short phrases, quickly attempt to express your answers randomly with as many responses as possible scattered on the paper.

GRAPHICS GALORE

Venn Diagram

Does anything about the transition make you feel any sense of loss? (You may want to ask your trans-identified partner to complete this graphic organizer with you or you can simply fill it in for them, based on the knowledge you already have.)

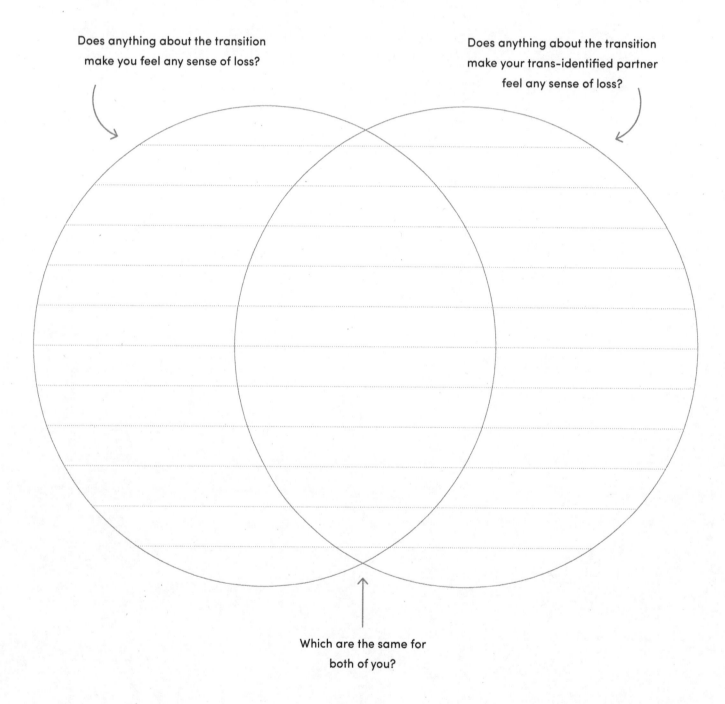

Does anything about the transition make you feel any sense of loss?

Does anything about the transition make your trans-identified partner feel any sense of loss?

Which are the same for both of you?

REFLECTIVE RESPONSES

1. What, if anything, makes you feel angry about the transition?

    . . . .

    . . . .

    . . . .

2. If you could negotiate, bargain, or change something about the transition or its process, what would it be?

    . . . .

    . . . .

    . . . .

3. Does anything about the transition make you feel sad or want to cry? If so, what and why?

    . . . .

    . . . .

    . . . .

4. When you think of the transition, is there something that makes you think or wish that your partner is just confused and not really transgender?

    . . . .

    . . . .

    . . . .

5. When you think of the transition, what aspects make you smile or want to celebrate?

    . . . .

    . . . .

    . . . .

6. What do you think you might miss the most once your partner transitions?

. . . .

. . . .

. . . .

7. What do you wish could remain the same once your partner transitions?

. . . .

. . . .

. . . .

8. Do you sometimes think: Is there something about me that I did or can change to make you stop transitioning? Explain your thoughts or concerns about what this may be or may have been.

. . . .

. . . .

. . . .

9. Does knowing your partner wants to transition foster any feelings of grief or loss, or feel like a type of death?

. . . .

. . . .

. . . .

10. Are you scared your partner will die from the surgery, hormones, or the violence of others?

. . . .

. . . .

. . . .

11. Will you share with your partner if you are scared they will die from the surgery, hormones, or the violence of others?

....

....

....

12. How will you discuss regretful verbalized statements you may have said to your partner during moments of extreme grief, which you may hope to be forgiven for saying?

....

....

....

13. How will you discuss regretful verbalized statements your partner may have said to you during moments of extreme grief?

....

....

....

14. Do you feel you will ever be able to catch up with acceptance as the transition presents many layers of the unknown, perhaps all at the same time?

....

....

....

15. Do you fear or think your life together was a lie?

....

....

....

16. Did you know or see the signs of your partner needing to transition, and ignore them?

. . . .

. . . .

. . . .

17. Do you feel your partner is transitioning to be hurtful to you?

. . . .

. . . .

. . . .

18. Do you feel your partner is being selfish?

. . . .

. . . .

. . . .

19. Do you feel your partner really cares about and/or really loves you?

. . . .

. . . .

. . . .

20. How do you think you will handle it if you notice that all anyone else ever seems to want to talk about is the transition?

. . . .

. . . .

. . . .

21. How do you think you will handle it when, or if, people are asking you inappropriate things about your partner's body and sparing your partner those questions?

....

....

....

22. Do you believe it would help if your partner could slow down the process of transitioning until you had enough time to understand it all and figure out if you are staying or leaving the relationship due to the transition?

....

....

....

23. What if you cannot remain in the relationship? Does it make you a bad person?

....

....

....

24. Do you believe your trans-identified partner or others would judge you in any way for leaving the relationship?

....

....

....

25. Do you believe your trans-identified partner or others would judge you in any way for staying in the relationship?

....

....

....

GRAPHICS GALORE

Web

Select one or more of the five stages of grief and then use the subtopics to express each thought that comes to mind in relation to that stage.

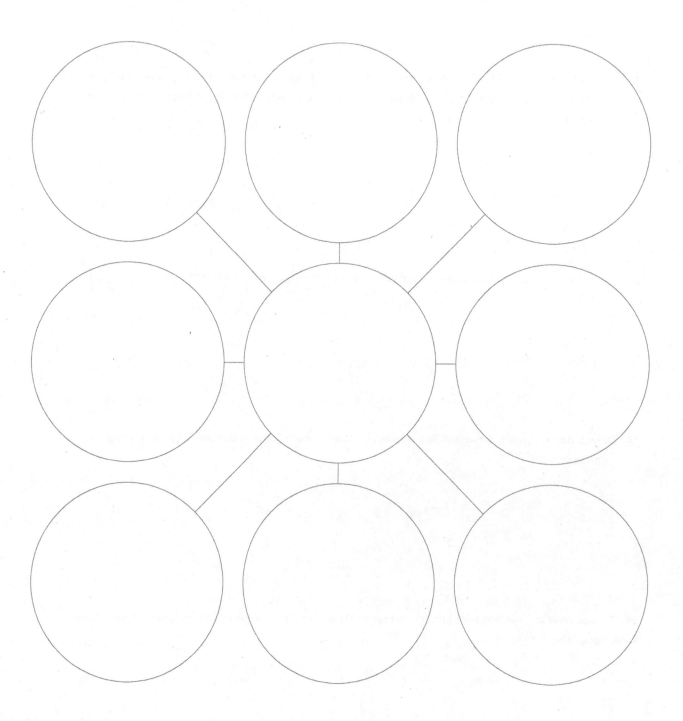

GRAPHICS GALORE

Timeline

Do you feel it is important to record and try to notice if there is any pattern or whether you tend to revert to a particular stage more often than another? This is simply to assist you in being more self-aware. Fill in daily, weekly, or monthly. (Denial, Anger, Bargaining, Depression, or Acceptance.)

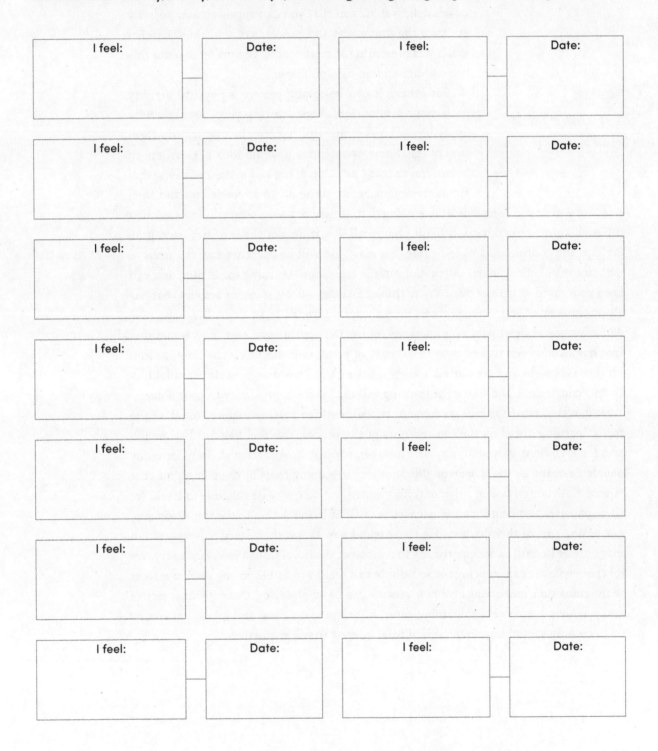

DESERVING DE-STRESS DELIGHTS

Something Novel

Trying something that is risky, new, or unlike you may not sound de-stressing, but in the end, it can become comforting when you are able to achieve things you thought you might not be capable of accomplishing. If you can overcome these fears or doubts, it may be enough to show you that you can approach and possibly embrace the unknowns and concerns of the transition. For me, it was presenting at conferences, beginning to write this book, and then finding a publisher.

> AFFIRMATIVE ANECDOTE
> *Pain, pain,*
> *Go away,*
> *Never come back*
> *Another day!*

For others, it can be taking part in a physical activity, gathering information about starting your own business, applying for a new job, or filling out the application form for college. Some people may have no idea even where to begin, and to that I say: Dream big and make a wish list that stems from your heart! Write down a few desires and then select one item you feel comfortable doing first. It may be as simple as dyeing your hair different colors or making a difficult phone call. Regardless of the venture, attempt it. Perhaps the confidence and self-pride you may gain will be exactly what you need to embrace the challenges and celebrations of the transition. Learning something new can keep your mind sharp and busy. Try to think of a class, hobby, sport, or activity that has always interested you. Some partners have always wanted to learn a new language, take dance lessons, or sign up for a photography course. Deep within you, you know something that has always been tucked away in the back of your mind and this is the time to clean off those cobwebs and get started. I suggest basing this choice on your time availability, budget constraints, and where the learning will take place in proximity to your home.

When the transition process for your trans-identified partner requires much of the focus, learning about all the ins and outs of the process can feel like a full-time job, and for a while it very well may be. However, it must be understood that, for many people, learning of the transition does not require coping tools or the gaining of core strength. Although taking a risk or trying something new may be valuable in itself, for these partners, working out ambivalences or self-doubt in relation to the transition may not be any part of their journey. For those who know this is their story, this suggestion may only be helpful as an opportunity to remember the novel things you want to try. Yet for those who are experiencing the self-doubt and feeling invisible on any level in respect to the transition, embarking on a new venture can be empowering. Once the dust settles and you have overcome that learning curve, it is time to de-stress and focus that energy on beginning something new that is of total interest to you to pursue!

Journal your reaction to this Deserving De-Stress Delight.

....

....

....

....

....

....

....

....

....

....

....

....

....

....

....

....

GRAPHICS GALORE

Box

Can you think of something that made you smile or celebrate today? Sometimes focusing on gratitude, while experiencing loss, reminds us that both can coexist!

1. I laughed at...	2. I saw beauty in...	3. Someone helped me to...
4. I helped someone to...	5. I learned...	6. I treated myself to...

GRAPHICS GALORE

T-Chart

Can you acknowledge how you feel today? Be gentle with yourself and be honest with your thoughts. This space focuses on acceptance. Each partner will approach this in a different way. For some, seeing the positive will be an easy task, but finding the negative may be more difficult. Yet for some people, the reverse may be true, where envisioning negative aspects of the transition may be more in the forefront and imagining positive statements may feel impossible at this time. This is all part of the acceptance stage and there is no timeline or expectation time frame that you need to adhere to. Fill in whatever comes to mind and do not judge your level of acceptance. It all takes time!

Positive (+) Aspects	Negative (−) Aspects	Neutral (=) Aspects

EMPATHY-EMBRACING EXERCISE

For some partners, the transition can be compared to mourning at different stages of the process. Remember that as heartbreaking as other losses or grieving periods have been in your life, you have overcome your pain and continued living. This exercise question intentionally reminds you that if you are mourning any aspect of the transition, it probably will not last forever.

Have you ever experienced an unexpected loss or grieved the passing of someone close to you? Who was it and how did you deal with the loss and/or grief?

> AFFIRMATIVE ANECDOTE
> *I miss*
> *My wife!*
> *I miss*
> *My husband!*
> *I miss...*

GRAPHICS GALORE

Bar Graph

To what degree are you experiencing these emotions? Based on a scale from 1 to 10, with 1 being the lowest and 10 being the highest, color or shade in your response. This visual will help you see where your greatest concerns lie and can help you to communicate this to your trans-identified partner, therapist, spiritual mentor, or for your own personal understanding. The bar graph results may vary as the transition progresses and your concerns or worries shift.

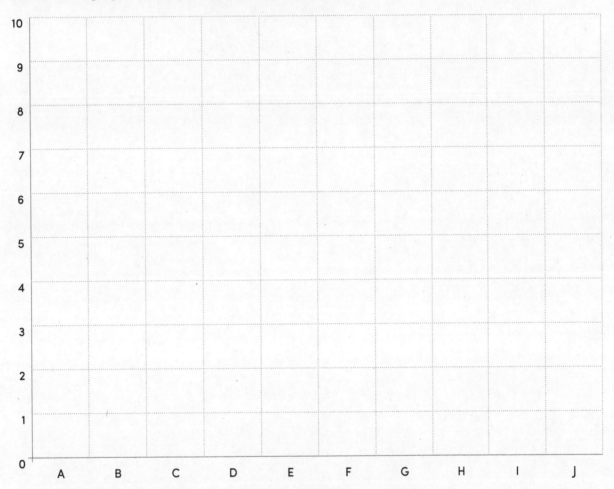

Use these ideas to fill in the bar graph or feel free to create your own!

A. Anger/Mad

B. Sadness/Depression

C. Denial/Disbelief

D. Confusion/Baffled

E. Fearful/Scared

F. Loneliness/Isolation

G. A Sense of Loss/Mourning

H. Joyfulness/Happiness

I. Balanced/Steadiness

J. Numbness/Hopelessness

GRAPHICS GALORE

Pie Graph

To what degree are you experiencing these emotions? Decide how important these statements are to you in relation to each other. Place the number that corresponds with a suggested topic within as many slices of the pie that conveys how each one matters to you. Only one number should be placed in each slice. You do not need to use all the topics but do fill in all the slices. Feel free to create your own topics and assign them their own number.

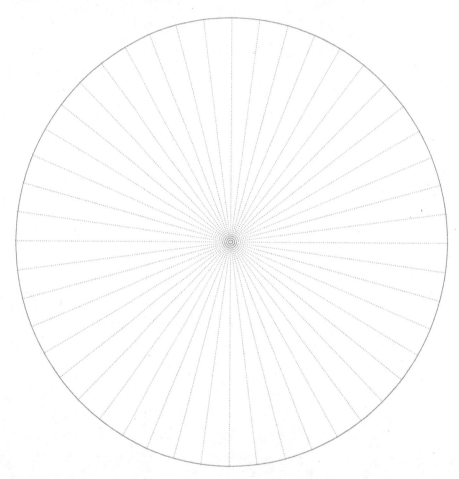

1. Anger/Mad

2. Sadness/Depression

3. Denial/Disbelief

4. Confusion/Baffled

5. Fearful/Scared

6. Loneliness/Isolation

7. A Sense of Loss/Mourning

8. Joyfulness/Happiness

9. Balanced/Steadiness

10. Numbness/Hopelessness

SAMPLER SHARE

Does knowing your partner wants to transition cause any feelings of grief, loss, or feel like a type of death?

I really don't feel that my experience fits into the five stages, maybe because I have known for such a long time, almost 16 years now. I've definitely had some anger, but not about her transitioning but more about specific things or actions that have occurred during the process. My experience has not been the experience of most partners and, perhaps somewhat surprisingly, has not been one where I viewed the transition of my spouse as the death of my husband and the subsequent birth of my wife, but rather it has been more tangential for me. As her transition moves forward, both mentally and physically, I see her growing into her skin and flourishing. I haven't felt a distinct end and a beginning but rather it has been like watching the tide come in.

> AFFIRMATIVE ANECDOTE
>
> *A sea of people,*
> *Which one are you?*
> *I used to know,*
> *I wish I still did!*

Small rolling waves in the early days correlating with those small first steps towards her feminization, things like growing out her hair and wearing her first skirts and dresses. As time has gone on, the waves have gathered strength and power as she has gained self-confidence and poise. I have seen this as she looks at her reflection in the mirror and sees a woman, and every time she is embraced and supported unconditionally by so many of our friends and family. At times the waves have crashed into the shore with a resounding roar, such as the day she got her new birth certificate with her true gender and name. Most days the waves lap at the shore, gently ebbing and flowing, always moving her forward towards her authentic self. Her transition has not felt like a death and re-birth of someone else, but rather it has felt like a force of nature, vast but navigable. This person whom I love unreservedly will now be a happier version of the amazing woman that she already is! She will finally be living her truth.

(Shared by Grace)

COUPLE COMMUNICATION CORNER

When partners or couples speak spontaneously out of anger or fear about the unknown, without thinking it through, they can sometimes regret the way they phrased it. Rehearsing what and how partners may want to ask or discuss with their trans-identified partner, and/or others, can help partners and couples before they actually communicate their thoughts. This gives the non-transitioning partner a moment to reflect and pause before they converse about emotional topics. Partners may choose to practice asking these questions with a trusted friend, family member, spiritual mentor, or therapist first. Explain your thoughts and feelings about these questions to each other. Do you and your trans-identified partner answer these questions in the same way or differently? Discuss your responses to understand how you view them and make time to celebrate all you learn from being willing to communicate with each other.

AFFIRMATIVE ANECDOTE

Minute by minute,
I try to understand.
Day by day,
Acceptance comes!
Season by season,
We celebrate!

---

1. Do you feel angry/mad about any part of the transition process?

The partner's thoughts: The trans person's thoughts:

. . . .

. . . .

. . . .

2. Do you feel sad/depressed about any part of the transition process?

The partner's thoughts: The trans person's thoughts:

. . . .

. . . .

. . . .

3. Do you feel you are in denial/disbelief about any part of the transition process?

The partner's thoughts: The trans person's thoughts:

. . . .

. . . .

. . . .

4. Do you feel confused/baffled about any part of the transition process?

The partner's thoughts: The trans person's thoughts:

. . . .

. . . .

. . . .

5. Do you feel fearful/scared about any part of the transition process?

The partner's thoughts: The trans person's thoughts:

. . . .

. . . .

. . . .

6. Do you feel lonely/isolated about any part of the transition process?

The partner's thoughts: The trans person's thoughts:

. . . .

. . . .

. . . .

7. Do you feel a sense of loss/mourning about any part of the transition process?

The partner's thoughts: The trans person's thoughts:

. . . .

. . . .

. . . .

8. Do you feel joyous/happiness about any part of the transition process?

The partner's thoughts:

· ·

· ·

· ·

The trans person's thoughts:

· ·

· ·

· ·

9. Do you feel in balance/a steadiness about any part of the transition process?

The partner's thoughts:

· ·

· ·

· ·

The trans person's thoughts:

· ·

· ·

· ·

10. Do you feel numb to/hopelessness about any part of the transition process?

The partner's thoughts:

· ·

· ·

· ·

The trans person's thoughts:

· ·

· ·

· ·

Chapter 5
IT CAN BE A FOREIGN LANGUAGE

VITAL VIGNETTE

The transition process involves understanding and relearning many aspects of daily life, which for me began in 2010. One that became essential for me to focus my energy on was the new vocabulary, which I humbly call a foreign language. There are commonly used words and subsets of these words that may be extremely relevant terms when your partner is transitioning. I attended a transgender-focused conference, and everyone was using vocabulary and terms that were foreign to me. I hardly had any idea what anyone was talking about and I felt like an outsider. In one workshop, someone handed out a sheet that contained vocabulary and terms, and I only knew five out of the thirty listed. In all honesty, I recall finding some of the vocabulary and terms offensive, but could acknowledge this was not the case for many people. I grew up in an era when "queer" was still considered a slur; however, now I understand that "queer" has been reclaimed and in this context, it refers to someone who is attracted to multiple genders and/or sexes. Many people were at complete ease with the words and phrases, so I knew it was something I would need to address and comprehend. I remember panicking and wondering how I was going to be able to grasp all of this and with great speed, so that I could feel as if I belonged.

> AFFIRMATIVE ANECDOTE
>
> *So many labels,*
> *Why do*
> *Any of*
> *Them matter?*
> *So many labels,*
> *Why?*
> *Do any of*
> *Them matter?*

Since the time that my partner came out, there has been much more talk of transgender people in the media, and the issues and terminology may be more widely known now. There may be some partners who are very familiar with the vocabulary and terms associated with transitioning, current lingo, and medical terminology, which I was not aware of and had never used before. For those who were or are more aware of these words and terms than I was, this chapter may simply serve as a review and personal reference resource, or it can be used to share with others who you feel may benefit from the information in this section of the workbook.

For those who are where I was then, this is what I did. I consciously began this venture by gathering vocabulary and terms I did not know the meaning of at that time. Out of respect for my partner, I wanted to be able to comprehend and communicate with people in the community and the medical world. I quickly realized it was a full-time job for me.

As an educator and lifelong learner, I searched for a way to achieve my objective, but I had to approach this learning in a way that was comfortable for me. As a result, I decided to apply all the games, methods, and skills I used in the classroom to help me grasp what I wanted to rapidly ingest. In hopes of helping others retain the vocabulary and terms, included in this chapter are the games and exercises I created for you to play and try as a tool to assist you in this process. If games are not your thing or if this seems too juvenile to you, I respect that and completely grasp why you may skip them. For those of you who love games and learn well from them, enjoy!

Since the list is truly extensive and continuously evolving, I am incorporating blank templates for you and suggest that you can refurbish the templates with words or terms that apply to your needs. I have also included basic directions to help guide you in playing and using the games and exercises. Again, please feel free to alter or change any method or suggestion to suit your needs, since the ultimate goal is to learn the vocabulary and terms.

You can use most of the games and exercises on your own, but some can be played with others. Using the tools can create a celebratory environment with family members or friends who want to learn the words and vocabulary, while also lending their support. The games and exercises are often used as a starting point to begin a dialogue or as a conversation piece. They can also be used to help educate everyone to grasp the common language, which is filled with valuable vocabulary and terms.

Through a fun and light-hearted gathering, partners, family members, and friends can form an encouraging team who can be the first line of support that a partner or couple may desperately need. It is also important to be patient with yourself when learning these terms and vocabulary. Besides much repetition and review, when time permits, I found that verbally using them periodically could be the best method. Just like any other language, the more you use the vocabulary and terms, the better you retain it.

Before they begin to learn the vocabulary and terms, many people may choose to review the terms first to evaluate which vocabulary and terms they know. Once the unknown words are identified and then learned, couples and/or individuals can personally assess which vocabulary or terms relate to or effectively represent them. This self-identification can be extremely powerful and enlightening. Using this personalized knowledge often helps when partners or couples are communicating with family members, friends, therapists, the medical community, and one another.

It is critical to note that this information is not meant to restrict, permanently label, or box anyone into something that does not feel right to them. Choosing language that feels right and appropriate is a private and personal choice, which can be always evolving and should never be used in a negative way against anyone, for any reason. The applicable vocabulary and terms must only be decided upon by the individuals who choose to use them for themselves, for whatever reason they deem relevant, and for nothing more. The sole purpose of these games and exercises is to create a common language in order to communicate and to educate in a gentle manner.

GRAPHICS AND GAMES GALORE

Splash

Can you jot down all of the vocabulary you can think of that is related to the transition process? By creatively splashing words and/or short phrases, quickly attempt to express your answers randomly with as many responses as possible scattered on the paper.

VOCABULARY MATCH QUESTIONNAIRE PRE-TEST

AFFIRMATIVE ANECDOTE

Racing, racing,
In my head.
Facing, facing,
Tons unsaid.
Bracing, bracing,
What's ahead?

It is as important to know what you know and then use that knowledge as a starting point to grow. After taking the pre-test, you will be able to understand what you still need to learn. The tools in this chapter should help you and enable you to internalize the vocabulary.

Match the vocabulary (the numbers) with the definitions (the letters) by drawing a line from a number to a letter, as a pre-test to see which words or terms you already know, and which words are new to you. Each number and letter should only be used once. What were the results? The answer keys are provided in the Answer Key Section in Chapter 15. I suggest you check your answers when you have taken the pre-test to see how well you did. Feel free to repeat this process at a later time; you may choose to use this activity to assess your progress by using this game as a post-test.

Matching Pre-Test #1

1. agender	A. Someone who does not feel sexual attraction to other people.
2. androgynous	B. A person who is attracted to both masculine and feminine people.
3. asexual	C. A feeling of enjoyment while knowing your partner is experiencing joy, usually when they are romantically or sexually involved with another person. Often used as a contrast to jealousy.
4. bigender	D. Someone who does not identify with or match any gender.
5. bilateral mastectomy	E. The belief that there are only two genders, male and female.
6. binary	F. A surgical procedure that permanently changes the genitals or internal reproductive organs.
7. binding	G. Someone who possesses both male and female characteristics.
8. bisexual	H. A surgical procedure that removes breast tissue from both sides of the chest and is part of the construction of a male chest for trans masculine people.
9. bottom surgery	I. Someone whose gender assigned at birth and gender identity are aligned.
10. cisgender	J. The advantages granted by society to people whose gender aligns with the gender assigned at birth.
11. cisgender privilege	K. Someone who experiences themselves as both male and female.
12. compersion	L. A practice of using material or clothing to constrict the breasts that enables a person to flatten their chest.

Retake this pre-test as a post-test to assess your personal progress and knowledge.

Match the vocabulary (the numbers) with the definitions (the letters) by drawing a line from a number to a letter, as a pre-test to see which words or terms you already know, and which words are new to you. Each number and letter should only be used once. What were the results? The answer keys are provided in the Answer Key Section in Chapter 15. I suggest you check your answers when you have taken the pre-test to see how well you did. Feel free to repeat this process at a later time; you may choose to use this activity to assess your progress by using this game as a post-test.

Matching Pre-Test #2

1. crossdresser	A. Surgery that brings the individual's body into alignment with their gender identity.
2. drag	B. A person who now identifies as male gendered but was assigned a female gender at birth.
3. facial feminization surgery	C. A gender identity and expression that encompasses a variety of aspects related to femininity, masculinity, and androgyny.
4. FTM/F2M/MTM/ female-to-male	D. One's internal sense of being masculine-identified, feminine-identified, neither, or both.
5. gatekeeper	E. The legal designation of one's gender on official documentation or records.
6. gender	F. The aspects that culture, society, and the individual deem as feminine, masculine, and androgynous.
7. gender-affirming surgery	G. Crossdressing for the purpose of performance and/or show.
8. gender dysphoria	H. A mental health or medical professional who controls access to medical treatment such as hormones and surgery.
9. gender expression	I. It is the manner in which a person demonstrates their masculinity and/or femininity that can include clothing, body, behavior, speech, gestures, and other forms of appearance.
10. gender fluid	J. A person who wears clothing and/or make-up of the gender other than they were assigned at birth.
11. gender identity	K. The uncomfortable and sometimes depressing feelings that occur in people when aspects of their body and behavior are not congruent with their gender identity.
12. gender markers	L. A variety of plastic surgery procedures to create a more feminine appearance to the features of the face.

Retake this pre-test as a post-test to assess your personal progress and knowledge.

Match the vocabulary (the numbers) with the definitions (the letters) by drawing a line from a number to a letter, as a pre-test to see which words or terms you already know, and which words are new to you. Each number and letter should only be used once. What were the results? The answer keys are provided in the Answer Key Section in Chapter 15. I suggest you check your answers when you have taken the pre-test to see how well you did. Feel free to repeat this process at a later time; you may choose to use this activity to assess your progress by using this game as a post-test.

Matching Pre-Test #3

1. gender nonconforming	A. A phrase for people who do not meet common gender norms.
2. genderqueer	B. A gender-neutral pronoun sometimes used to replace "her" and "him."
3. hir	C. The bottom surgery for a trans woman that involves the removal of testicles.
4. intersex	D. A type of relationship where a person is sexually and/or romantically involved with only one person at a time.
5. LGBTQQIA+ (also LGBTQ and LGBTQ+)	E. A person who now identifies as female gendered but was assigned a male gender at birth.
6. metoidioplasty	F. An all-encompassing abbreviation which stands for lesbian, gay, bisexual, transgender, queer, questioning, intersex, allies, plus others.
7. misogyny	G. Someone who identifies outside of the gender binary.
8. monogamous	H. The act of disclosing someone's sexuality and/or gender identity without their knowledge and/or permission.
9. MTF/M2F/FTF/male-to-female	I. A group of medical conditions where someone can be born with ambiguous genitalia and internal sex organs or chromosomal differences that are not clearly male or female.
10. nonbinary	J. A disdain, hatred, or mistrust of all people female and feminine.
11. orchiectomy	K. A gender-affirming bottom surgery for trans men which releases the micro phallus and can include urethra lengthening.
12. outing	L. A gender that is not exclusively male or exclusively female.

Retake this pre-test as a post-test to assess your personal progress and knowledge.

Match the vocabulary (the numbers) with the definitions (the letters) by drawing a line from a number to a letter, as a pre-test to see which words or terms you already know, and which words are new to you. Each number and letter should only be used once. What were the results? The answer keys are provided in the Answer Key Section in Chapter 15. I suggest you check your answers when you have taken the pre-test to see how well you did. Feel free to repeat this process at a later time; you may choose to use this activity to assess your progress by using this game as a post-test.

Matching Pre-Test #4

1. packing	A. The ability for a person to be read as their affirmed gender by those who are unaware that the individual's identity is transgender.
2. pan hysterectomy	B. The practice of others using or referring to a person in the way an individual desires to be addressed, when pronouns are involved.
3. pansexual	C. A word used to describe a person who is in a sexual and/or romantic relationship with someone.
4. partner	D. The act of a person who is attempting to figure out their own sexuality and/or gender.
5. passing	E. A surgical procedure that creates a scrotal sac and can include testicular implants.
6. phalloplasty	F. A gender-neutral pronoun sometimes used to replace "she" and "he."
7. polyamorous	G. The use of prosthetics and/or other materials to enable an individual to possess the appearance and feeling of having a penis and testicles.
8. preferred gender pronouns	H. A type of bottom surgery that usually includes removing the uterus, ovaries, and fallopian tubes and which could involve the removal of the cervix.
9. questioning	I. The pattern of thoughts, feelings, and arousal that determine sexual preferences.
10. scrotoplasty	J. A type of relationship where a person is sexually and/or romantically involved with more than one person at the same time.
11. sexuality	K. Someone who is attracted to people of various genders.
12. sie/ze	L. A type of bottom surgery that entails the construction of a penis and can include the construction of testicles and the implant of an erection device.

Retake this pre-test as a post-test to assess your personal progress and knowledge.

Match the vocabulary (the numbers) with the definitions (the letters) by drawing a line from a number to a letter, as a pre-test to see which words or terms you already know, and which words are new to you. Each number and letter should only be used once. What were the results? The answer keys are provided in the Answer Key Section in Chapter 15. I suggest you check your answers when you have taken the pre-test to see how well you did. Feel free to repeat this process at a later time; you may choose to use this activity to assess your progress by using this game as a post-test.

Matching Pre-Test #5

1. stealth	A. A word that may also be used as a gender-neutral pronoun to describe a single individual.
2. they	B. A person who is in a relationship with someone who identifies as transgender or gender nonconforming.
3. top surgery	C. An overarching word which can be used for people whose gender expression and/or gender identity does not align with their sex assigned at birth.
4. tracheal shave	D. Julia Serano, an activist for the trans community, coined this word to describe a form of misogyny that is focused towards trans women.
5. transgender/trans-identified	E. The surgical construction of a vagina for both transgender and cisgender women.
6. transitioning	F. A word used for a transgender person who chooses to keep their trans status private.
7. trans misogyny	G. A surgical procedure made to create a masculine-appearing chest.
8. trans partner	H. An Indigenous North American identity embraced by some individuals who incorporate a variety of gender roles, identities, and expressions by embodying both masculine and feminine spirits and traits.
9. transphobia	I. The social and medical actions a person takes to explore and/or affirm their gender identity.
10. transsexual	J. Prejudice, fear, disdain, or discrimination in respect of gender nonconforming and transgender people.
11. two-spirit	K. A surgical procedure that reduces the thyroid cartilage, which makes up the Adam's apple.
12. vaginoplasty	L. A person who identifies within the gender binary (either male or female) and may have medical procedures to bring their body in line with their identity. However, not all transgender people who have medical transitions identify as transsexual.

Retake this pre-test as a post-test to assess your personal progress and knowledge.

REFLECTIVE RESPONSES

1. How do you prefer to learn all the words/terms?

    ....

    ....

    ....

2. Which words/terms describe or apply to you now?

    ....

    ....

    ....

3. Which words/terms describe or apply to your partner now?

    ....

    ....

    ....

4. Which words/terms describe or apply to you as a couple now, and how will you decide this?

    ....

    ....

    ....

5. Which words/terms, if any, confuse or upset you and why?

    ....

    ....

    ....

6. Which words/terms, if any, do you want to share with others?

. . . .

. . . .

. . . .

7. How will you decide who you will share which words and/or terms with, and when?

. . . .

. . . .

. . . .

8. Are there any words/terms that will be shifting as the transition evolves? If so, which ones and what is the tentative timing of the shift?

. . . .

. . . .

. . . .

9. Are there any particular words/terms your partner and/or you prefer never to use in reference to either one of you? If so, which ones and why?

. . . .

. . . .

. . . .

10. Which words/terms are/were completely new to you?

. . . .

. . . .

. . . .

VOCABULARY FOR ALL GAMES

agender	crossdresser	gender nonconforming	packing	stealth
androgynous	drag	genderqueer	pan hysterectomy	they
asexual	facial feminization surgery	hir	pansexual	top surgery
bigender	FTM/MTM/F2M	intersex	partner	tracheal shave
bilateral mastectomy	gatekeeper(s)	LGBTQ/LGBTQ+/LGBTQQIA+	passing	trans-identified/transgender
binary	gender	metoidioplasty	phalloplasty	transitioning
binding	gender-affirming surgery	misogyny	polyamorous	transmisogyny
bisexual	gender dysphoria	monogamous	preferred gender pronouns	trans partner
bottom surgery	gender expression	MTF/FTF/M2F	questioning	transphobia
cisgender	gender fluid	nonbinary	scrotoplasty	transsexual
cisgender privilege	gender identity	orchiectomy	sexuality	two-spirit
compersion	gender markers	outing	sie/ze	vaginoplasty

How many of the words above can you find in the word search on the next page? Once found, circle or highlight them! (HINT: The following vocabulary words do not appear in the Word Search: LGBTQ+, LGBTQQIA+, F2M, & M2F. Can you find the bonus word: queer!)

Word search

```
S T H E Y D G N I M R O F N O C N O N R E D N E G
M T M S U O N Y G O R D N A G A T E K E E P E R S
S G E N D E R M A R K E R S U O P R E D N E G I Y
N K W T I T W O S P I R I T G N I T U O Y S A C N
U G A R D V T T R A C H E A L S H A V E R B D I Y
O M P A X C R C Q T B G L T O P S U R G E R Y S G
N E A N G J A E F S U O R O M A Y L O P G G P G O
O T N S N R N T R E B I N D I N G R L H R A Y E S
R O H I I Y S S E X S G N M X S V A K A U I T N I
P I Y D N T M A D U Y Q H T A E U N C L S R I D M
R D S E O S I M N A D U E F H X G T J L M O T E V
E I T N I A S L E L K E L M E U B R P O O H N R A
D O E T T L O A G I O E Q S R A I A T P T P E P G
N P R I I P G R S T U R A V X L G P C L T S D R I
E L E F S O Y E N Y I N T E R S E X R A O Y I I N
G A C I N T N T A Y A O Z B R Z N C O S B D R V O
D S T E A O Y A R R E N T R A P D V S T W R E I P
E T O D R R M L T N P F H T L A E T S Y A E D L L
R Y M O T C E I H C R O B I N A R Y D I O D N E A
R G Y C I S P B K G L R E D N E G A R Q E N E G S
E Y R E G R U S G N I M R I F F A R E D N E G E T
F A C I A L F E M I N I Z A T I O N S U R G E R Y
E F T M S U O M A G O N O M F N O I S R E P M O C
R R E E U Q R E D N E G Y T C I S G E N D E R Z W
P A S S I N G R T U I E M D I U L F R E D N E G O
G N I K C A P G E N D E R E X P R E S S I O N Z G
P L A U X E S S N A R T A S D F Y R A N I B N O N
E J Z B I S E X U A L R E N T R A P S N A R T J M
Z G N I N O I T S E U Q X T R A N S P H O B I A Z
```

The answer key for the word search is in the Answer Key Section in Chapter 15. Good luck and have fun!

DESERVING DE-STRESS DELIGHTS

Date with Yourself

Make a date with yourself, which is what I fondly coined "Getting to Know Yourself." Making a date with yourself can be quite a liberating and exhilarating experience but also feel strange and scary. Taking time to reflect and rejuvenate from all the decisions and questions that require your energy can be draining. Being the type of person who craves the company of others, it surprised me when I suddenly had the desire to spend periods of time by myself. Perhaps it was the searching for answers or the overwhelming thoughts, but I remember thinking my transgender partner seemed to know what they wanted and needed, yet I was so unsure of what I wanted or needed.

> AFFIRMATIVE ANECDOTE
>
> *My senses*
> *Are overwhelmed,*
> *Shock has set in,*
> *Fear is loud,*
> *Concerns abundant.*
> *How did I not know?*
> *Now I do!*
> *What next?*

Friends and family would often express their opinions of what they would do if this was their journey. They were all well intentioned, but in the end it was me who had to explore my options. Out of this unknowing, I decided that I would make dates with myself and try to figure out what was correct for me. I made a list of the things I enjoyed and took myself to them. I wrote in solitude or reflected as I experienced the event or activity. Little by little, I was able to look within myself and find the answers and results that worked for me.

Many people have shared a similar need that I experienced. Some people took mini-vacations alone, while others told those in their lives that they were away on vacation, but in actuality stayed home and would not respond to any outside communication. Those with money obstacles searched for free events that were happening in their area. One person shared that they went alone for a quiet picnic lunch by a lake for several hours. All of these self-dates are offered only as examples of how beautiful the experience can be to explore your own truth through "Getting to Know Yourself" dates. I suggest you find what you love to do and then discover those hidden spaces and bravely unwrap them. As you date yourself from time to time, you can find exactly what you seek. The answers will come, because they are all inside of you right now!

Journal your reaction to this Deserving De-Stress Delight.

....

....

....

....

....

....

....

....

....

....

....

....

....

....

....

....

....

....

....

....

....

....

GRAPHICS AND GAMES GALORE

ABC Game

Write all or some of the vocabulary words on index cards. Use the vocabulary listed in the chart on page 99. Mix the vocabulary words up and place them in alphabetical order. This will help you become more familiar with the words.

Memory Game

Use the vocabulary listed in the chart on page 99. Then copy and glue/tape the definitions from the glossary in Chapter 15 on to index cards, too. Next, use the 12 Pre-Test game words from #1, #2, #3, #4, or #5 and their matching meanings on index cards to play this game.

Place the 12 words and 12 definitions face down on a flat surface, in no particular order. Player one turns over two cards and reads them aloud. If they match, then keep the matching pair and go again. If they do not match, turn them back over and the next player turns two cards over and reads them aloud. If they match, then keep the matching pair and go again. If the new cards do not match, turn them back over and the next player turns two cards over and reads them aloud. This process continues until all pairs are matched. The player with the most pairs wins the game. An alternative is to play this game with two sets of vocabulary words with no definitions. You may elect to play with only the vocabulary you do not know, in order to master them and/or use any combination of words and definitions provided on pages 104–111.

Solo Memory Game

If playing alone, line any 12 vocabulary words face up on a flat surface and hold their matching definition cards in your hand. Turn over one index definition card at a time and place it under the corresponding vocabulary word until all words have a match.

Memory Cards

agender	androgynous	asexual	bigender
bilateral mastectomy	Someone who does not identify with or match any gender.	Someone who possesses both male and female characteristics.	Someone who does not feel sexual attraction to other people.
Someone who experiences themselves as both male and female.	A surgical procedure that removes breast tissue from both sides of the chest and is part of the construction of a male chest for trans masculine people.	binary	binding
bisexual (bi)	bottom surgery	cisgender	The belief that there are only two genders, male and female.

A practice of using material or clothing to constrict the breasts that enables a person to flatten their chest.

A person who is attracted to both masculine and feminine people.

A surgical procedure that permanently changes the genitals or internal reproductive organs.

Someone whose gender assigned at birth and gender identity are aligned.

cisgender privilege

compersion

crossdresser

drag

facial feminization surgery

The advantages granted by society to people whose gender aligns with the one assigned at birth.

A feeling of enjoyment while knowing your partner is experiencing joy, usually when they are romantically or sexually involved with another person; often used as a contrast to jealousy.

A person who wears clothing and/or make-up of the gender other than the one they were assigned at birth.

Crossdressing for the purpose of performance and/or show.

A variety of plastic surgery procedures made to create a more feminine appearance to the features of the face.

FTM/MTM/F2M female-to-male

gatekeeper

gender	gender-affirming surgery	gender dysphoria	A person who now identifies as male gendered but was assigned a female gender at birth.
Mental health or medical professional who controls access to medical treatment such as hormones and surgery.	The aspects that culture, society, and the individual deem as feminine, masculine, and androgynous.	Surgeries that bring the individual's body into alignment with their gender identity.	The uncomfortable and sometimes depressing feelings that occur in people when aspects of their body and behavior are not congruent with their gender identity.
gender expression	gender fluid	gender identity	gender markers
gender nonconforming	The manner in which a person demonstrates their masculinity and/or femininity, which can include clothing, body, behavior, speech, gestures, and other forms of appearance.	A gender identity and expression that encompasses a variety of aspects related to femininity, masculinity, and androgyny.	One's internal sense of being masculine-identified, feminine-identified, neither, or both.

The legal designation of one's gender on official documentation or records.	Someone who does not meet common gender norms.	genderqueer	hir
intersex	LGBTQQIA+ (and LGBTQ/LGBTQ+)	metoidioplasty	Someone who identifies outside of the gender binary.
A gender-neutral pronoun sometimes used to replace "her" and "him".	A group of medical conditions where someone can be born with ambiguous genitalia and internal sex organs or chromosomal differences that are not clearly male or female.	An all-encompassing abbreviation which stands for lesbian, gay, bisexual, transgender, queer, questioning, intersex, allies, plus others.	A type of gender-affirming bottom surgery for trans men that releases the micro phallus and can include urethra lengthening.
misogyny	monogamous	MTF/FTF/M2F male-to-female	nonbinary

orchiectomy	A disdain, hatred, or mistrust of all people female and feminine.	A type of relationship where a person is sexually and/or romantically involved with only one person at a time.	A person who now identifies as female gendered but was assigned a male gender at birth.
A gender that is not exclusively male or exclusively female.	Bottom surgery for trans women that involves the removal of testicles.	outing	packing
pan hysterectomy	pansexual	partner	The act of disclosing someone's sexuality and/or gender identity without their knowledge and/or permission.
The use of prosthetics and/or other materials to enable an individual to possess the appearance and feeling of having a penis and testicles.	A type of bottom surgery which usually includes removing the uterus, ovaries, and fallopian tubes and that could involve the removal of the cervix.	Someone who is attracted to people of various genders.	A word used to describe a person who is in a sexual and/or romantic relationship with someone.

passing	phalloplasty	polyamorous	preferred gender pronouns
queer	questioning	The ability for a person to be read as their affirmed gender by those who are unaware the individual's identity is transgender.	A type of bottom surgery that entails the construction of a penis and can include the construction of testicles and the implant of an erection device.
A type of relationship where a person is sexually and/or romantically involved with more than one person at the same time.	The practice of others using or referring to a person in the way an individual desires to be addressed, when pronouns are involved.	The act of a person who is attempting to figure out their own sexuality and/or gender.	scrotoplasty
sexuality	sie/ze	stealth	they

A surgical procedure that creates a scrotal sac and can include testicular implants.	The pattern of thoughts, feelings, and arousal that determine sexual preferences.	A gender-neutral pronoun sometimes used to replace "she" and "he".	A transgender person who chooses to keep their trans status private.
This word may also be used as a gender-neutral pronoun to describe a single individual.	top surgery	tracheal shave	trans-identified and transgender
transitioning	transmisogyny	A surgical procedure to create a masculine-appearing chest.	A surgical procedure that reduces the thyroid cartilage, which makes up the Adam's apple.
Someone whose gender expression and/or gender identity does not align with their sex assigned at birth.	The social and medical actions a person takes to explore and/or affirm their gender identity.	Julia Serano, an activist for the trans community, coined this word to describe a form of misogyny that is focused towards trans women.	trans partner

transphobia	transsexual	two-spirit	vaginoplasty

A person who is in a relationship with someone who identifies as transgender or gender nonconforming.	Prejudice, fear, disdain, or discrimination in respect of gender nonconforming and transgender people.	A person who identifies within the gender binary (either male or female) and may have medical procedures to bring their body in line with their identity.	An Indigenous North American identity embraced by some individuals who incorporate a variety of gender roles, identities, and expressions by embodying both masculine and feminine spirits and traits.

The surgical construction of a vagina for both transgender and cisgender women.	Someone who is attracted to multiple genders and/or sexes.

Blank Cards

Create your own Memory Cards to add to the ones above. Feel free to make as many copies as you need to help you learn the vocabulary and definitions.

GRAPHICS AND GAMES GALORE

Crossword Puzzle (Definition Hints Below!)

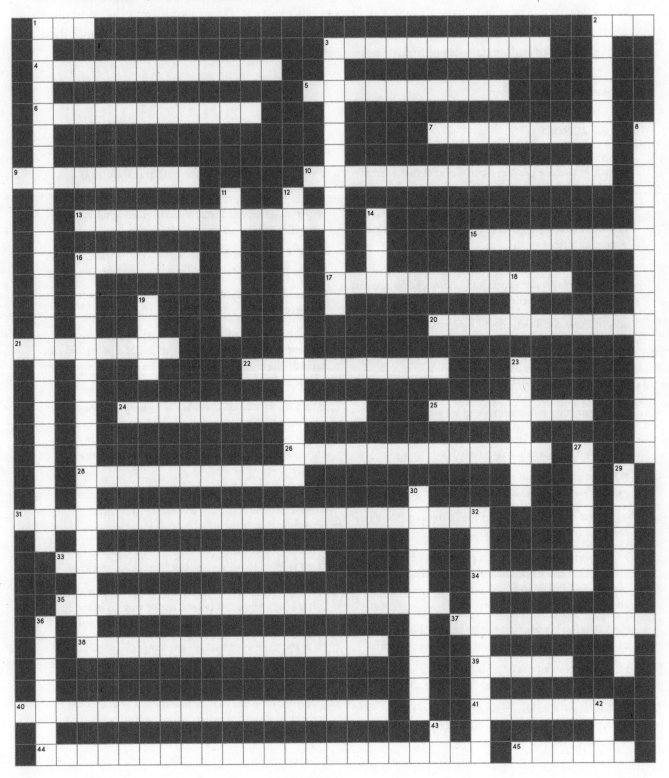

How to Do the Crossword Puzzle

Read the clues that correspond with the "across" and "down" numbers and fill in the puzzle with the answers to the clues listed below. All the answers are words from the vocabulary chart on page 99 above. The answer key is provided in the Answer Key Section in Chapter 15. (These words from the vocabulary chart are *not* in the crossword puzzle: agender, asexual, bottom surgery, identity, gender, gender fluid, pansexual, questioning, trans-identified, trans partner, and two-spirit.)

Crossword Puzzle Clues

Clues: ACROSS

1. A 3-letter abbreviation that means a person who now identifies as male gendered but was assigned a female gender at birth.

2. A 3-letter abbreviation that means a person who now identifies as female gendered but was assigned a male gender at birth.

3. An 11-letter overarching word which can be used for people whose gender expression and/or gender identity does not align with their sex assigned at birth.

4. A 12-letter word that means a person who wears clothing and/or make-up of the gender other than they were assigned at birth.

5. A 10-letter word that means a mental health or medical professional who controls access to medical treatment such as hormones and surgery.

6. An 11-letter word that means someone who possesses both male and female characteristics.

7. A 9-letter word that means a gender that is not exclusively male or exclusively female.

9. A 9-letter word that means the pattern of thoughts, feelings, and arousal that determine sexual preferences.

10. A 15-letter phrase that means a type of bottom surgery that usually includes removing the uterus, ovaries, and fallopian tubes and which could involve the removal of the cervix.

13. A 13-letter phrase that means the legal designation of one's gender on official documentation or records.

15. A 9-letter word that means someone whose gender assigned at birth and gender identity are aligned.

16. A 6-letter word that means the aspects that culture, society, and the individual deem as feminine, masculine, and androgynous.

17. A 12-letter word that means the surgical construction of a vagina for both transgender and cisgender women.

20. An 11-letter word that means someone who identifies outside of the gender binary.

21. An 8-letter word that means someone who experiences themselves as both male and female.

22. A 10-letter phrase that means a surgical procedure made to create a masculine-appearing chest.

24. A 12-letter word that means a type of bottom surgery that entails the construction of a penis and can include the construction of testicles and the implant of an erection device.

25. An 8-letter word that means a group of medical conditions where someone can be born with ambiguous genitalia and internal sex organs or chromosomal differences that are not clearly male or female.

26. A 13-letter word coined by Julia Serano, an activist for the trans community, to describe a form of misogyny that is focused towards trans women.

28. An 11-letter word that means the bottom surgery for trans women that involves the removal of testicles.

31. A 23-letter phrase that means the practice of others using or referring to a person in the way an individual desires to be addressed, when pronouns are involved.

33. A 13-letter word that means the social and medical actions one takes to explore and/or affirm their gender identity.

34. A 6-letter word that means the act of disclosing someone's sexuality and/or gender identity without their knowledge and/or permission.

35. A 19-letter phrase that means a surgical procedure that removes breast tissue from both sides of the chest and is part of the construction of a male chest for trans masculine people.

37. A 10-letter word that means a feeling of enjoyment while knowing your partner is experiencing joy, usually when they are romantically or sexually involved with another person. Often used as a contrast to jealousy.

38. A 15-letter phrase that means the uncomfortable and sometimes depressing feelings that occur in people when aspects of their body and behavior are not congruent with their gender identity.

39. A 5-letter abbreviation which stands for lesbian, gay, bisexual, transgender, and queer.

40. An 18-letter phrase that means the advantages granted by society to people whose gender aligns with the one assigned at birth.

41. A 7-letter word that is used for a transgender person who chooses to keep their trans status private.

44. A 22-letter phrase that means surgery that brings the individual's body into alignment with their gender identity.

45. A 6-letter word that means the belief that there are only two genders, male and female.

Clues: DOWN

1. A 25-letter phrase that means a variety of plastic surgery procedures made to create a more feminine appearance to the features of the face.

2. An 8-letter word that means a disdain, hatred, or mistrust of all female and feminine people.

3. A 13-letter phrase that means a surgical procedure that reduces the thyroid cartilage, which makes up the Adam's apple.

8. A 16-letter phrase that means the manner in which a person demonstrates their masculinity and/or femininity and which can include clothing, body, behavior, speech, gestures, and other forms of appearance.

11. A 7-letter word that means the ability for a person to be read as their affirmed gender by those who are unaware the individual's identity is transgender.

12. A 14-letter word that means a gender-affirming bottom surgery for trans men, which releases the micro phallus and can include lengthening of the urethra.

14. A 4-letter word that means crossdressing for the purpose of performance and/or show.

16. A 19-letter phrase that means people who do not meet common gender norms.

18. A 3-letter gender-neutral pronoun sometimes used to replace "she" and "he."

19. A 4-letter word that may also be used as a gender-neutral pronoun to describe a single individual.

23. A 7-letter word used to describe a person who is in a sexual and/or romantic relationship with someone.

27. A 7-letter word that means a practice of using material or clothing to constrict the breasts that enables a person to flatten their chest.

29. A 10-letter word that means a type of relationship where a person is sexually and/or romantically involved with only one person at a time.

30. An 11-letter word that means a type of relationship where a person is sexually and/or romantically involved with more than one person at the same time.

32. A 12-letter word that means a surgical procedure that creates a scrotal sac and can include testicular implants.

36. A 7-letter word that means the use of prosthetics and/or other materials to enable an individual to possess the appearance and feeling of having a penis and testicles.

42. A 3-letter gender-neutral pronoun sometimes used to replace "her" and "him."

43. A 2-letter gender-neutral pronoun sometimes used to replace "she" and "he."

GRAPHICS AND GAMES GALORE

Bingo Game Directions

All players write in or copy the Memory Cards and place cards of eight vocabulary words in the empty spaces. Place one coin or placeholder in the center of the Bingo Board. The caller, a person who reads the definitions aloud, states the meanings. If the meanings match the definition being read, a player, the one with the Bingo Board below, places a coin or placeholder on the corresponding word. If a player's board contains three placeholders in a row, they are the winner. An alternative is to have the caller state the vocabulary word and the player marks the word on the card. Another option is to have the caller state the vocabulary words and the player marks the definitions in the corresponding eight blank spaces.

> AFFIRMATIVE ANECDOTE
> *Options galore,*
> *Sometimes*
> *Too abundant!*

Supplies: Each player, other than the caller, begins with a Bingo Board and nine coins or other placeholders. You may copy the Bingo Board from the workbook for the sole purpose of playing this game. Suggestion: Feel free to make 6–10 copies of the Bingo Board below!

Bingo Board

	Free Space	

SAMPLER SHARE

How or when did you learn about transgender vocabulary before, during, or after your relationship? Explain how and what you learned.

I began learning while attending an Institute drop-in center program. I was 18–19. I then went to school for LGBT studies. This all predated my relationship.

(Shared by Veronica)

COUPLE COMMUNICATION CORNER

Which games, if any, would you like to invite your trans-identified partner or other friends and/or family to either try alone or play with you?

1.   Pre-Test Vocabulary Match #1 and/or try as a post-test?

   The partner's thoughts: The trans persons's thoughts:

   . . . .

   . . . .

2.   Pre-Test Vocabulary Match #2 and/or try as a post-test?

   The partner's thoughts: The trans persons's thoughts:

   . . . .

3.   Pre-Test Vocabulary Match #3 and/or try as a post-test?

   The partner's thoughts: The trans persons's thoughts:

   . . . .

4.   Pre-Test Vocabulary Match #4 and/or try as a post-test?

   The partner's thoughts: The trans persons's thoughts:

   . . . .

5.   Pre-Test Vocabulary Match #5 and/or try as a post-test?

   The partner's thoughts: The trans persons's thoughts:

   . . . .

6.   Word search?

   The partner's thoughts: The trans persons's thoughts:

   . . . .

7. Crossword?

The partner's thoughts: The trans persons's thoughts:

....

....

8.   Memory Game or Solo Memory Game?

The partner's thoughts: The trans persons's thoughts:

....

9. Bingo?

The partner's thoughts: The trans persons's thoughts:

....

10. ABC Game?

The partner's thoughts: The trans persons's thoughts:

....

Chapter 6

MEDICAL AND SOCIAL OPTIONS: SORTING IT OUT!

VITAL VIGNETTE

The choices connected to medical options are as varied as the people questioning what is correct for them. Will your partner want or need to transition medically and/or socially? If so, how and to what extent will you be involved? Whether this is all extremely new to a partner or not, the decisions can be beyond comprehension for some and very frightening for a variety of reasons. Transitioning without any medical interventions is a real possibility and one that many people can begin or end with, but since this is something that could play an important role in the relationship, communication is critical. Adding hormones to the equation is a layer that can have both a physical and emotional impact on the dynamics of a couple. The sensory changes that can occur are abundant, and many partners, aware of the challenges or not, can find it all overwhelming. Possible changes can affect genitals, skin texture, vocal pitch, personal scent, the gaining or loss of hair in different locations, and mood behaviors. There is no crystal ball that can guarantee the extent and rate of these changes, nor can anyone state exactly how the organs in the body will respond internally. Gathering information from reliable sources, acquiring the advice of medical professionals, and speaking with others who have gone through the hormone process can be the most help.

> AFFIRMATIVE ANECDOTE
>
> *Major surgeries,*
> *Body parts*
> *Come and go.*
> *Powerful hormones,*
> *Body hair*
> *Comes and goes.*
> *Important memories,*
> *Body scents*
> *Come and go.*

Couple all of this with surgery and it can all become too much to grasp, especially if communication is not paramount. For many partners, being included in all aspects of the physical transition can be a lifesaver and a way to bond with the person in transition. Giving value to the non-transitioning partner's voice in the decision making and hearing their concerns is a critical form of respect that must be acknowledged and cannot be underestimated. Once aware of the wants and needs of the transitioning person, the partner may need to take time, before anything physical begins, to figure out what they are comfortable being present for and what they are not. The non-transitioning partner may also require the option of changing their mind, because some things have to be experienced and no one can know how they will feel about a situation until they are going through it.

Some partners are 100% on board; others may need to honor their own timeline, even if it does not match the desires of the person in transition. If these two voices do not align, important conversations will become even more critical. The more transparent and informed a couple is, the better the tools they have to discuss and communicate what each person wants, needs, and can contribute. Simple things like checking in as a medical change occurs may be helpful, as each person expresses how they feel about what is happening physically. Being prepared is also crucial. Surgeries may have complications, hormone levels need monitoring, and finances can be greatly drained. Having multiple plans in place for all the many layers can help in moments of urgency, and having the partner be part of this planning can be invaluable. Partners need to give themselves permission to set boundaries and take the time to understand what is and is not acceptable to them. For some people, their threshold can be very high and what they believe they can participate in may be abundant. For others, however, much or a portion of the medical and/or social transition may be too much, and not participating in certain aspects may be the option that works best for them. Either way, there is no correct-or incorrect way to navigate the transition, and neither partner is at fault. It is as important to know what you cannot handle as it is to know what you can handle. This is why no one can be an island in respect of the medical and/or social aspects of the transition.

Whenever possible, it takes a team effort. Knowing this puts less stress on everyone. In the end, having the medical and/or social transition occur with as much ease and safety as possible is the ultimate goal. Being prepared can look very different in every situation.

When shopping for clothing or getting a haircut, perhaps one of you could visit the clothing store prior to purchasing anything to see if the employees will be respectful. If you find someone who appears to be an ally, remember to note when they work by asking that ahead of time. It can also be advantageous to inquire about specific needs ahead of time, via email or over the phone. It is acceptable to research whether certain conveniences are readily available, such as whether a particular store has the sizes you will need in stock or if the dressing rooms are private. For some people it is empowering to try things on in the store; for others, shopping online is the better fit.

When investigating hormones, understand the possible side effects of different levels of usage and how they will be both monitored and ordered. Knowing the limitations of the hormones for various ages or stages and how to manage them throughout medical interventions, or, for example, what pregnancy options there might be, are major considerations that may need to be addressed in a responsible way. During the interview process with medical doctors or facilities it is recommended that you and/or your partner write down questions prior to meeting with a surgeon. Be certain that both of you have determined and reviewed the questions ahead of time.

It can also be helpful to discuss who will ask which question and who will write down the answers. It is important to find out if the surgeon will welcome the non-transitioning partner into the consultation and examination if you both prefer this courtesy. Find out how the medical professionals' communication will proceed throughout the procedures before, during, and after surgery. Inquire how many surgeries the doctor has done and what types. You can even ask to view photos of past surgeries. Some doctors may share a list of people who have offered to speak with those who have used them for the same type of surgery.

Every single part of sorting out the medical and/or social options is extremely important and should never be taken lightly or as a matter of fact. There are real risks, emotional roller coasters, fearful unknowns, and extremely difficult decisions that can make you feel as if you are drowning. Working as a team, communicating regularly, and creating support teams during this part of the process are the best assurances for success in navigating this stage of the transition. Above all else, be true to yourself and your needs!

GRAPHICS GALORE

Splash

Can you record the medical interventions and social changes that you believe a trans-identified person can consider based on the knowledge you have now? By creatively splashing words and/or short phrases, quickly attempt to express your answers randomly with as many responses as possible scattered on the paper.

GRAPHICS GALORE

T-Chart

How has my knowledge of medical options and/or procedures changed throughout the transition?

These are medical procedures I know about in relation to transition	These are medical procedures I want to know about in relation to transition	These are medical procedures I learned about in relation to transition

REFLECTIVE RESPONSES

> AFFIRMATIVE ANECDOTE
>
> *Who is that talking?*
> *Who am I seeing?*
> *Who am I feeling?*
> *Who am I smelling?*
> *What is your name?*
> *Hello? Ohhh...it's you!*

1. Do you think you will be comfortable being there with your partner if they decide to medically and/or socially transition? If yes, to what extent will you be involved with this aspect of the transition?

....

....

....

2. Does your partner expect or want you to be part of the process?

....

....

....

3. How do you feel about being part of the process or not?

....

....

....

4. Do you feel comfortable with the medical interventions and/or social changes that your trans-identified partner needs to do?

....

....

....

5. What do you think you will do if you do not feel comfortable with the medical interventions and/or social changes?

. . . .

. . . .

. . . .

6. Will you go with your partner to doctor appointments?

. . . .

7. If yes, which doctor appointments will you go to?

. . . .

. . . .

. . . .

8. How will you decide which appointments you will go to and which ones you will not?

. . . .

. . . .

. . . .

9. If not, how do you feel about not going to the doctor appointments?

. . . .

. . . .

. . . .

10. What questions, if any, will you ask the doctors?

. . . .

. . . .

. . . .

11. What questions, if any, will your partner ask?

....

....

....

12. What questions, if any, will you ask together?

....

....

....

13. How do you plan to find out what you will need to know in order to help with the medical post-op caretaking?

....

....

....

14. What is the emergency contact information you will need if something goes wrong?

....

....

....

15. How should things look medically within 24 hours of the surgery?

....

....

....

16. What do you need to look for to know if something is wrong within 24 hours of the surgery?

. . . .

. . . .

. . . .

17. Who will be your support team during the surgical portion of the transition and what does that look like for you?

. . . .

. . . .

. . . .

18. Who will be your support team throughout the recovery period, so you are not/do not feel alone throughout the post-surgery period once you leave the medical facility?

. . . .

. . . .

. . . .

19. If needed, who will relieve you, so you can sleep or eat during the post-surgery period?

. . . .

. . . .

. . . .

20. Could your partner die as a result of the surgery? What are your thoughts about this concern?

. . . .

. . . .

. . . .

21. What are the potential complications? What are your thoughts about these concerns?

....

....

....

22. How will you find out if your medical insurance will pay for the surgery?

....

....

....

23. How will you find out if your medical insurance will pay for the medicine/drugs/hormones?

....

....

....

24. What medical interventions or social changes do you believe you may witness to your partner's body and/or behavior as your partner transitions?

....

....

....

25. Can the medical interventions and/or social changes wait? If so, which changes can wait and which cannot wait according to your trans-identified partner?

....

....

....

GRAPHICS GALORE

Web

What type of medical interventions and/or social changes do you feel are realistic options for your trans-identified partner? (Feel free to incorporate responses from the Splash or not.) If you find it easier, create two different webs, one titled "Medical Interventions" and the other titled "Social Changes."

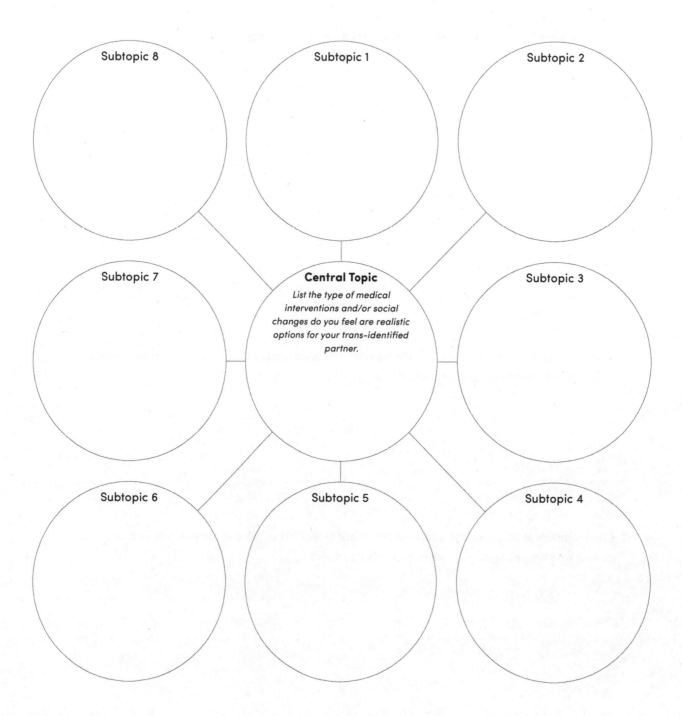

GRAPHICS GALORE

Venn Diagram

Which medical interventions and social changes do you feel or know...

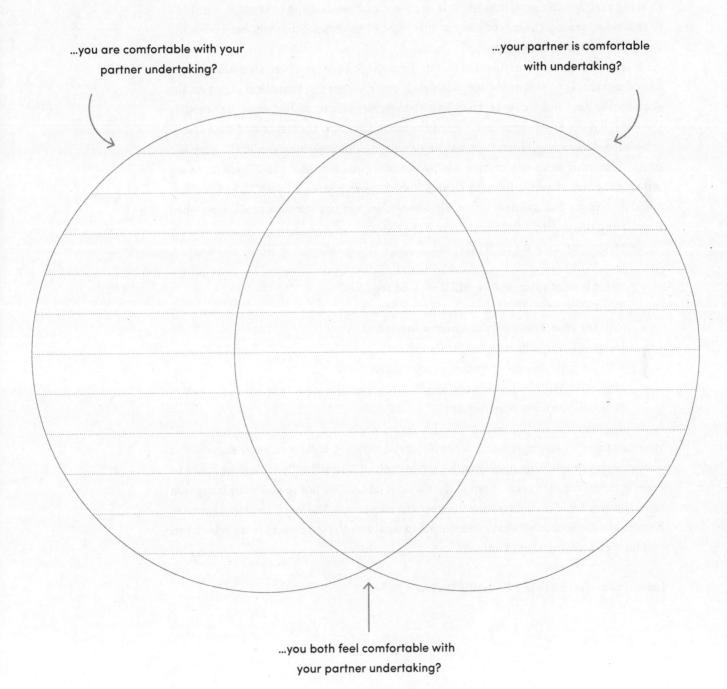

...you are comfortable with your partner undertaking?

...your partner is comfortable with undertaking?

...you both feel comfortable with your partner undertaking?

DESERVING DE-STRESS DELIGHTS

Date Your Partner

Often, a great deal of the time spent with your trans-identified partner can become focused on the transition. Hours after hours can quickly turn into days after days of going to doctors and therapists, filling out forms, changing markers, discussing and sometimes fighting over options, explaining details to others, and researching next steps. While all of this is happening, the two of you can lose sight of the couple that you once were and grow further and further apart.

It is critical to nurture the relationship throughout the transition. One healthy way to address this is to schedule dates with each other, where the transition is put on the shelf for the date. Some days this will be extremely difficult to do, but those are probably the days that the relationship will need it the most. Plan how the structured time can be scheduled. Some couples elect one evening a week to do something you both enjoy as a unit, while other couples alternate having the other one plan the date. These dates are only for the two of you—not with family, friends, work parties, or your kids. The dates could involve sex and intimacy or not. That is another part you may want to discuss when negotiating the ground rules in relation to the dates.

Questions you may ask each other are:

- What type of things do we still like to do together?
- What topics are off the table during the dates?
- Will sex or intimacy play any role in the dates?
- What will our budget be for the dates?
- Will we plan the dates together or separately?
- How often will the dates occur?
- How will the dates be scheduled?

Whether you will stay together as a couple or not may not be known yet. I suggest you continue communicating openly with each other and intentionally create the space to experience dating each other. Even as the changes unfold, try not to allow the transition to be the only topic of conversation between the two of you. The key is to make the dates happen and for both of you to be committed to whatever the ground rules are, which you will have created together as a team.

Journal your reaction to this Deserving De-Stress Delight.

. . . .

. . . .

. . . .

AFFIRMATIVE ANECDOTE

Your amazing chest,
Brave and bold,
Just like you!

GRAPHICS GALORE

Box

What medical changes have you and/or your trans-identified partner researched?

Type of change?	Date it was researched:	Who researched it?	Important information to record?
Type of change?	Date it was researched:	Who researched it?	Important information to record?
Type of change?	Date it was researched:	Who researched it?	Important information to record?
Type of change?	Date it was researched:	Who researched it?	Important information to record?

GRAPHICS GALORE

AFFIRMATIVE ANECDOTE

Your clothes,
Your things!
My clothes,
My things!
No sharing,
For today!

Timeline

Record information pertaining to any medically scheduled interventions your trans-identified partner is planning to undertake. (I wish I had kept a log of all the critical happenings that occurred throughout the transition process, but I did not. I have created a tool that can help you keep a record of these moments as time goes by. Complete the timeline as you find out different, relevant information about the transition. You may need or choose to use this information to discuss these events with a therapist, for your own reference, or for medical needs.)

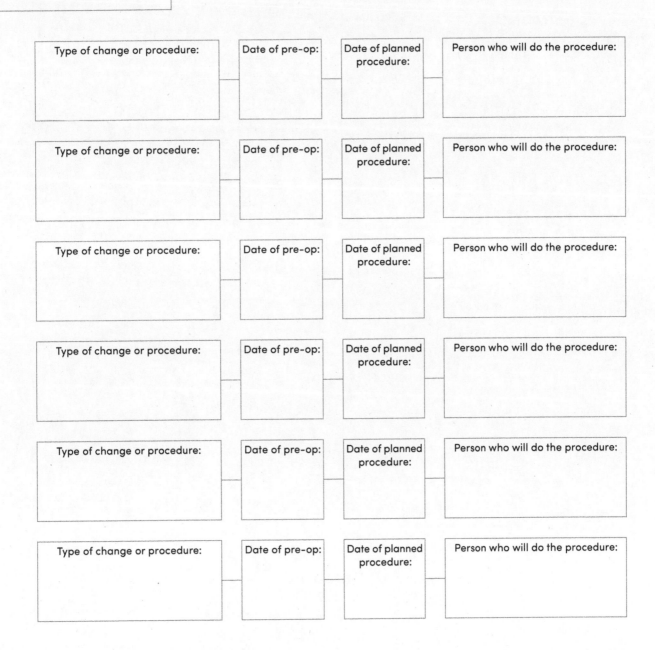

Type of change or procedure:	Date of pre-op:	Date of planned procedure:	Person who will do the procedure:
Type of change or procedure:	Date of pre-op:	Date of planned procedure:	Person who will do the procedure:
Type of change or procedure:	Date of pre-op:	Date of planned procedure:	Person who will do the procedure:
Type of change or procedure:	Date of pre-op:	Date of planned procedure:	Person who will do the procedure:
Type of change or procedure:	Date of pre-op:	Date of planned procedure:	Person who will do the procedure:
Type of change or procedure:	Date of pre-op:	Date of planned procedure:	Person who will do the procedure:

EMPATHY-EMBRACING EXERCISE

For partners to be able to understand, even on some level, the reality of dysphoria that is often part of the transition process, I have posed this exercise question. It enables a partner to look at the parts of their own body that feel wrong and/or that they believe do not belong on their body. By incorporating this exercise, a partner has an opportunity to reflect on what makes them feel uncomfortable with their own body and have at least some level of understanding of the struggle their trans-identified partner often faces on a daily basis.

If you could have surgery or take hormones to physically change or alter one or two things on your body, what would it/they be and why?

....

....

....

....

....

....

....

....

....

....

....

....

....

GRAPHICS GALORE

Bar Graph

To what degree does/did these social and/or medical interventions matter to you? Based on a scale from 1 to 10, with 1 being the lowest and 10 being the highest, color or shade in your response. This visual will help you to see where your greatest concerns lie and can help you communicate this to your trans-identified partner, therapist, spiritual mentor, or for your own personal understanding. The bar graph results may vary as the transition progresses and your thoughts may shift.

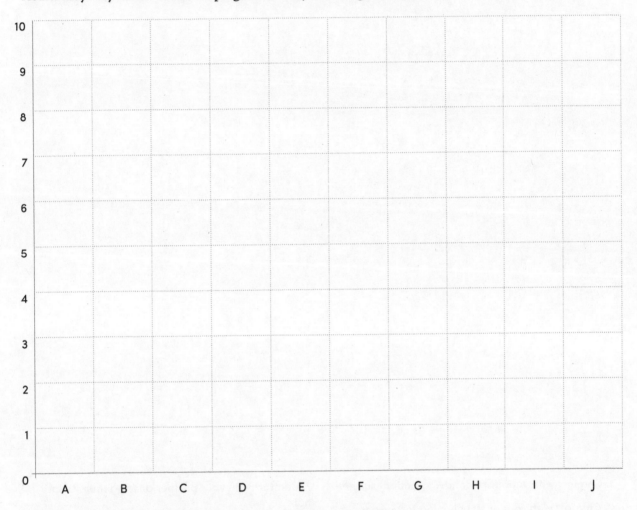

Use these ideas to fill in the bar graph or feel free to create your own!

A. Comfort with your partner having bottom surgery.

B. Comfort with your partner having top surgery.

C. Comfort with your partner taking hormones.

D. Comfort with your partner dressing in a way that is more aligned with their affirmed gender.

E. Comfort with your partner's scent being different than it was before taking hormones.

F. Comfort with your partner's vocal range changing.

G. Comfort with your partner altering their facial hair.

H. Comfort with your partner's facial structure looking differently than before this medical intervention began.

I. Comfort with your partner adding or stopping the use of make-up.

J. Comfort with your partner using accessories differently than before the transition.

GRAPHICS GALORE

Pie Graph

To what degree does/did these social and/or medical interventions matter to you? Decide how important are these topics to you, in relation to each other? Place the number that corresponds with a suggested topic within as many slices of the pie that conveys how each one matters to you. Only one number should be placed in each slice. You do not need to use all the topics but do fill in all the slices. Feel free to create your own topics and assign them their own number.

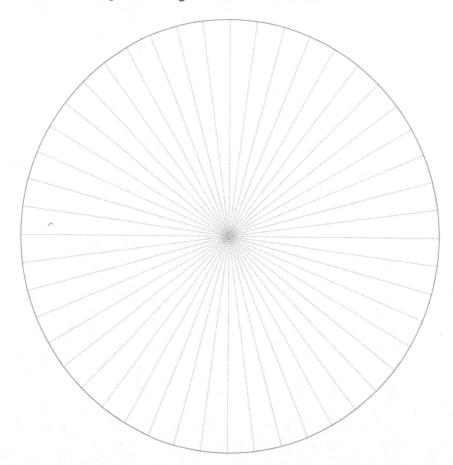

1. Comfort with your partner having bottom surgery.

2. Comfort with your partner having top surgery.

3. Comfort with your partner taking hormones.

4. Comfort with your partner dressing in a way that is more aligned with their affirmed gender.

5. Comfort with your partner's scent being different than it was before taking hormones.

6. Comfort with your partner's vocal range changing.

7. Comfort with your partner altering their facial hair.

8. Comfort with your partner's facial structure looking differently than before this medical intervention began.

9. Comfort with your partner adding or stopping the use of make-up.

10. Comfort with your partner using accessories differently than before the transition.

SAMPLER SHARE

Who will be your support team during the surgical portion of the transition and what does that look like for you?

AFFIRMATIVE ANECDOTE

I know you are in there,
But some days
I just can't find you.

My partner's procedure took longer than is typical for top surgery, as he elected to have male body contouring done at the same time as his periareolar mastectomy. My partner and I planned to arrive together at the hospital early; one friend would join us right before he was taken into surgery, and another close friend planned to arrive about three hours into the surgery. The surgeon who performed his procedures has staff who are well trained in providing trans-affirming care, and this made an enormous difference to both of our experiences. Their LGBTQ Coordinator was a great resource and was available during my partner's surgery to answer questions and update us.

(Shared by Ivy)

What medical interventions and/or social changes do you believe you may witness to your partner's body or behavior as your partner transitions?

We took baby steps at first; starting with laser hair removal, nail polish on her toes, a little dressing up, but only within the walls of our home. She decided on her new name. Then we told a few people. Life continued on over the months but it was hard on both of us. In our own ways, each of us has been and continues to live a double life. It's exhausting. As time has passed, her rate of transition has really ramped up in the past six months. She's amassed quite a nice wardrobe. She's had make-up lessons and grown out her hair. We're going out together in public as two women. She's filed her paperwork to change her gender marker and name on her birth certificate. She's now living essentially full-time as female. We're not all the way out yet, but we'll get there. A few more years and then the surgeries will happen. We have a plan. It's taking extraordinary patience to work through it, far longer than we would like or would have chosen, but that's what circumstances dictate for us right now. We'll get there together in the end, stronger than we've ever been, happier than we've ever been and with a love between us that can conquer anything!

(Shared by Grace)

COUPLE COMMUNICATION CORNER

When partners or couples speak spontaneously out of anger or fear about the unknown, without thinking it through, they can sometimes regret the way they phrased it. Rehearsing what and how partners may want to ask or discuss with their trans-identified partner, and/or others, can help partners and couples before they actually communicate their thoughts. This gives the non-transitioning partner a moment to reflect and pause before they converse about emotional topics. Partners may choose to practice asking these questions with a trusted friend, family member, spiritual mentor, or therapist first.

Explain your thoughts and feelings about these questions to each other. Do you and your trans-identified partner answer these questions in the same way or differently? Discuss your responses to understand how you view them and make time to celebrate all you learn from being willing to communicate with each other.

1. Does your partner plan on discussing the medical interventions and/or social changes they are considering before any of them begin and are they willing to take your feedback into consideration or do they feel this is their decision to make alone without your input?

    The partner's thoughts: The trans persons's thoughts:

    . . . .

    . . . .

    . . . .

2. Does your partner plan on having bottom surgery? If so, in what time frame and what type?

    The partner's thoughts: The trans persons's thoughts:

    . . . .

    . . . .

    . . . .

3. Does your partner plan on having top surgery? If so, in what time frame and what type?

    The partner's thoughts: The trans persons's thoughts:

    . . . .

    . . . .

    . . . .

4. Does your partner plan on beginning hormones? If so, in what time frame and what type?

The partner's thoughts: The trans persons's thoughts:

. . . .

. . . .

. . . .

5. Does your partner plan on dressing differently? If so, in what time frame and how?

The partner's thoughts: The trans persons's thoughts:

. . . .

. . . .

. . . .

AFFIRMATIVE ANECDOTE

You smile,
Now I smile,
You feel complete,
Now, we feel complete!

6. Does your partner plan on having vocal training? If so, in what time frame and what type?

The partner's thoughts: The trans persons's thoughts:

. . . .

. . . .

. . . .

7. Does your partner plan on changing their hairstyle? If so, in what time frame and to what style?

The partner's thoughts: The trans persons's thoughts:

. . . .

. . . .

. . . .

8. Does your partner plan on changing their facial structure? If so, in what time frame and how?

The partner's thoughts:

· ·

· ·

· ·

The trans persons's thoughts:

· ·

· ·

· ·

9. Does your partner plan on using or not using make-up now? If so, in what time frame and how?

The partner's thoughts:

· ·

· ·

· ·

The trans persons's thoughts:

· ·

· ·

· ·

10. Does your partner plan on using or not using accessories now? If so, in what time frame and how?

The partner's thoughts:

· ·

· ·

· ·

The trans persons's thoughts:

· ·

· ·

· ·

Chapter 7

FRIENDS AND FAMILY: WILL THEY STAY, OR WILL THEY GO?

VITAL VIGNETTE

Discussing the transition with families and friends can be one of the most nerve-racking and confrontational parts of the transition itself. It can also be a time when families and friends can easily embrace and celebrate the transition. None of us live in a bubble, and therefore the love, support, and opinions of others can play a vital role in how the process unravels. As you approach coming out to family and friends, pre-planning and discussing the way you and your trans-identified partner elect to share this part of the transition can be critical. That being said, these conversations can also make things much more complicated and frustrating.

We each enter the relationship with our own history and family and/or friend dynamics, which can vary dramatically. Some may carry more baggage, unknowns, and complexities than others. While many families and friends may offer unconditional love regardless of the circumstances, others may not. There are families and friends who offer advice, incorporate religion into the conversation, or may find it difficult to separate how the information you are explaining will affect them and their personal lives. In many experiences, it can be a combination of all these. As hard as it is, the focus must address your needs and wants, too. At times, the support team of your family and friends may be a major safe haven for you, for in most instances you are their priority. Your wellbeing will be first and foremost with them, with your needs being the prize. This is a time where you truly want to evaluate the relationships you have fostered separate and apart from your trans-identified partner. You will have to search for what you value, whom you trust, and why they matter to you. Deciding when, where, why, and with whom you discuss specific topics or feelings will become essential decisions you will need to determine for yourself.

> AFFIRMATIVE ANECDOTE
>
> *Our needs*
> *May require us to say*
> *Goodbye today,*
> *But in time,*
> *Our needs*
> *May say hello again,*
> *In a loving embrace!*

Processing what is best for you as you soul-search and engage in much self-reflection all takes time. You will want to assess each relationship in a way that you may never have evaluated it before. It is a job that can only be done by you and you alone. Start with one person on your list of family or friends and build a team from there. Make the time to figure out what you value in a situation of need or crisis. You will have to find a balance that feels right, safe, and comfortable for you. Begin with one person, by trusting your instinct. Above all else, search for that place within yourself that has the loudest voice leading you to that one person or two who will have your back and best interest at heart.

I found privately answering the questions below were key for me to navigate the next step of creating my support network. You, and perhaps your partner, will need to make time to decide who will be a part of your separate support teams and who will be on the team for both of you as a couple. It is also important to communicate who is off limits for each of you to share with, and what, if anything, is off limits to discuss with anyone. Once these discussions take place, either verbally or written, both you and your partner in transition will have to decide what you can and cannot agree to at this time. I strongly suggest that you do not make any final decisions out of anger or fear. It may all feel urgent and not fast enough, or it may feel as if things are speeding out of control and you do not know how much longer you can last without speaking with a family member or friend. The order in which you share what is going on, and with whom, may require an abundance of energy and much care from both of you. Remember, it is completely acceptable to embrace the support of family and friends, as their support and focus will be primarily on you.

GRAPHICS GALORE

Splash

Can you list all of your closest friends and family members? By creatively splashing words and/or short phrases, quickly attempt to express your answers randomly with as many responses as possible scattered on the paper.

GRAPHICS GALORE

Venn Diagram

Select and record 15–20 of your closest friends or family members. (You can elect to have your trans-identified partner fill out their column or you may choose to do it alone; that choice is yours.)

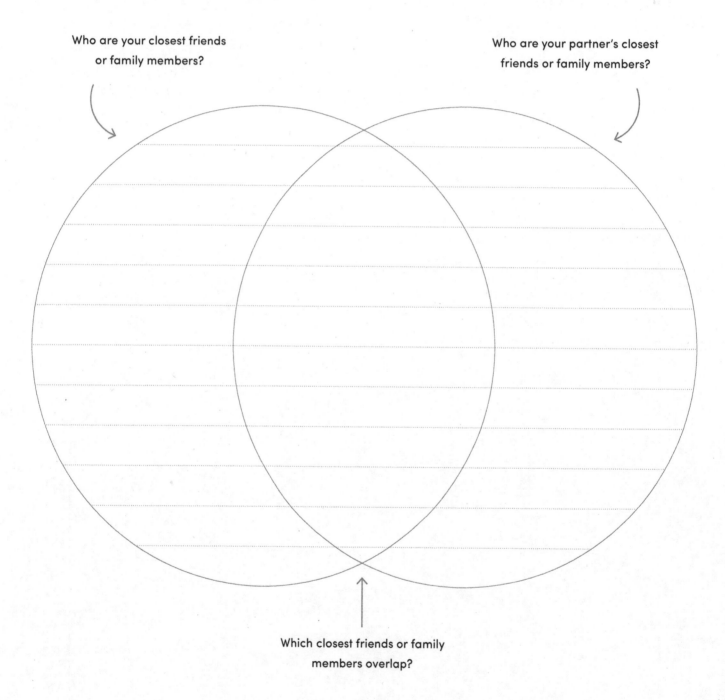

Who are your closest friends or family members?

Who are your partner's closest friends or family members?

Which closest friends or family members overlap?

REFLECTIVE RESPONSES

1. Which family members and friends will you each tell about the transition alone?

   . . . .

   . . . .

   . . . .

2. Which family members and friends will you tell about the transition together?

   . . . .

   . . . .

   . . . .

3. What, where, and how will you both tell family members and friends about the transition?

   . . . .

   . . . .

   . . . .

4. Will your own children, nephews, nieces, or grandchildren need to know about the transition?

   . . . .

   . . . .

   . . . .

5. How do you believe the transition will impact your children, nephews, nieces, or grandchildren?

   . . . .

   . . . .

   . . . .

6.   When necessary, which one of you will set up the appointments with each family member and/or friend?

....

....

....

AFFIRMATIVE ANECDOTE

Will you be there when I am sad?
Will you be there when I am scared?
Will you be there when I am mad?
Will you be someone who cared?

7.   How will you each answer the appropriate and inappropriate questions of others?

....

....

....

8.   Do you want the friends or family members on either of your lists to support you during any medical interventions and/or social changes? How will they know?

....

....

....

9.   Are there people who you absolutely do not want to know about the transition? Does this mean that you cannot tell certain people because of concerns that those unwanted people would find out? Who and why?

....

....

....

10.   If these are different, how will you choose to honor both of your preferences when you share the information about the transition with family and friends?

....

....

11. What thoughts, feelings, fears, or concerns do you both feel you should share with your family members and friends?

....

....

....

12. What thoughts, feelings, fears, or concerns do you both feel you should not share with your family members and friends?

....

....

....

13. Do you know anyone else who has gone through having their partner transition, with whom you feel safe to discuss the transition at this time?

....

....

....

14. Do you prefer to reach out to someone in person, on the phone, by email, or another way?

....

....

....

15. What do you believe is at risk if you tell others?

....

....

....

16. Who do you fear will leave or keep their distance for a while?

....

....

....

17. What ground rules will be agreed upon between your partner and you before, during, or after discussing the transition with a third party? Who will determine and explain the ground rules?

....

....

....

18. Will you have a follow-up meeting with your partner after you meet with a particular person to discuss what transpired? With which person or people? When and where? Is your partner in transition willing to do the same with and for you?

....

....

....

19. Who will be creating and negotiating the ground rules throughout the process in relation to family and friends? What will you/both of you say and not say?

....

....

....

20. Do you feel the dynamics will be different when engaging with each of your friends, families, and other couples, now that your partner is trans-identified? How and why or why not?

....

....

GRAPHICS GALORE

Web
Can you list all of the various groups of important friends and family members you can think of at this moment?

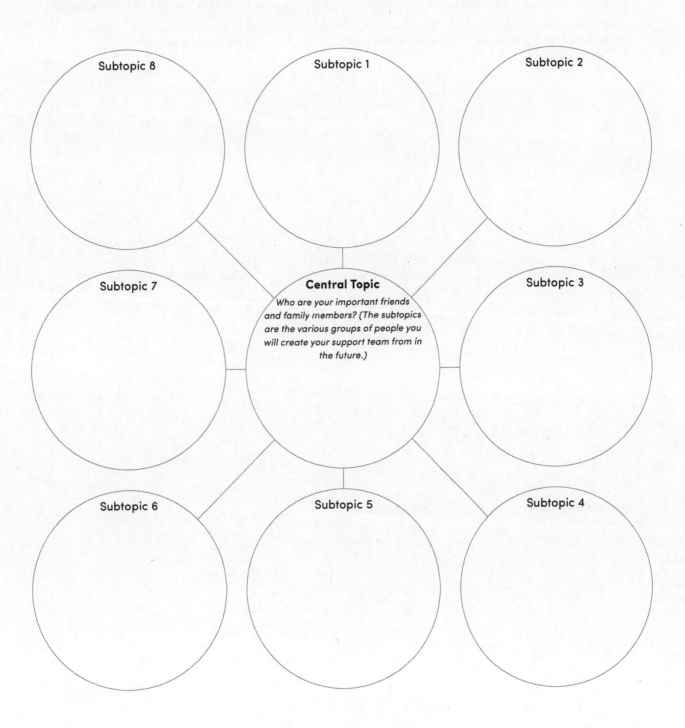

GRAPHICS GALORE

Box

Can you list all of the people in each of these categories: Immediate Family Members, All Cousins, Aunts and/or Uncles, Childhood Friends, College Friends, Inner Circle Friends, Medical Support, etc.? (Feel free to only use your grouping ideas! Use these or base them on your Web categories listed above.)

Immediate Family Members:	All Cousins:	Aunts and/or Uncles:
Childhood Friends:	College Friends:	Inner Circle Friends:
Medical Support:	Your ideas...:	

DESERVING DE-STRESS DELIGHTS

Time with Friends and Family

When partners need support, they often turn to close friends and trusted family members. Arranging a date with friends or family can help you feel less isolated and help you remember you do not have to be alone throughout the transition or even once the focus of the transition is part of the past. Laughing, sharing, and experiencing moments with those who know you well and love you unconditionally can be the best medicine of all. Perhaps you will want to ask them not to discuss the transition sometimes and request that you simply talk about other topics. Yet, other times, the transition may be exactly what you need to focus on. Most supportive people will respect your lead, but the responsibility to communicate your desires is yours. Be direct and let them know. If they are not made aware of your needs, they will be unable to help you as well as they could. Plan activities and celebrations that make you look forward to spending time with them and value what they have to offer in the form of friendship and care. You deserve it!

> AFFIRMATIVE ANECDOTE
>
> *Life has been*
> *So rough,*
> *I want to be*
> *Real tough,*
> *But tell me,*
> *When is enough*
> *ENOUGH???*

Journal your reaction to this Deserving De-Stress Delight.

....

....

....

....

....

....

....

....

....

....

....

....

....

....

....

....

....

....

....

....

....

....

....

....

....

....

....

GRAPHICS GALORE

T-Chart

Who do you want to tell about the transition?

Before the transition begins...	During the transition...	After you consider the transition over...

GRAPHICS GALORE

Timeline

Who will you tell about the transition? Who will tell them? When and where? What will you tell them? (Your response may vary for different people.)

Who will you tell?	Who will tell them?	When will you tell them?	Where will you tell them?	What will you tell them?
Who will you tell?	Who will tell them?	When will you tell them?	Where will you tell them?	What will you tell them?
Who will you tell?	Who will tell them?	When will you tell them?	Where will you tell them?	What will you tell them?
Who will you tell?	Who will tell them?	When will you tell them?	Where will you tell them?	What will you tell them?
Who will you tell?	Who will tell them?	When will you tell them?	Where will you tell them?	What will you tell them?
Who will you tell?	Who will tell them?	When will you tell them?	Where will you tell them?	What will you tell them?
Who will you tell?	Who will tell them?	When will you tell them?	Where will you tell them?	What will you tell them?

EMPATHY-EMBRACING EXERCISE

For many transgender people, the fear of losing the love and/or support of family and friends can prevent them from disclosing their affirmed gender.

Was there ever a time in your life that you feared losing the love and/or support of family and friends if you disclosed something personal about yourself? If so, what was it and did you disclose it? If not, why? If yes, what was the outcome?

AFFIRMATIVE ANECDOTE

Will people talk about me?
Will people laugh at me?
Will people pity me?
Will people leave me?
Will people care about me?
Will people judge me?
Will people fear me?
Will people love me?
People, support me!

GRAPHICS GALORE

Bar Graph

To what degree does/did it matter to you, who and how you tell these people about the transition? Based on a scale from 1 to 10, with 1 being the lowest and 10 being the highest, color or shade in your response. This visual will help you see where your greatest concerns lie and can help you communicate these to your trans-identified partner, therapist, spiritual mentor, or for your own personal understanding. The bar graph results may vary as the transition progresses and your thoughts may shift.

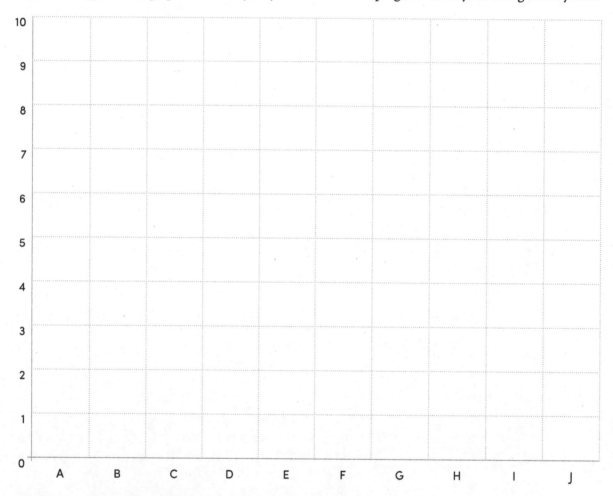

Use these ideas to fill in the bar graph or feel free to create your own!

A. Telling your family about the transition alone.

B. Telling your family about the transition with your partner there.

C. Having your partner tell their family about their transition alone.

D. Having your partner tell their family about their transition with you.

E. Having only one of you tell the children about the transition alone.

F. Having both of you tell the children about the transition together.

G. Telling your friends about the transition alone.

H. Telling your friends about the transition with your partner there.

I. Having your partner tell their friends about the transition alone.

J. Having your partner tell their friends about the transition with you.

GRAPHICS GALORE

Pie Graph

To what degree does/did it matter to you, who and how you tell these people about the transition? Decide how important are these topics to you, in relation to each other? Place the number that corresponds with a suggested topic within as many slices of the pie that conveys how each one matters to you. Only one number should be placed in each slice. You do not need to use all the topics but do fill in all the slices. Feel free to create your own topics and assign them their own number.

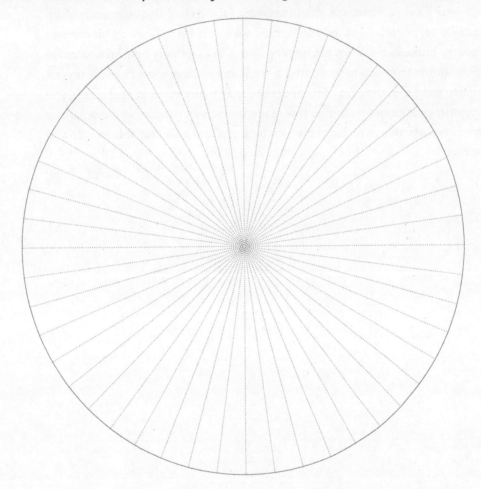

1. Telling your family about the transition alone.

2. Telling your family about the transition with your partner there.

3. Having your partner tell their family about their transition alone.

4. Having your partner tell their family about their transition with you.

5. Having only one of you tell the children about the transition alone.

6. Having both of you tell the children about the transition together.

7. Telling your friends about the transition alone.

8. Telling your friends about the transition with your partner there.

9. Having your partner tell their friends about the transition alone.

10. Having your partner tell their friends about the transition with you.

SAMPLER SHARE

Do you want the friends or family members on either of your lists to support you during any medical interventions and/or social changes? How will they know?

About a month prior to my partner's surgery, he created a spreadsheet that was shared with friends, so they were able to see exactly when help was needed and "sign up" for a visit, make a meal, or help with a specific task. I felt very well supported by friends and the hospital staff, and we were all calm, happy, and excited for him when we were finally able to visit him in recovery. Friends had also generously given us gifts of car service rides and food delivery, so we were able to focus on his comfort and recovery immediately after his surgery. This was extremely helpful and made it possible for me to return to work after a week and to have some time for myself. I was able to leave the house for a few hours each day to run errands, see friends, and go to my own appointments. I think this made recovery better for both my partner and myself as I was able to recharge my own batteries and be better able to help and care for him.

(Shared by Ivy)

COUPLE COMMUNICATION CORNER

When partners or couples speak spontaneously out of anger or fear about the unknown, without thinking it through, they can sometimes regret the way they phrased it. Rehearsing what and how partners may want to ask or discuss with their trans-identified partner, and/or others, can help partners and couples before they actually communicate their thoughts. This gives the non-transitioning partner a moment to reflect and pause before they converse about emotional topics. Partners may choose to practice asking these questions with a trusted friend, family member, spiritual mentor, or therapist first.

Explain your thoughts and feelings about these questions to each other. Do you and your trans-identified partner answer these questions in the same way or differently? Discuss your responses to understand how you view them and make time to celebrate all you learn from being willing to communicate with each other.

1. What will you say or do if a person asks what transitioning is?

    The partner's thoughts: The trans persons's thoughts:

    ....

    ....

    ....

2. What will you say or do if a person asks what the transition process will entail for you?

    The partner's thoughts: The trans persons's thoughts:

    ....

    ....

    ....

AFFIRMATIVE ANECDOTE

It comes
In waves.
Some days I get
Pulled under;
Other days,
I am able
To ride them.
On the
Best of days
I can hear
And see
The beauty!

3. What will you say or do if a person asks what is the correct pronoun/name to use?

    The partner's thoughts: The trans persons's thoughts:

    ....

    ....

    ....

4. What will you say or do if a person asks what they can tell others about the transition?

The partner's thoughts: The trans persons's thoughts:

. . . .

. . . .

. . . .

5. What will you say or do if a person asks how they can help with the transition?

The partner's thoughts: The trans persons's thoughts:

. . . .

. . . .

. . . .

6. What will you say or do if a person asks what type of surgeries will be involved, if any?

The partner's thoughts: The trans persons's thoughts:

. . . .

. . . .

. . . .

7. What will you say or do if a person asks what type of hormones will be involved, if any?

The partner's thoughts: The trans persons's thoughts:

. . . .

. . . .

. . . .

AFFIRMATIVE ANECDOTE

Sometimes friends
Become family.
We welcome
The unconditional
Love.

8. What will you say or do if a person makes inappropriate statements about the transition?

The partner's thoughts: The trans persons's thoughts:

....

....

....

9. What will you say or do if a person asks inappropriate questions about the transition?

The partner's thoughts: The trans persons's thoughts:

....

....

....

10. What will you say or do to explain what are inappropriate questions about the transition?

The partner's thoughts: The trans persons's thoughts:

....

....

....

Chapter 8

WORK: IN OR OUT?

VITAL VIGNETTE

In many instances, the focus of coming out or staying in at work is thought of solely in relation to the person who is in transition. In reality, both the partner and the person in transition need to ask themselves the same question: Should we let people at work know about the transition or not? There are numerous reasons that might support either stance, but it is important that the partner examines their own choices. Similar inquiries come into play when both parties ponder the best and most appropriate choice with respect to outing their partner's transition in the workplace.

AFFIRMATIVE ANECDOTE

Why do you Need to know THAT?

The first question you may want to pose to yourself is: Why would I need or want to come out at work about my partner's transition? For some, it can be a personal choice or preference whether to share your trans-identified partner's transgender status. For others, it could become necessary for several reasons. Is the person who is in transition on your medical insurance? If the answer is yes, and your partner is planning on medically transitioning by using any portion of the medical insurance to pay for it, then it may become necessary for you to consult the human resources department or medical insurance company. This is a very personal decision that you may need to discuss and decide together. It is important to ask a person who knows your rights prior to speaking to anyone in the workplace, so that you have the most accurate legal advice available to you.

It should be noted that many people may not have medical insurance through their employer and therefore cannot address their insurance needs in reference to transition-related care with the help of a human resources liaison or other representative. If you do not have this benefit, you may be able to access medical insurance provided by state or federal programs; therefore, it is important to investigate these options. In some cases, you may be able to speak with someone about these issues over the phone or via email; however, it may be necessary to discuss this topic in person. I would suggest that you investigate if there is a local NGO (non-governmental organization) that could assist you with this process, especially if doing it alone feels too overwhelming or confusing.

I am not a legal expert and I do not know the laws in your country, city, province, state, or town, so with that in mind, before you even take the step of inquiring, you should consult someone who knows your legal rights and the laws that will affect your employment, safety, and wellbeing. These legal rights, insurance policies, and laws could affect you and your coverage. Whether you plan specifically to disclose your partner's plans to transition medically or simply inquire about policies, before you do so, consult a lawyer, agency, or someone you completely trust and know is giving you the most up-to-date advice based on facts and not opinion. Although people often have the best of intentions, unless their information is credible and accurate, I would suggest not taking their advice, since it can possibly affect more areas of your life than you may realize.

Research the legal rights in your city or state that protect you at your place of employment, then decide, as a couple, whether you should share the transition with your employer, based on current material and legal advice. You may also want to inquire about insurance coverage and what the rules are for medical and family leave. Under some circumstances, unions and/or companies have negotiated policies already put in place for time off or leaves of absence. If you are comfortable and it is legally recommended, you can inquire about these options. Asking about your options, in a protected environment, does not mean you must do what they offer or recommend. It is simply fact-finding and nothing more. Knowledge is power, and gathering information to find out what works best for you is key, once you have the facts. If and when you feel comfortable moving forward, based on legal advice, you may opt to speak with your employer, the human resource liaison, benefits manager, or someone who can help navigate the process of using insurance, and then do so. I would suggest getting it all in writing, rather than simply verbal approval over the phone or in person. In addition, every conversation, including the person's name, contact number, and any information they provide, should all be documented in writing. There is space for recording these interactions in this chapter. You will want to record the date, time, phone number, extension, name of the person you spoke to (full name if possible), their position or title, and exactly what was discussed, including your questions and the person's reply.

If you are unclear about their response or unsure of any detail, ask them to rephrase their answer or to repeat what they previously stated. It is typically advisable to ask for a supervisor up front, and continue to follow up with the same person, if possible. This requires keeping track of names and extensions for any supervisors you may speak with and inquiring when they are most often available to answer your questions, and what is the best time to call back. Some insurance companies or doctor's offices will only speak to the person who was transitioning and/or the person who is the primary policyholder. If that is the case and you both have the time, it may be best to call together. When time is a factor, you can divide up the tasks. It is smoother and easier if these decisions and choices are clear before any inquiries are made or any information gathering begins.

You may be surprised to find out how many people have never heard the words "transgender" or "transitioning" when it pertains to health benefits and rights. In some instances, you could be told that there is no policy put in place with respect to this inquiry. In fact, if there is a policy, sometimes the person helping you is unsure of the specifics, so they will have to research it and get back to you. If this happens, record this fact and ask them when they will follow up on this. Then make a phone or in-person appointment to continue the conversation, so you can obtain the critical information you need. Emphasize the urgency of the situation and, whenever possible, ask if there is someone you can speak to at that moment who may be able to assist you better. Before you end your conversation, thank them for all their help in regard to this matter and let them know how much you appreciate all their assistance with this inquiry.

Since this process can be emotionally draining, you may need to take breaks and nurture yourself as much as possible. There can be an extra layer of exhaustion for the partner since, as you may be moving forward with the logistics, you may still feel internally conflicted, confused, scared, and worried. Within this duality you may have to muster up the energy and intellect to defend, explain, pursue, and forge ahead if you have made the commitment to be involved and assist. Moreover, your trans-identified partner may need your assistance, especially if they are covered as a dependent under your insurance policy. The partner can feel unsure of what to say when interacting with a person who is unaware of the meaning of "transgender" or "transitioning." To make things easier, perhaps you can write out a short response ahead of time that reflects your voice, for the sake of efficiency and consistency, so you will know exactly how to reply, should this occur. In addition, I did not want to come across as resentful or as annoyed as I felt about the fact that I had to educate them about what I thought was their responsibility. Once I accepted the fact that educating the public, as well as friends and family, is one more role that the partner will learn comes with the territory of being in a transgender relationship, I became at peace with this reality.

Once you obtain legal advice and acquire the facts about what is covered and what you can afford financially, you may both choose to decide what you will do next.

Questions that may come to mind include:

- Do you both believe it is best and necessary to disclose your trans-identified partner's transgender status to a co-worker, employee, client, boss, and/or employer?

- Do you both want to speak with your employer/boss as a team to show unity?

- Would you prefer to go alone (and why or why not)?

- Do you want to bring along a person who knows your legal rights, such as a union representative, to an in-person appointment?

- How much time will you need off from work based on the information you have obtained? Be prepared to discuss this if necessary, since it is a commonly asked question.

- What documentation will be needed to prove why you are taking time off from work?

- Will the time off affect your employment and/or promotions?

- Do insurance benefits have any exclusions in your policy for transgender care? If so, what are those exclusions, and where are they referred to in the certificate of coverage?

The answers to these questions may influence how you proceed. Take the time to process the replies, either alone or with your partner in transition.

Deciding to tell or not to tell co-workers, employees and/or clients is another choice you should make in consultation with your partner who is transitioning. Some people feel strongly about not outing their transitioning partner without their permission, while others suggest doing what you need to feel whole and at peace. However, I strongly recommend you discuss this with your trans-identified partner and come up with a solution that meets the needs of both of you. Your decision could have consequences that may not be able to be undone. I suggest considering this carefully and then making the choice that works for both of you.

If you are selecting the path to come out at work, perhaps for support or the need to be transparent, carefully choose those who you feel will keep your confidence and respect your relationship needs. As with family members and friends, who may be co-workers, employees, clients, bosses, and/or employers too, start with one and pre-plan where, what, and when you will tell them. Be prepared for any questions they may have and consider how you will address any probing and/or inappropriate questions. Remember that you may be asked to educate and explain many facts and details that are extremely personal and not what you may have anticipated as part of sharing information with a co-worker, employee, client, boss, and/or employer. I suggest setting up boundaries in reference to questions and emphasizing the crucial role of confidentiality. Knowing these guidelines and boundaries for both yourself and your partner could be critical before discussing the transition with anyone in the workplace.

It is important to know that there are many transgender people and partners who want to remain "stealth" or simply not disclose about the transition. This is something that needs to be discussed and thoroughly communicated before you take any steps in relation to work. There are numerous considerations, and each person will have to make this decision for themselves. With whom, what, where, when, why, and how you come out at work, in respect to the transition and based on legal advice, is a decision that requires planning, preparation, information gathering, soul-searching, and crucial communication with everyone involved. There are no rules and very often partners struggle with how to share about the life changes at work while at the same time attempting to comprehend them for themselves. Remember, if you do not know the answer to a question, it is acceptable to let those in the workplace know you need to think about it before you respond!

GRAPHICS GALORE

Splash

Can you list all of your clients, employees, co-workers, bosses, and/or employers? By creatively splashing words and/or short phrases, quickly attempt to express your answers randomly with as many responses as possible scattered on the paper. Suggestion: Do not edit or leave out anyone who comes to mind. Feel free to list people from different departments or from various levels of the organization.

GRAPHICS GALORE

Box

Can you divide up, by categorizing, the clients, employees, co-workers, bosses, and/or employers you have listed from the Splash? (There are optional columns to include input from your partner.)

Those people, from the Splash graphic organizer or not, that you think you feel comfortable telling about the transition.	Those people, from the Splash graphic organizer or not, that you think you do not feel comfortable telling about the transition.	Those people, from the Splash graphic organizer or not, that you are unsure of telling about the transition, but may do so.
Those people, from the Splash graphic organizer or not, that you believe your partner would be comfortable telling about the transition. (Optional)	Those people, from the Splash graphic organizer or not, that you do not believe your partner would be comfortable telling about the transition. (Optional)	Those people, from the Splash graphic organizer or not, that you are unsure your partner would be comfortable telling about the transition. (Optional)

REFLECTIVE RESPONSES

1. With whom will you discuss your legal rights, laws, and employment before you take any action to discuss the transition with anyone at work in regard to insurance, job security, and/or any relevant factors, in order to legally protect both you and your partner in transition?

    . . . .

    . . . .

    . . . .

2. What information did you acquire and what did you decide to do based on these legal facts?

    . . . .

    . . . .

    . . . .

3. If it is legally advisable to inquire, what information did both of you acquire from the human resources liaison, benefits manager, and/or medical insurance company in regard to the rights, policies, and financial options in relation to the transition?

    . . . .

    . . . .

    . . . .

4. Who are the clients, employees, co-workers, bosses, and/or employers you and your partner believe you will each tell separately and/or together about the transition first and why?

    . . . .

    . . . .

    . . . .

5. Where and what will you both tell clients, employees, co-workers, bosses, and/or employers about the transition?

....

....

....

6. If necessary, when will you and/or your partner set up the appointments with each client, employee, co-worker, boss, and/or employer? Will these appointments be done separately or together?

....

....

....

7. What thoughts, feelings, fears, or concerns do you each have about discussing the transition at your respective workplaces?

....

....

....

8. What have you and your partner decided not to share about the transition with any client, employee, co-worker, boss, and/or employer?

....

....

....

9. What is the timeline or order for each co-worker, client, and/or employee?

....

....

....

10. What is the timeline or order for each boss and/or employer?

. . . .

. . . .

. . . .

GRAPHICS GALORE

Web

Who are the people or the resources each of you will consult or have consulted to find out your legal rights, the laws, and/or company policies to protect your employment at your current job?

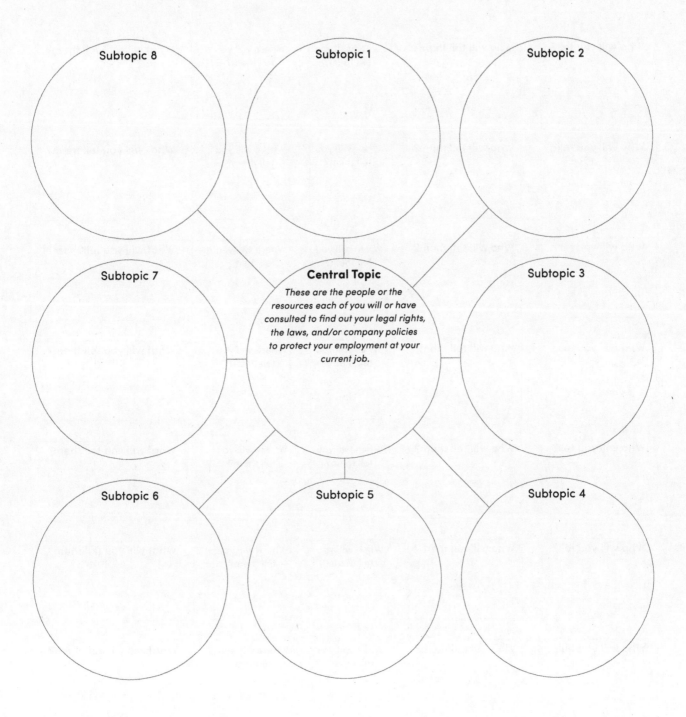

Subtopic 8

Subtopic 1

Subtopic 2

Subtopic 7

Central Topic
These are the people or the resources each of you will or have consulted to find out your legal rights, the laws, and/or company policies to protect your employment at your current job.

Subtopic 3

Subtopic 6

Subtopic 5

Subtopic 4

GRAPHICS GALORE

Timeline

Who will you tell about the transition? Who will tell them? When and where? What will you tell them? Feel free to use the information gathered from the other graphic organizers to fill this in. (Your response may vary for different people.)

Who will you tell?	Who will tell them?	When will you tell them?	Where will you tell them?	What will you tell them?

DESERVING DE-STRESS DELIGHTS

Experience a Sport

Participating in or watching others take part in a sport or physical activity can allow anger or nervous energy to disperse in a healthy way. One bonus of either joining a team sport or cheering for a team is the camaraderie of it all. It offers you the inherent feelings of belonging and being united. The individuals you engage with in this activity can become yet another layer of support for you without them even knowing! They can play the role of a safe haven where your interactions can be entirely on the sport and not the transition. Perhaps they will not even be people who know about or understand anything in relation to the transition. This may become one area in which you can easily separate from all the ups and downs of the transition and simply experience the joy of the sport or physical activity.

> AFFIRMATIVE ANECDOTE
>
> *Why do you think*
> *My sex life,*
> *My spouse's genitalia,*
> *Is any of*
> *Your business?*

For some people, being connected to a physical sport or activity can also provide a level of meditation that may have a calming or comforting effect on their body and mind.

Journal your reaction to this Deserving De-Stress Delight.

....

....

....

....

....

....

....

....

....

....

....

....

....

....

....

....

....

....

....

....

....

....

....

....

....

....

GRAPHICS GALORE

T-Chart

What are the legal rights, company policies, and laws for the area you and your partner in transition reside in with relation to protection of employment and/or medical insurance coverage? (Complete this graphic organizer based on legal advice, any other credible sources, and/or research you acquire.) Be sure to state the legal location you each reside in when gathering facts!

What are the legal rights in regard to disclosing the transition?	What are the laws in regard to disclosing the transition?	What are the company's policies in regard to disclosing the transition?

GRAPHICS GALORE

Venn Diagram

What are you comfortable sharing with clients, employees, co-workers, bosses, and employers in respect to discussing the transition with those in the workplace?

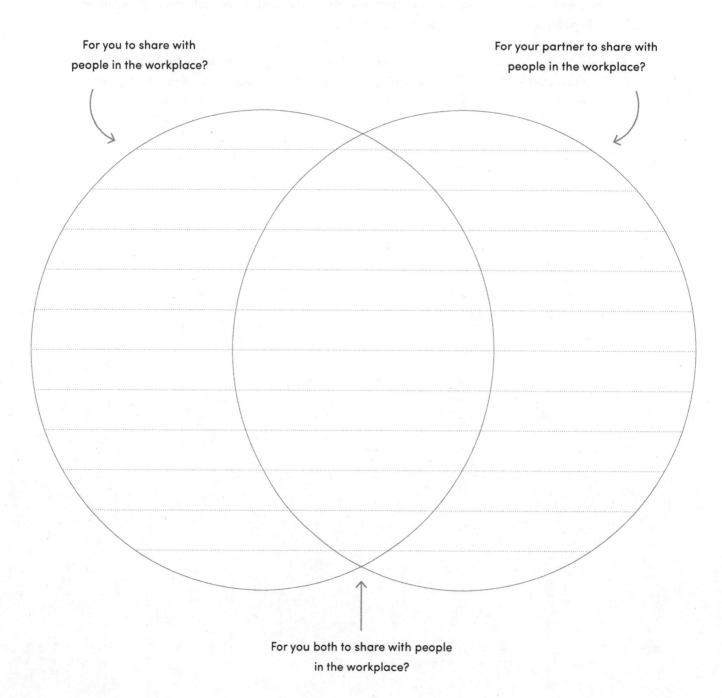

For you to share with people in the workplace?

For your partner to share with people in the workplace?

For you both to share with people in the workplace?

EMPATHY-EMBRACING EXERCISE

For many transgender people, the fear of losing the respect and/or support of those in the workplace can prevent them from disclosing their affirmed gender.

AFFIRMATIVE ANECDOTE

Hard choices!
Does anyone know
How hard?

Was there ever a time in your life that you feared losing the respect and/or support of those in the workplace if you disclosed something personal about yourself? If so, what was it and did you disclose it? If not, why? If yes, what was the outcome?

....

....

....

....

....

....

....

....

....

....

....

....

GRAPHICS GALORE

Bar Graph

To what degree does/did it matter to you, who and how you tell these people about the transition? Based on a scale from 1 to 10, who and how you tell these people about the transition, with 1 being the lowest and 10 being the highest? Color or shade in your response. This visual will help you to see where your greatest concerns lie and can help you communicate this to your trans-identified partner, therapist, spiritual mentor, or for your own personal understanding. The bar graph results may vary as the transition progresses and your thoughts may shift.

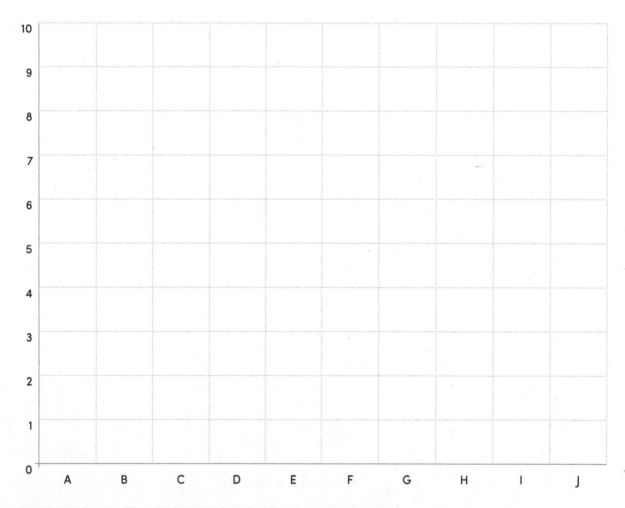

Use these ideas to fill in the bar graph or feel free to create your own!

A. Telling your clients, employees, co-workers about the transition alone.

B. Telling your clients, employees, co-workers about the transition with another person present.

C. Your concerns about how your clients, employees, co-workers may react to you at the time you disclose the transition.

D. Your concerns about how your clients, employees, co-workers may treat you once you disclose the transition.

E. Your concerns about how sharing the transition with people will affect your future with the employer.

F. Telling your boss and/or employer about the transition alone.

G. Telling your boss and/or employer about the transition with another person present.

H. Your concerns about how your boss and/or employer may react to you at the time you disclose the transition.

I. Your concerns of how your boss and/or employer may treat you once you disclose the transition.

J. Your concerns about being able to take time off work when you feel it is critical to do so, without a negative outcome.

GRAPHICS GALORE

Pie Graph

To what degree does/did it matter to you, who and how you tell these people about the transition? Decide how important to you are each of these topics or matters, in relation to each other? Place the number that corresponds with a suggested topic within as many slices of the pie that conveys how each one matters to you. Only one number should be placed in each slice. You do not need to use all the topics but do fill in all the slices. Feel free to create your own topics and assign them their own number.

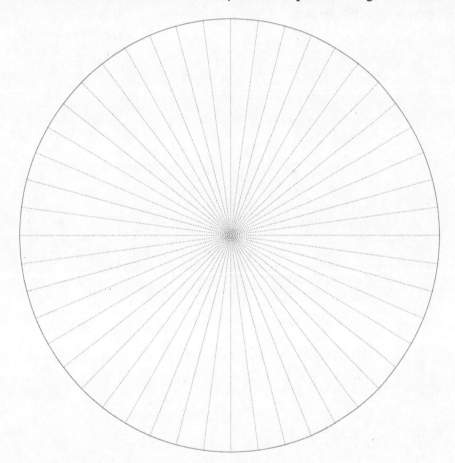

1. Telling your clients, employees, co-workers about the transition alone.
2. Telling your clients, employees, co-workers about the transition with another person present.
3. Your concerns about how your clients, employees, co-workers may react at the time you disclose the transition.
4. Your concerns about how your clients, employees, co-workers may treat you once you disclose the transition.
5. Your concerns about how sharing the transition with people will affect your future with the employer.

6. Telling your boss and/or employer about the transition alone.
7. Telling your boss and/or employer about the transition with another person present.
8. Your concerns about how your boss and/or employer may react at the time you disclose the transition.
9. Your concerns about how your boss and/or employer may treat you once you disclose the transition.
10. Your concerns about being able to take time off work when you feel it is critical to do so, without a negative outcome.

SAMPLER SHARE

What thoughts, feelings, fears, or concerns do you each have about discussing the transition at your respective workplaces?

I fear that she will be outed before she wants to be. I worry if she is outed at work that her safety could be compromised (she has had a long and respected career in a very male-dominant profession). I am concerned that her final few years in the career she loves will be marred with hurtful transphobic vitriol instead of kudos and respect for 30 years of public service.

(Shared by Grace)

COUPLE COMMUNICATION CORNER

When partners or couples speak spontaneously out of anger or fear about the unknown, without thinking it through, they can sometimes regret the way they phrased it. Rehearsing what and how partners may want to ask or discuss with their trans-identified partner, and/or others, can help partners and couples before they actually communicate their thoughts. This gives the non-transitioning partner a moment to reflect and pause before they converse about emotional topics. Partners may choose to practice asking these questions with a trusted friend, family member, spiritual mentor, or therapist first.

> AFFIRMATIVE ANECDOTE
>
> *You are rude.*
> *There are unsaid rules...*
> *Figure them out!*

Explain your thoughts and feelings about these questions to each other. Do you and your trans-identified partner answer these questions in the same way or differently? Discuss your responses to understand how you view them and make time to celebrate all you learn from being willing to communicate with each other.

1. What will you say or do if a person at work asks what transitioning is?

    The partner's thoughts: The trans persons's thoughts:

    . . . .

    . . . .

    . . . .

2. What will you say or do if a person at work asks what the transition will entail for you?

    The partner's thoughts: The trans persons's thoughts:

    . . . .

    . . . .

    . . . .

3. What will you say or do if a person at work asks what is the correct pronoun/name to use for your partner?

The partner's thoughts: The trans persons's thoughts:

·   ·

·   ·

·   ·

4. What will you say or do if a person at work asks what they can tell others about the transition?

The partner's thoughts: The trans persons's thoughts:

·   ·

·   ·

·   ·

5. What will you say or do if a person at work asks how they can help with the transition?

The partner's thoughts: The trans persons's thoughts:

·   ·

·   ·

·   ·

6. What will you say or do if a person at work asks what type of surgeries will be involved, if any?

The partner's thoughts: The trans persons's thoughts:

·   ·

·   ·

·   ·

7. What will you say or do if a person at work asks what type of hormones will be involved, if any?

The partner's thoughts:

The trans persons's thoughts:

. . . .

. . . .

. . . .

8. What will you say or do if a person at work makes inappropriate statements about the transition?

AFFIRMATIVE ANECDOTE

*We must
Teach others
So one day
Everyone
Will have
Learned!*

The partner's thoughts:

The trans persons's thoughts:

. . . .

. . . .

. . . .

9. What will you say or do if a person at work asks inappropriate questions about the transition?

The partner's thoughts:

The trans persons's thoughts:

. . . .

. . . .

. . . .

10. What will you say or do to explain to people at work what are inappropriate questions about the transition?

The partner's thoughts:

The trans persons's thoughts:

. . . .

. . . .

. . . .

Chapter 9

INSURANCES, GENDER MARKERS, AND DOCUMENTS... OH MY!

VITAL VIGNETTE

Gender markers, name changes, and insurances can either be viewed as an important friend or as a frustrating foe. Some days they can be both at the same time. Here, as with many other decisions, you will need to communicate with your transitioning partner as to what, if any, your role will be in regard to any aspect of changing or sustaining the gender marker on each and every document. For those of you who are unsure of what a gender marker is, it is the gender designation on all official documents, usually stating male or female gender. Some countries have begun adding a third option, but this is rare. In most cases, your transitioning partner will need to take much of the responsibility, and you will have to determine what you will need to do to protect yourself and your future in connection to your current documentation. Every single part of this will take time, documentation, patience, and endurance.

> AFFIRMATIVE ANECDOTE
> *New name,*
> *Take hormones,*
> *Schedule surgery,*
> *Change gender markers.*
> *So much to do,*
> *So much time!*

It can become frustrating, heartbreaking, and overwhelming rather quickly. This chapter requires the establishment of timelines and commitment. Fear and worry can also be present throughout the procedures necessary for you and your transitioning partner to feel safe, protected, and respected. Many of the issues or suggestions discussed in this chapter will involve legality and rights, which can vary from country to country, state to state, province to province, and so on and so on. These topics will require you to dot your i's and cross your t's because you may be dealing with people and institutions that will not always have the most current information or the personnel who will care about the criticalness of all that you will have to do.

As far as banks are concerned, most are not overly concerned about gender markers. They will honor the documentation required to change the name on accounts once you provide a copy of the legal name change order. Sometimes all the individuals who are on the account will need to be present for changes to be made. I suggest inquiring about the bank's policy before you plan on making these changes.

Some insurance companies may require name changes and other legal changes, while for other insurance companies it may be advantageous for the partner in transition to keep things exactly as they presently are, in order for medications, surgeries, or other procedures to be covered. For example, a trans woman who has a history of prostate cancer may need to retain a male gender marker on their health insurance in order to have treatment covered by their insurance company, should there be a need for such medical intervention in the future. These specifics and details are critical and must be researched and discussed in advance. After seeking legal advice, the best sources for these types of inquiries will most likely be talking to the human resources liaison of your employer, researching the insurance company's policies, or speaking to your medical provider.

The importance of preparing for incapacitation and death by completing proper documents cannot be overstated. These are extremely uncomfortable and difficult topics for many people under the most benign of conditions, but discussing these matters while navigating the transition can add an even more challenging dynamic to an already complicated matter. Having this documentation put in place is especially critical for those in transition who may be considering multiple surgeries or invasive procedures.

It is imperative that these topics are painstakingly discussed, thoroughly addressed, and legally documented. Knowing who will be in charge of making the most vital decisions pertaining to each other's remains and what the exact wishes are is paramount. Should the person in transition become incapacitated at any time for any reason, these documents could save an abundance of heartache and anguish at a time of great confusion and anxiety. As unbearable and unpleasant as it is to discuss, all couples must address the particulars of creating a will, healthcare proxy, and appointment of an agent to control the disposition of remains. Every detail needs to be formally written down and legally filed. Healthcare proxies must state the specifics of the person's wishes, should this documentation be necessary. Once it is determined what each person deems necessary and desires, it must be written down on the healthcare proxy. If the current documentation does not reflect the trans-identified person's name and/or gender marker listed on these forms, the logistics of legally clarifying wishes and desires at the time of death or incapacitation can become a nightmare for all involved.

I strongly recommend you consult a knowledgeable estate-planning lawyer who is aware of current laws and practices in the jurisdiction in which you both live prior to any medical and/or legal changes. In regard to name changes, it is strongly recommended that you get multiple (at least ten) certified copies of name change orders. If the name change is sealed, it is even more important to buy multiple certified copies, because it can be quite difficult or even impossible to get it unsealed and obtain more copies later. Banks and social security, for example, will only accept certified copies, not just photocopies. In "friendly" states, it is possible to get a name change order sealed to help with privacy and safety. It is worth petitioning for it. This saves the trouble and expense of publishing a public notice in a newspaper, especially since many newspapers now have online archives and the name/gender change information becomes public record and comes up in Google searches. Also, for most people, social security needs to be the first stop because their other benefits may also depend on having documentation of the name change request from social security. Lastly, it is important to note that sometimes having a criminal record or severe financial debt may complicate your ability to legally change your name. Once more, I would strongly suggest consulting a competent lawyer about this prior to doing anything, should this apply to you.

There may come a time when you feel completely panicked and want to scream. If this happens, as it sometimes does, perhaps this may be an ideal time to try one of the Deserving De-Stress Delights. You can and will be able to do all that is necessary, but you must take breaks and long pauses when it all feels too much. Knowing this ahead of time helps, and relying on your support team, as well as each other, will get you through it.

On a positive note, once these changes in legal documentation have been completed to the best of your ability, you will sleep better and feel a sense of relief that will be worth the headache and energy it will require. I have created the best forms and tools I could possibly think of for this chapter and you are welcome to copy or enhance anything you need to have your needs met. In addition, I have made a comprehensive list of documents that may be of use for couples who are facing the need to begin gender marker changes. I cannot stress enough that you should be consulting legal experts, accountants, financial institutions, and any other professional who can advise you about the laws that pertain to changing a gender marker, before you proceed with anything permanent or anything that can possibly affect you in a negative way.

In summary:

1. Always record the name of the person you spoke to, the time, date, and details of what you discussed.

2. For each formal change, find out the documentation you will need and record it.

3. Find out if you need to do it in person, or if you are able to do it by phone, fax, email, or snail mail; keep records of when forms are submitted and to whom.

4. Record whether you will both need to be present to change any document/s or whether only one of you is required to be present to make these changes.

5. Based on the above (#1–#4), make a list and then create a plan for addressing each change.

6. Label physical folders for each name or gender marker change and attach the sheet from the graphic organizer in this chapter on the front. Place everything you need for this change in a physical folder or in a safe and private computer file. I suggest keeping both hard copies and digital copies in a password-protected file. Make copies of forms ahead of time and review what is needed prior to beginning the process. Consider making two physical copies of everything!

7. Decide on a realistic schedule that is both practical and makes sense time-wise.

8. Schedule a weekly date together to discuss what tasks have been accomplished and what tasks still have to be completed. You may need to decide who is responsible for what task and by what date it needs to be done. Updating, reviewing, and altering original plans can be critical to reaching your goals.

9. Make notes of when you will need legal advice, a notary, or the assistance of a professional before you proceed in addressing a gender marker on a particular document. Some documents will require a notary, so create a list of the days and times one is available and their cost.

10. Ask for help and support if it becomes too much or overwhelming. Sometimes, simply having a person sit with you when you call or fax something feels better.

11. Create boundaries for yourself, such as allocating a specific amount of time for each task or deciding to begin and end at specific times.

12. If you are unsure whether you received the correct information, then ask to speak with someone else, or call back again and ask the same questions of another person. Perhaps you can have your partner call again, with you present, to find out if they get the same answers to the same questions.

13. You may need a witness or two when signing legal documents, so compile a list of the names of people with whom you are comfortable doing this, and then create a list of their typical dates and times of availability. You may have the same names as your partner in transition or not.

14. Take the time to celebrate what you have completed by making a date with yourself, with family or friends, and/or with your partner in transition in order to acknowledge all you have achieved. It will re-energize both of you!

GRAPHICS GALORE

Splash

On which documents do you think your partner's name (if it applies) and/or gender marker will need to be changed as a result of the transition? By creatively splashing words and/or short phrases, quickly attempt to express your answers randomly with as many responses as possible scattered on the paper.

GRAPHICS GALORE

Box

Which documents will need the gender marker and/or name changed on them?

Highlight or circle your choices below. I strongly suggest you discuss this with your trans-identified partner and/or a person who knows the legality and requirements for the town, city, state, province, and country that you and your trans-identified partner legally reside in!

Will	Healthcare proximity	Remains form	Driver's license
Pension	IRA	403B	Mortgage/s
Funeral plots	All utilities	Birth certificate	Long-term insurance
Short-term insurance	Medical insurance	Passport	Other people's will
Life insurance	Maintenance	All doctor offices	Dentist
Library cards	Credit cards	All diplomas	Old/current colleges
School records/ transcripts	Memberships: gym	Memberships: museum	Bank accounts
Post office/mailbox signs	Religious institutions	Door buzzer	Children's school
Children's birth certificate	Adoption papers	Marriage certificates	Check books
All online presence/ accounts	Administration for Children's Services	Funeral plans	Door labels of apartment
Male/female actuary stuff	Car insurance	Prescription cards	Medical cards
All loans: car, school, etc.	Motor vehicle	At pharmacy	Warranties
Emergency info for kids	Business cards	Accountant	IRS info/taxes
Business/corporation info	Email address info	Voice message	Current court cases
All emergency info for you	Grocery store	Weight loss programs	Professional licenses
Hair/barber/nail salons	Department stores	Netflix/Amazon accounts	Trusts
Address label info	Hotel accounts	Parole/probation officer	
Additional ideas:			

REFLECTIVE RESPONSES

1. Do you want to be involved with helping to make the name and/or gender marker changes?

   . . . .

   . . . .

   . . . .

2. Which documents do you believe will be affected when changing the name and/or gender marker? Does your partner want you to assist with any of those? If so, with which ones?

   . . . .

   . . . .

   . . . .

3. Which documents will not be affected by the name and/or gender marker changes and will stay the same for now?

   . . . .

   . . . .

   . . . .

4. What will you need to bring to each appointment and who will gather those items?

   . . . .

   . . . .

   . . . .

5. Which name and/or gender marker changes require specific paperwork and who will gather those materials?

....

....

....

6. What organizations or services can help support you with your questions?

....

....

....

7. How will this transition affect your rights and/or marriage due to local laws?

....

....

....

8. What or how will the gender marker and/or name change affect you financially?

....

....

....

9. Do you know a lawyer or another individual who can help you with all of this?

....

....

....

10. What are the most important pieces of knowledge you feel helped you and/or may help others as your partner transitioned in relation to insurances, changing the gender marker, and documentation?

....

....

....

GRAPHICS GALORE

Venn Diagram

Which documents should have the gender marker and/or name changed and...

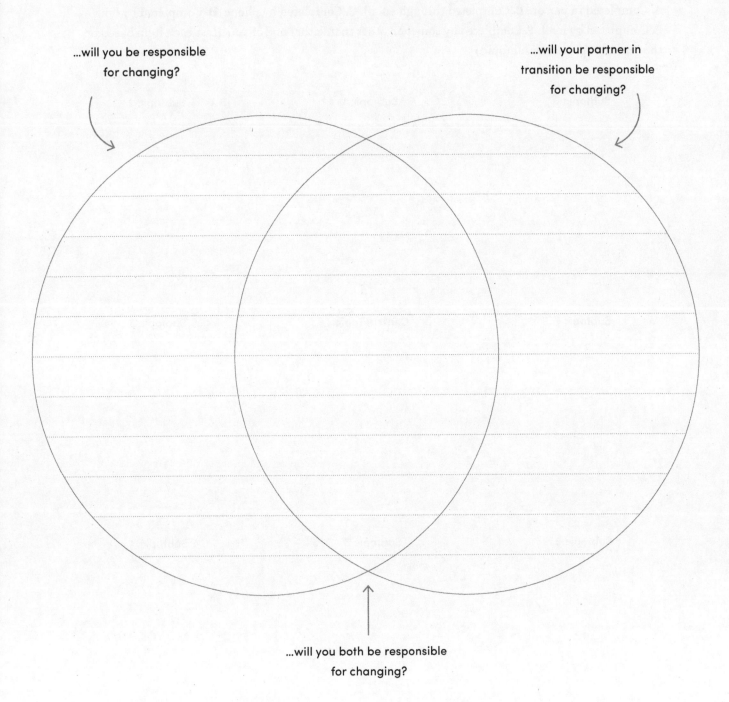

...will you be responsible for changing?

...will your partner in transition be responsible for changing?

...will you both be responsible for changing?

GRAPHICS GALORE

Web

By what means will the gender marker be changed on documents? I suggest you complete six separate webs to help you by using the titles listed below as a guide and place each title (A–F) one at a time in the center on your own.

A. Completed in person. **B.** Completed through email. **C.** Completed by phone. **D.** Completed by fax. **E.** Completed by mail. **F.** Completed by someone other than either one of you. (List each item based on the central topic in the subtopic.)

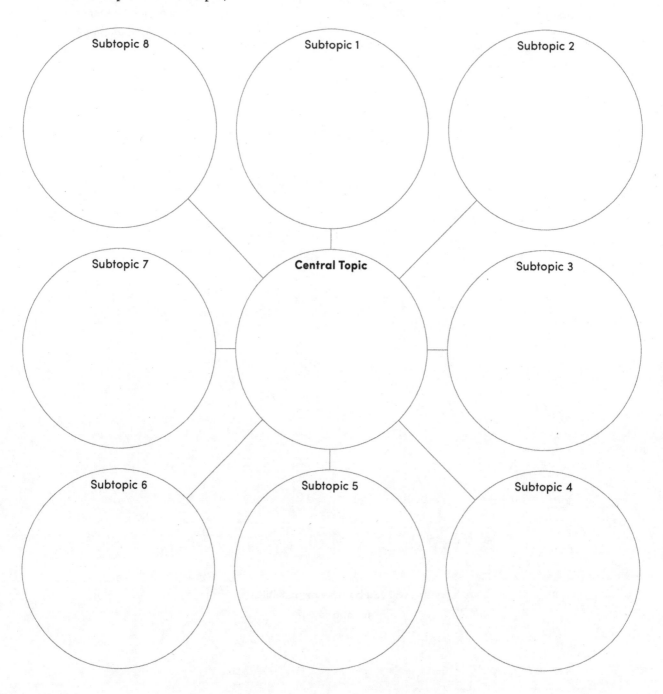

DESERVING DE-STRESS DELIGHTS

Arts Appreciation

For many partners, the arts can allow them to identify with what they are experiencing in relation to their own life. For some partners, going to a museum, theater, or concert can give them a chance to look at the transition from a different perspective. For others, painting, singing, or acting can offer a release of emotions or supply a sense of comforting joy. These types of activities can give partners the permission to feel deeply, but still allow them simply to breathe when events feel overwhelming. Looking at a piece of art or a photograph or watching a play can often transport partners to another place or mindset. After attending one of these events, a partner may choose to share the feelings that can surface through journaling or by discussing them with another person. Whether through studying a piece of artwork or participating in a theatrical performance, these experiences can provide a cathartic opportunity for partners to gain insight about the transition. For many partners, the arts can inspire and help them feel emotions they have avoided expressing. What can be evoked is something quite personal and unexpected, but extremely healing!

> AFFIRMATIVE ANECDOTE
>
> *You scream HURRY, I scream WAIT! You cry FASTER, I just CRY!*

Journal your reaction to this Deserving De-Stress Delight.

....

....

....

....

....

....

....

....

GRAPHICS GALORE

Timeline

What is the best timeline order for the gender marker and/or name to be changed on this document?

Type of document the gender marker and/or name will be changed on:	Start date:	Follow-up date:	Date done:
Type of document the gender marker and/or name will be changed on:	Start date:	Follow-up date:	Date done:
Type of document the gender marker and/or name will be changed on:	Start date:	Follow-up date:	Date done:
Type of document the gender marker and/or name will be changed on:	Start date:	Follow-up date:	Date done:
Type of document the gender marker and/or name will be changed on:	Start date:	Follow-up date:	Date done:
Type of document the gender marker and/or name will be changed on:	Start date:	Follow-up date:	Date done:
Type of document the gender marker and/or name will be changed on:	Start date:	Follow-up date:	Date done:

GRAPHICS GALORE

T-Chart

What are the pieces of information you and/or your partner may need to record in relation to changing the gender marker and/or name? This form is created to assist you!

Feel free to make copies and use this form for each document that will need to have the gender marker and/or name changed on it.

What type of procedure or documentation am I/we preparing to discuss?		How did I/we communicate with the agency? Phone, email, mail, fax, or in person?	
How much time do I/we have to finish this today?		Will I/we need someone to be with me when I/we call? Who?	
Agency/doctor's name called?		Email of agency	
Date of contact		Fax number	
Phone number: Extension:		What address is the information to be mailed to?	
Who made call?		Who I/we spoke to?	
Where will I/we get any forms I/we will need?		What costs, if any?	
What are any deadlines?		Do I/we need a notary?	
Date it must/will it be done by?		Will I/we need a witness?	
Do I/we need authorization from insurance or anywhere else?		Is a letter required, and if so, from whom?	
What documents do I/we need to complete before this document can be changed?		What will the letter need to state?	
What was said, discussed, and transpired?		Will I/we need a lawyer for any of these changes?	

Who will be in charge of changing the gender marker after the information is gathered?		How many copies of this updated document can we receive? What is the cost?	
Is there any old documentation that must be shown before this document can be changed?		What day will the agency or doctor be contacted again to make sure it is done and received?	
Where will this information be filed or stored?		Who will finalize that this transaction is completed?	

Record any additional information or other questions below.

AFFIRMATIVE ANECDOTE

Include me,
Talk to me,
I am here!

....

....

....

....

....

....

....

....

....

....

....

EMPATHY-EMBRACING EXERCISE

Dealing with insurance companies can be extremely exhausting and overwhelming. Without the proper documentation, this task can become painfully draining and frustrating. Try to imagine how any errors in forms or incomplete paperwork could delay or prevent any critical surgery or medicine you may need to feel whole. That is exactly how it feels for a transgender person when they are at the mercy of insurance companies for the financial funding of these necessary procedures or medicines.

Has there been a time in your life when you were financially dependent on an organization or a person to support something that was crucial to your health, wellbeing, or betterment of life? If so, what was it and did you disclose it? If not, why? If yes, what was the outcome?

AFFIRMATIVE ANECDOTE
Choices.
Challenging at times,
Not always fair.

GRAPHICS GALORE

Bar Graph

To what degree do these legal and/or official topics matter to you? Based on a scale from 1 to 10, with 1 being the lowest and 10 being the highest, color or shade in your response. This visual will help you see where your greatest concerns lie and can help you to communicate this to your trans-identified partner, therapist, clergy, or for your own personal understanding. The bar graph results may vary as the transition progresses and your thoughts may shift.

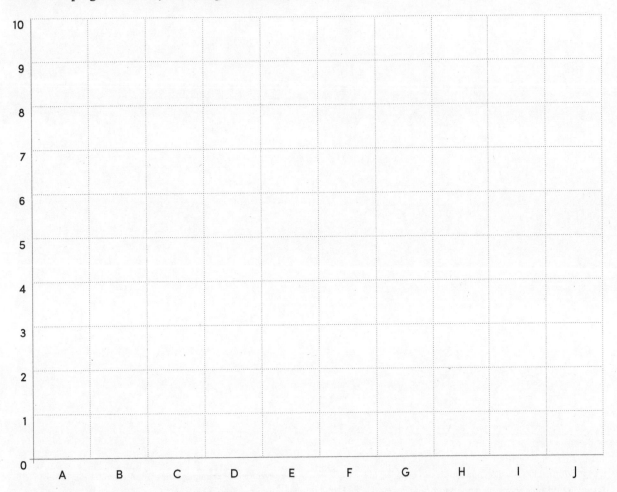

Use these ideas to fill in the bar graph or feel free to create your own!

A. Legally/officially changing name/pronoun assigned at birth.

B. Legally/officially changing name and/or gender marker on birth certificate.

C. Legally/officially changing name and/or gender marker on passport.

D. Legally/officially changing name and/or gender marker on social security card/country documents.

E. Legally/officially changing name and/or gender marker on all medical/hospital records.

F. Legally/officially changing name and/or gender marker on all licenses/diplomas/certifications/college transcripts.

G. Legally/officially changing name and/or gender marker on all insurance policies/pensions/financial documents/leases/mortgages.

H. Legally/officially changing name and/or gender marker on all store cards/credit cards/memberships/utilities/online accounts.

I. Legally/officially changing name and/or gender marker on all wills/trusts/emergency documents related to illness and/or death.

J. Legally/officially changing name and/or gender marker on all documents in relation to children.

GRAPHICS GALORE

Pie Graph

To what degree do these legal and/or official topics matter to you? Decide how important these statements are to you in relation to each other. Place the number that corresponds with a suggested topic within as many slices of the pie that conveys how each one matters to you. Only one number should be placed in each slice. You do not need to use all the topics but do fill in all the slices. Feel free to create your own topics and assign them their own number.

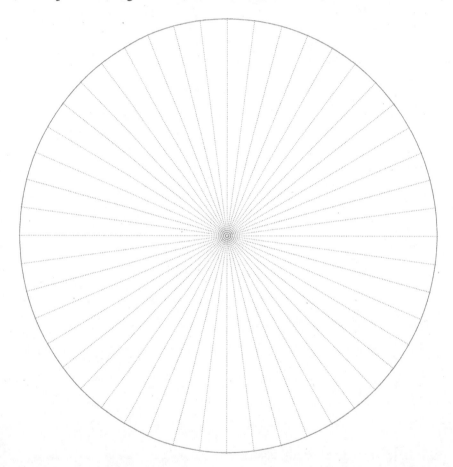

1. Legally/officially changing name/pronoun assigned at birth.

2. Legally/officially changing name and/or gender marker on birth certificate.

3. Legally/officially changing name and/or gender marker on passport.

4. Legally/officially changing name and/or gender marker on social security card/country documents.

5. Legally/officially changing name and/or gender marker on all medical/hospital records.

6. Legally/officially changing name and/or gender marker on all licenses/diplomas/certifications/college transcripts.

7. Legally/officially changing name and/or gender marker on all insurance policies/pensions/financial documents/leases/mortgages.

8. Legally/officially changing name and/or gender marker on all store cards/credit cards/memberships/utilities/online accounts.

9. Legally/officially changing name and/or gender marker on all wills/trusts/emergency documents related to illness and/or death.

10. Legally/officially changing name and/or gender marker on all documents in relation to children.

SAMPLER SHARE

What are the most important pieces of knowledge you feel helped you and may help others as your partner transitioned in relation to insurances, changing the gender marker, and documentations?

The most complicated and time-consuming issue was actually completing a name change, which required my partner to take time off from work and go to the courthouse. My partner handled the name change and updating his documents on his own. We were fortunate to have resources like Sylvia Rivera Law Project and Transgender Legal Defense and Education Fund (TLDEF), both of which give step-by-step instructions for legal name changes on their websites and offer technical assistance and legal clinics for the purposes of name changes. Our state also requires that name changes be published in a newspaper, which can be a huge barrier for transgender people—the publication can be expensive and many newspapers publish their content online, making the information searchable and publicly available. Fortunately, my partner requested and was granted a waiver from publication, in order to protect his privacy and safety. Once his legal name change was completed, there were no issues with changing his name and gender marker on his driver's license or changing his name on our bank account. The name change and gender marker change on his insurance policy and ID card took slightly longer.

One piece of advice that we have for others, with regard to insurance and transition, is to expect the unexpected. Although my partner and I both have experience navigating the healthcare system, he received multiple denials for a gender-affirming procedure. This led to a complex appeal process that took additional time and expense, and mental and emotional energy to complete. We had not fully resolved the issue until two days before his surgery, which led to a great deal of anxiety and stress. It helped that my partner and I had access to a credit union and were able to obtain the additional funds necessary to cover his procedures at a low interest rate. I would tell others that they should expect delays and complications with insurance, but also assure them that these issues can be worked through with additional support from community-based organizations and legal professionals and cooperation with their medical providers.

(Shared by Ivy)

COUPLE COMMUNICATION CORNER

The wording shared in the Couple Communication Corner of this chapter differs from the other chapters. Though the other chapters pose questions to discuss with one another and/or others, this chapter offers statements. These statements were originally planned to be used as a helpful script when you and/or your partner in transition may be attempting to communicate with others on the phone when trying to change or get information on how to change your trans-identified partner's gender marker on a document. Its purpose was to be used as a "How To Do" tool intended to make this task easier. If you are unsure of your safety or protections at work or any agency, I suggest you check with an experienced legal organization that can advise you on which information to share with the individual or company you are about to contact. However, should you decide to use the statements, I have made the script simpler to navigate by separating each sentence into individual steps. Feel free to combine these steps to form a script or use them one at a time as provided, to practice using with or without each other. Explain your thoughts and feelings about these statements to each other and decide which statements, if any, will be used. Do you and your trans-identified partner respond to these statements in the same way or differently? Discuss your responses to understand how you view them and make time to celebrate all you learn from being willing to communicate with each other.

1. Initial attempt: Hello, my name is _____ and I want to update my records/documents. You have my spouse listed as male/female, but my spouse is actually female/male and should be recorded as female/male. (Please note that some jurisdictions allow a third option other than female/male.) Can you help me with this? If not, would you please connect me with someone who can? (Get the name and phone number/extension for each interaction.)

   The partner's thoughts: The trans persons's thoughts:

   . . . .

   . . . .

2. If you are getting nowhere with this person, then thank them for their time and help and...

   The partner's thoughts: The trans persons's thoughts:

   . . . .

   . . . .

3. Then state you are requesting to speak with their supervisor or the highest-ranking person available. Once you reach this person, repeat statement #1 again.

    The partner's thoughts: The trans persons's thoughts:

    ....

    ....

4. If the supervisor or highest-ranking person is unavailable to speak with you, you can request to have that person call you back or ask for their direct number and ask them when they will be able to be reached. Record that number and get the information of the person who gave you this information so that you can state that person recommended you contact them. Put the person who will call you back in your phone so that, when they call you back, it shows up and you know it is them.

    The partner's thoughts: The trans persons's thoughts:

    ....

    ....

5. If you are speaking with the supervisor or higher-ranking person and they are questioning how there can be such an error, make the point that you need to know how to get this changed. Ask what documentation the company needs to prove your partner's gender. Record this information and thank them for their help.

    The partner's thoughts: The trans persons's thoughts:

    ....

    ....

6. If they can change it over the phone, with no further steps needed, ask them to email or mail you the corrected documentation as proof and thank them for their assistance.

    The partner's thoughts: The trans persons's thoughts:

    ....

    ....

7. If they state they will need to get back to you, ask exactly when that will be; ask if they will call you back with the update or whether you need to call back. Lastly, ask if they need any information from you, what that is, and what is the best or most effective way to get this information to them.

The partner's thoughts:

The trans persons's thoughts:

. . . .

. . . .

. . . .

. . . .

8. If the person presses you and you feel you need to explain about the transition, make sure it is an appropriate person to share this with and state that the information you are sharing is confidential.

> AFFIRMATIVE ANECDOTE
>
> *Your ignorance*
> *Is NOT*
> *My responsibility!*

Decide how you and your partner want to define the transition/transgender. (I stated that my partner is transgender and legally transitioned. I stated I have all the legal documentation to prove this fact and that I was advised to contact them.) Ask what forms they may or may not need to change this document. Who do you send it to? What else do you need? What is the time frame in which this will be completed? Who are you talking to?

The partner's thoughts:

The trans persons's thoughts:

. . . .

. . . .

. . . .

. . . .

9. If you do not feel that you're getting anywhere, contact a legal or advocacy organization that can help you with this.

The partner's thoughts:

The trans persons's thoughts:

. . . .

. . . .

. . . .

. . . .

10. Much information about changing the gender marker can be found online. Some key words to use: changing gender marker(s)/transition/transgender. Also, include the country or state in which you and your trans-identified partner reside. In addition, ask others what they did, whom they used to help them, and what steps they took to change the gender marker!

The partner's thoughts:

The trans persons's thoughts:

. . . .

. . . .

Chapter 10

PRIVILEGE: LOSS OR GAIN?

VITAL VIGNETTE

"Privilege" may be an unfamiliar concept, which you may not have previously considered. Privilege is a special advantage or right granted to a particular person or group. It was something that rarely, if ever, crossed my mind before transitioning affected any part of

AFFIRMATIVE ANECDOTE

How can Someone so Visible Feel so invisible?

my life. I had heard of privilege or the lack of it in relation to sexual orientation, class, race, religion, ethnicity, ability, age, aesthetics, size, and gender, but it was not something I ever expected would become another layer of the transition. How you are treated now will determine the reality or perception of whether you have gained or lost privilege. A way the loss or gaining of privilege can manifest is how no longer being viewed as you were once seen, in relation to respect, can affect your feelings of visibility and value to those around you. Some forms of privilege implicitly confer a level of worthiness upon a person by society that can be either extremely harmful or ego-boosting to individuals, depending on their situation. As a result of the transition, this ranking is often re-evaluated throughout each experience and every situation, requiring a reassessment of the role privilege plays in your life.

The major question I continuously ask myself in relation to privilege is: How does privilege impact my life? This question is followed by two other questions: What am I losing or gaining as a result of the transition? Is there something that can be done about privilege to make me feel better or more whole around this issue? Much of the gain or loss depends on how you were publicly perceived prior to the transition compared with afterwards. In every case, the gaining or loss of privilege may be subtle, ambivalent, or blatant, and only you can decide how it feels for you.

These scenarios are based on situations partners have shared with me. For some trans people and their partners, living with the fear of the transgender person being racially profiled can cause a realistic terror for both them and their partner, as they feel a tremendous loss of a specific freedom. A partner was horrified as they witnessed their spouse, who was once read as a black woman, being stopped by the police as they walked down the street together. This was an action that had never happened to them prior to passing as their affirmed male gender. The transgender partner was being profiled simply because they were now seen as a black man. For a trans woman and her wife, a simple luncheon with their children can become extremely uncomfortable as the hostess asks, "Which one of the women is the mother?" In this situation the trans woman is gaining the privilege of being seen as a cisgender woman but losing privilege as the hostess is implying they both cannot be the mother, exhibiting the heteronormative bias that many a lesbian and gay couple experience on a daily basis. In addition, the effects this type of repetitive ignorance may have upon the witnessing children can also create a feeling of loss in terms of privilege and pain for the entire family. Imagine how frustrating it is for previously labeled lesbian couples to now have to endure a salesperson explaining to the trans masculine partner how an appliance works, while their partner is disregarded by the misogynist act of ignoring the female spouse. It can be demoralizing for a lesbian partner to realize she has lost her privilege of being seen as an intellectual equal simply because her trans-identified partner has transitioned and gained privilege. Furthermore, both partners can be in a position to apply for the same job, but the trans man could now be hired for a higher salary over an equally or even more qualified partner. Just as unnerving is when a couple is asked at check-in at a hotel if they want separate beds, even though the reservation clearly states a king-sized bed, because the use of testosterone may give the visual appearance of a younger-looking man with someone assumed to be their parent.

Tragically, the loss of privilege coupled with transmisogyny is felt when a trans woman is both fetishized and insulted by her male co-workers for transitioning, and no longer valued for her superior skills at the job she held for years prior to the transition. Conversely, the privilege of being safe, when a couple who previously presented as gay men can now openly walk hand in hand in a location where they could have been attacked prior to the trans woman's transition, can be exhilarating. In another situation, a couple, one of whom is a cisgender male and one of whom is nonbinary, attends a party and the bartender uses male pronouns for the nonbinary spouse. Since the cisgender spouse has more privilege in this situation, he corrects the bartender and tells the bartender to refer to his nonbinary partner by using the pronoun "they." In most cases, cisgender people are able to correct or request the way the transgender or nonbinary partner is being addressed and will receive much less resistance or fear for their safety than the person who is being misgendered. It is important to note that some transgender and nonbinary people prefer others to not correct anyone if they are gendered incorrectly or the wrong name is used. Out of respect to them, it is a subject that must be discussed with your trans-identified or nonbinary-identified partner, prior to intervening. The examples of the loss and gaining of privilege are endless and are as varied as are the couples that are in transition.

A common loss of privilege, which lesbians speak of as a result of their partner transitioning, is no longer being read or seen as queer or part of the LGBTQQIA+ community.

In addition, they often feel their strong feminist voices are either diminished or ignored. It cannot be overstated that for some queer, gay, and lesbian couples, especially for the partners, the pain and loss of privilege of their queer, gay, or lesbian identity that is felt when they are being thought of or read as a straight couple can be extremely distressing. For other couples in the same scenario, some embrace the new labeling and experience a freedom as others see them as a heterosexual couple. The reverse can be also true; for formerly straight-labeled couples, being seen as gay or lesbian can now be viewed as a loss of privilege as both partners begin to feel the prejudice and bias of homophobia. The emotions and complexity of privilege in an abundance of situations is difficult to understand until it is personally experienced.

The subject of privilege, for both the non-transitioning partner and the transgender partner, can affect a plethora of circumstances including public safety especially in relation to bathroom use, medical and health services, the way friends and family interact and react to them individually and as a couple, work challenges, legal rights, finances, and inheritance. One safety concern that has been discussed at conferences I have been involved with addresses being screened at security points at the airport. It is a topic rarely mentioned but it could affect individuals and/or couples when they travel. The scanning machines often flag if a trans man is "packing" or if a trans woman has not had bottom surgery. The results for some have caused extreme embarrassment, hostile harassment, or being forced to deal with legal battles. This possible reality should be discussed before travel begins so that all individuals have a plan for how to both protect the parties involved and what to do if a problem arises. It is highly recommended that each individual and/or couple run through exactly what they are going to say and/or do, should a screener announce, "There is a bodily anomaly." It is critical that you are aware of what legal rights you have in every country you visit where a security screening may be necessary. Some transgender folks acquire a letter from a medical professional explaining that they are transgender with the proper wording, which may help them educate the screener, if these challenges occur. In addition, some people elect to bring the phone numbers and/or email addresses of legal defense lawyers, in case they feel that they need immediate legal advice or assistance. If financially able, some transgender folks have found obtaining global entry is a way to avoid being required to do a full body scan. Should this be an option for the trans-identified person, it is important to research which countries do not honor global entry policies; in order to, have all of the facts. There are some individuals who choose not to travel to particular countries or investigate which documentation they may need, in case they do experience a problem with the scanning procedures at the airport or at any other venue which has this practice.

The loss of privilege can be accompanied by shame, fear, anger, humiliation, confusion, and feelings of inferiority. In contrast, the gaining of privilege can evoke feelings of pride, safety, joy, validation, and empowerment. No individual or couple can be prepared for all the possible encounters that may occur in relation to privilege. Nor can you understand how you will feel or react each and every time someone affects your loss or gaining of privilege. The best way to approach these situations, which can be paralyzing, enraging, or empowering, is to have a plan. Decide ahead of time how you will address the situation if either one or both of you are mistreated or overlooked. Verbally rehearse what will be said if one of you is treated with less respect by a salesperson, medical professional, or others. In addition, when an unexpected privilege-related issue arises, and you are unsure of what to say, perhaps you will have to put it aside and discuss what your best approach may be the next time a similar scenario arises. As emotionally challenging as it may be to ignore the action of another person's ignorance, it is always crucial to make safety your first concern. This is even more critical if the person in transition is visibly trans and/or their gender can possibly be misread. The reality is that the loss and gaining of privilege demands to be acknowledged in how it affects couples when the transition is now part of their experience. It must especially be recognized that it plays a major factor in contributing to the self-worth, wellbeing, confidence, and lives of the non-transitioning partners on a number of levels.

GRAPHICS GALORE

Splash

When you think of privilege, what words come to mind for you? By creatively splashing words and/or short phrases, quickly attempt to express your answers randomly with as many responses as possible scattered on the paper.

GRAPHICS GALORE

Box

What societal privileges do/did you have prior to the transition in relation to: sexual orientation, class, race, religion, ethnicity, ability, age, aesthetics, size, and gender? Record your responses below.

Sexual Orientation	Class	Race	Religion	Ethnicity

Ability	Age	Asthetics	Size	Gender

REFLECTIVE RESPONSES

1. Do you feel, as the partner of a now trans-identified person, that you have gained or lost privilege in any way or in any area of your life?

   ....
   ....
   ....

2. How does it feel to share or not to share the bathroom with your trans-identified partner in public bathrooms?

   ....
   ....
   ....

3. Have any safety issues/concerns arisen in relation to the bathroom now?

   ....
   ....
   ....

4. How do people in stores (e.g. when appliance shopping) treat you as an individual, and as part of a couple, now that the transition is taking or has taken place?

   ....
   ....
   ....

5. How do people in restaurants treat you as an individual, and as part of a couple, now that the transition is taking or has taken place?

   ....
   ....

6. Are you able to walk hand in hand in public with your partner? How does this feel?

. . . .

. . . .

. . . .

AFFIRMATIVE ANECDOTE

Change takes time,
So many changes.
Only time will tell,
How many changes,
And how much time.

7. How do you feel people in the LGBTQQIA+ community view you as an individual, and as part of a couple, now that the transition is taking or has taken place?

. . . .

. . . .

. . . .

8. Is your trans-identified partner able to be viewed as their affirmed gender by others? Do you view this as a loss or gaining of privilege?

. . . .

. . . .

. . . .

9. Has the appearance of your related ages changed since the transition, due to hormone use? Does this even matter to you? How does this feel to you?

. . . .

. . . .

. . . .

10. How do friends and family treat you in social circles as an individual and as part of a couple, now that the transition is taking or has taken place?

. . . .

. . . .

11. How do people involved with legal rights or laws in your area treat you as an individual and as part of a couple, now that the transition is taking or has taken place?

. . . .

. . . .

. . . .

12. How do your children, nieces, nephews, students, or other children engage with you and treat you as an individual and as part of a couple, now that the transition is taking or has taken place?

. . . .

. . . .

. . . .

13. How do people at work treat you as an individual and as part of a couple, now that the transition is taking or has taken place?

. . . .

. . . .

. . . .

14. How do people in financial institutions treat you as an individual and as part of a couple, now that the transition is taking or has taken place?

. . . .

. . . .

. . . .

15. How do people in doctor's offices, hospitals, and the medical profession treat you as an individual and as part of a couple, now that the transition is taking or has taken place?

. . . .

. . . .

. . . .

16. How do people who you/your partner bump into from your/their past treat you as an individual and as part of a couple, now that the transition is taking or has taken place?

. . . .

. . . .

. . . .

17. How are gender roles and biased attitudes the same or different at home and/or in the presence of others for you as an individual and as part of a couple, now that the transition is taking or has taken place?

. . . .

. . . .

. . . .

18. How do people in clothing or make-up departments treat you as an individual and as part of a couple, now that the transition is taking or has taken place?

. . . .

. . . .

. . . .

19. How do you feel privilege has been affected in relation to safety issues/concerns for you as an individual, your trans-identified partner alone, and as a couple?

. . . .

. . . .

. . . .

20. How does it feel for you if your partner vacations with friends of the same or different gender now and shares a room with that person, now that they have transitioned?

. . . .

. . . .

. . . .

GRAPHICS GALORE

Bar Graph

To what degree are your concerns regarding how any changes in privilege may impact you and/or your relationship, as a result of the transition, matter to you? Based on a scale from 1 to 10, with 1 being the lowest and 10 being the highest, color or shade in your response. This visual will help you see where your greatest concerns lie and can help you to communicate this to your trans-identified partner, therapist, clergy, or for your own personal understanding. The bar graph results may vary as the transition progresses and your thoughts may shift.

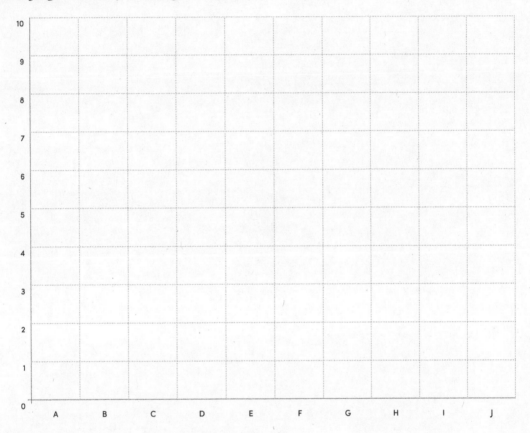

Use these ideas to fill in the bar graph or feel free to create your own!

A. The importance of the gaining or loss of privilege in relation to safety issues.

B. The importance of the gaining or loss of privilege in relation to shopping or eating in restaurants.

C. The importance of the gaining or loss of privilege in relation to social circles with family and friends.

D. The importance of the gaining or loss of privilege in relation to receiving any medical treatment and with medical professionals.

E. The importance of the gaining or loss of privilege in relation to inclusion in the LGBTQQA+ community.

F. The importance of the gaining or loss of privilege in relation to being affectionate in public.

G. The importance of the gaining or loss of privilege in relation to legal rights and laws.

H. The importance of the gaining or loss of privilege in relation to financial institutions.

I. The importance of the gaining or loss of privilege in relation to travel and vacation opportunities.

J. The importance of the gaining or loss of privilege in relation to employment and career opportunities.

GRAPHICS GALORE
Pie Graph

To what degree are your concerns regarding how any changes in privilege may impact you and/or your relationship, as a result of the transition, matter to you? Decide how important these statements are to you in relation to each other. Place the number that corresponds with a suggested topic within as many slices of the pie that conveys how each one matters to you. Only one number should be placed in each slice. You do not need to use all the topics but do fill in all the slices. Feel free to create your own topics and assign them their own number.

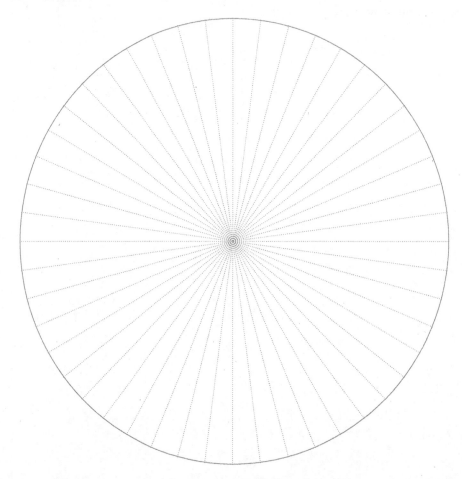

1. The importance of the gaining or loss of privilege in relation to safety issues.

2. The importance of the gaining or loss of privilege in relation to shopping or eating in restaurants.

3. The importance of the gaining or loss of privilege in relation to social circles with family and friends.

4. The importance of the gaining or loss of privilege in relation to receiving any medical treatment and with medical professionals.

5. The importance of the gaining or loss of privilege in relation to inclusion in the LGBTQQA+ community.

6. The importance of the gaining or loss of privilege in relation to being affectionate in public.

7. The importance of the gaining or loss of privilege in relation to legal rights and laws.

8. The importance of the gaining or loss of privilege in relation to financial institutions.

9. The importance of the gaining or loss of privilege in relation to travel and vacation opportunities.

10. The importance of the gaining or loss of privilege in relation to employment and career opportunities.

DESERVING DE-STRESS DELIGHTS

Playtime

Play can be a time dedicated to pure happiness, laughter, and fun! How appealing can this be to any partner? For me, a light-hearted game day with friends was the perfect remedy for the isolation and sadness I experienced when the heaviest of the mourning period affected me during the transition. Even for those who are completely at peace with the transitioning process, the interpersonal interactions with others can certainly be a pick-me-up experience that warms the soul. I recall playing Mahjong with friends for hours, and another time participating in a water balloon fight with students. The goal is for partners not only to give themselves permission to play games or relive enjoyable children's activities that soothe their heart, but to schedule in what I lovingly coined "Forced Fun"! I recommend that whatever makes a partner feel free and smile must be a positive, intended part of their routine. Many trans partners find that this time of "Forced Fun" can serve as a release of tension, fear, and anxiety or an opportunity to experience the gifts and joys in relation to the transition.

Journal your reaction to this Deserving De-Stress Delight.

> AFFIRMATIVE ANECDOTE
>
> *One foot*
> *In front*
> *Of the other,*
> *The weight*
> *Of the world*
> *On my shoulders,*
> *I shift*
> *The load*
> *And forge ahead.*

....

....

....

....

....

....

....

....

....

....

....

....

....

....

....

....

....

....

GRAPHICS GALORE

Web

Since the transition, what important topics or areas of your life have been affected in relation to privilege?

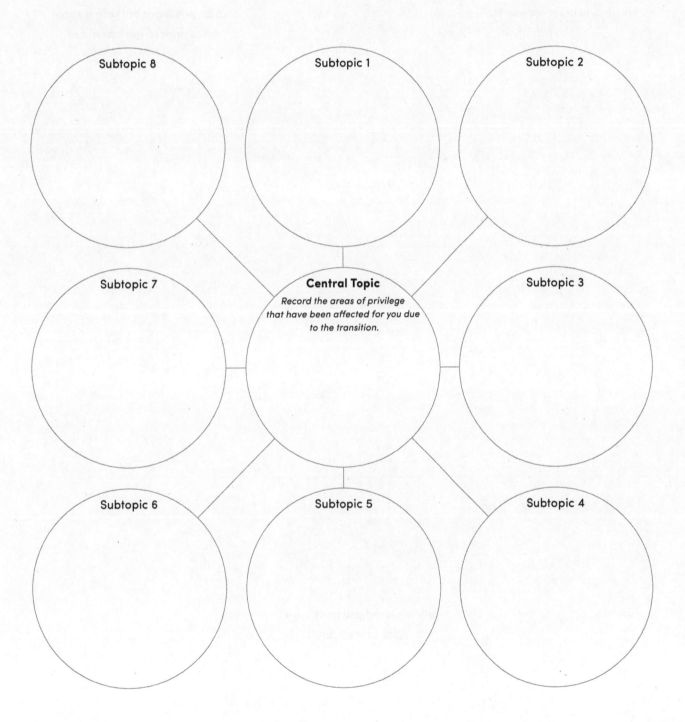

Subtopic 8

Subtopic 1

Subtopic 2

Subtopic 7

Central Topic
Record the areas of privilege that have been affected for you due to the transition.

Subtopic 3

Subtopic 6

Subtopic 5

Subtopic 4

GRAPHICS GALORE

Venn Diagram

How has privilege presented in both of your lives prior to the transition? (Feel free to redo this exercise again during and after the transition).

Which privileges did you have prior to the transition?

Which privileges did your partner have prior to the transition?

Which privileges did you both have in common prior to the transition?

EMPATHY-EMBRACING EXERCISE

Identifying what privilege means to a partner and then assessing whether the transition affects their privilege is a conversation that this exercise question brings to the forefront. It can be a subtle presence of positive or negative shifts. Many partners and even trans-identified partners say that they see a change in privilege as an unexpected result of the transition, in relation to how others treat them.

AFFIRMATIVE ANECDOTE

*I long
For yesterday.*

Has there been a time in your life when you felt a loss or gaining of privilege based on your gender, prior to the transition? If so, what was it and how did it affect your life? If it did not affect your life, why do you think it did not?

....

....

....

....

....

....

....

....

....

....

....

....

GRAPHICS GALORE

Timeline

Recording when you lost or gained any privilege, as an individual or as a couple, throughout the transition process can help you notice if the loss or gaining of privilege has or is happening at a rapid or slow pace.

Date:	What privilege did both or one of you lose or have gained?	Did you lose or gain it personally or as a couple?

Date:	What privilege did you lose or gain?	Did you lose or gain it personally or as a couple?

Date:	What privilege did you lose or gain?	Did you lose or gain it personally or as a couple?

Date:	What privilege did you lose or gain?	Did you lose or gain it personally or as a couple?

GRAPHICS GALORE

T-Chart

How do you believe your individual privilege has been affected as a result of the transition? Feel free to answer this in relation to your relationship or not!

What are some positive changes you have experienced in relation to privilege?	What are some negative changes you have experienced in relation to privilege?	What areas have not changed in relation to privilege?

SAMPLER SHARE

Do you feel, as the partner of a now trans-identified person, that you have gained or lost privilege in any way or in any area of your life?

I had been out as a lesbian for almost 20 years when my partner transitioned and I feel rooted in my queer identity. Being femme, though, often masked my queerness, and sometimes my partner was mistaken for a man, so sometimes I felt I passed as straight, while still living with the fear of homophobic violence. Since transitioning I sometimes avoid using gendered terms so that I don't have to feel like I am deceiving people—in other words, I am afraid of identifying myself as straight by gendering my partner as male because it feels like a lie, or not the whole truth. I have gained privilege to identify as straight if I want to, which is more privilege than I had before for sure and is a powerful feeling. But I feel both ends of the spectrum have been padded—my privilege and my oppression—because my fear of violence against my family is heightened by the state of oppression that trans communities are under right now. It feels like I went back 20 years and am educating people all over again, except this time around, on transgender issues.

(Shared by Yvette)

COUPLE COMMUNICATION CORNER

When partners or couples speak spontaneously out of anger or fear about the unknown, without thinking it through, they can sometimes regret the way they phrased it. Rehearsing what and how partners may want to ask or discuss with their trans-identified partner, and/or others, can help partners and couples before they actually communicate their thoughts. This gives the non-transitioning partner a moment to reflect and pause before they converse about emotional topics. Partners may choose to practice asking these questions with a trusted friend, family member, spiritual mentor, or therapist first.

Explain your thoughts and feelings about these questions to each other. Do you and your trans-identified partner answer these questions in the same way or differently? Discuss your responses to understand how you view them and make time to celebrate all you learn from being willing to communicate with each other.

1. Are you able to discuss with your partner the way you feel privilege may have changed for you and/or as a couple in relation to bathroom use and any safety concerns?

The partner's thoughts: The trans persons's thoughts:

. . . .

. . . .

2. Are you able to discuss with your partner the way you feel privilege may have changed for you and/or as a couple in relation to shopping in stores together?

The partner's thoughts: The trans persons's thoughts:

. . . .

. . . .

3. Are you able to discuss with your partner the way you feel privilege may have changed for you and/or as a couple in relation to eating in restaurants together?

The partner's thoughts: The trans persons's thoughts:

. . . .

. . . .

4. Are you able to discuss with your partner about the way you feel privilege may have changed for you and/or as a couple in relation to showing affection in public?

The partner's thoughts: The trans persons's thoughts:

....

....

5. Are you able to discuss with your partner the way you feel privilege may have changed for you and/or as a couple in relation to being part of the LGBTQQIA+ community?

The partner's thoughts: The trans persons's thoughts:

....

....

6. Are you able to discuss with your partner the way you feel privilege may have changed for you and/or as a couple in relation to social circles of friends and family?

The partner's thoughts: The trans persons's thoughts:

....

....

7. Are you able to discuss with your partner the way you feel privilege may have changed for you and/or as a couple in relation to hospitals and/or with medical personnel?

| AFFIRMATIVE ANECDOTE | The partner's thoughts: | The trans persons's thoughts: |

Wheels keep spinning,
I hold on for dear life,
Jumping off is
Not an option.
The earth rotates,
Gravity's pull is critical,
Taking small steps
Is the only choice!

The partner's thoughts: The trans persons's thoughts:

....

....

....

....

8. Are you able to discuss with your partner the way you feel privilege may have changed for you and/or as a couple in relation to legal rights and laws?

The partner's thoughts:

The trans persons's thoughts:

. . . .

. . . .

. . . .

9. Are you able to discuss with your partner the way you feel privilege may have changed for you and/or as a couple in relation to work and/or finances?

The partner's thoughts:

The trans persons's thoughts:

. . . .

. . . .

10. Are you able to discuss with your partner the way you feel privilege may have changed for you and/or as a couple in relation to gender roles and/or biased attitudes?

The partner's thoughts:

The trans persons's thoughts

. . . .

. . . .

Chapter 11

LET'S TALK ABOUT FINDING A THERAPIST

VITAL VIGNETTE

Many times, feelings of concern or confusion are alleviated if the partner discovers a knowledgeable and experienced therapist. The search may not be difficult if you know how to look. As may be expected, it can be much easier to find a qualified therapist who is familiar with LGBTQQIA+ issues if you live in an urban or metropolitan area. The number of providers in this specialty is exploding. Training is occurring in many parts of certain countries, including rural areas. Some people who cannot find a trained provider in their area will travel great distances to work in person with a therapist. If this is not an option for you, partners may choose to speak remotely with a therapist or rely more on peer support through the Internet, support groups, conferences, etc.

> AFFIRMATIVE ANECDOTE
>
> *Sometimes*
> *I just stare.*
> *Is this my life?*
> *Is this our life?*
> *Sometimes*
> *I stare*
> *Into space,*
> *Searching,*
> *For me,*
> *For us.*

Sometimes, there are LGBTQQIA+-experienced therapists who have very little training in regard to the "T." Then, add in the fact that you are looking for a therapist who understands the unique requirements of the partner of someone who is in transition, and the pool can become narrower still. There are a multitude of things I would suggest that a partner should keep in mind when attempting to find a therapist who will suit your personal needs. I strongly recommend that you interview the therapist on the phone as a first screening. Second, I would set up an initial in-person consultation, but use this opportunity to grasp the therapist's knowledge and awareness of the issues that matter most to you. Even if a therapist states that they are experienced in working with the LGBTQQIA+ community on a website or a referral list, this does not automatically mean they have had any specific training in transgender issues. It could simply mean that they are open to providing services to transgender clients and/or their families, but have no experience or clinical training in relation to transgender matters or the needs of partners. It is completely acceptable to ask if the therapist is knowledgeable about vocabulary, inquire how many partners they have worked with or have as clients, and question their training and certifications that align with your needs. Equally important, you may have other core issues that must be addressed, in addition to the transition, such as a history of abuse, addictions, trauma, panic attacks, or depression.

Many partners have stated that the transition triggered past trauma they had buried, especially now that they are in a relationship with a person who presents as a different gender from when they became a couple. Others have discussed how their addictions to food and/or other substances became challenging while the transition process was the focal point of their relationship. In some cases, partners are seeking not only a therapist who has experience with the array of circumstances facing the non-transitioning partner, but also one who is familiar with mental illness, trauma, or a myriad of critical issues that must also be addressed.

During your interviewing and initial consultation process, if at any time you feel that the therapist is inappropriate with their line of questioning or statements, such as blaming your actions for your partner's need to transition, or that they have a bias that contradicts your beliefs, you do not need to use this therapist. Trust your gut, and if any part of the interview feels uncomfortable, find a different therapist who fits your needs. However, it is important to note that many difficult and unexpected issues can arise during therapy. You should question the therapist to clarify the communication. There can be miscommunication. Also, if you do not like the therapist after a first visit, there is no need to go back. But if you are uncomfortable with your current therapist, I suggest you discuss any issues with the therapist before terminating working with them. It is important to note that an experienced therapist whose cultural background, race, ethnicity, religion, gender, age, ability, size, or LGBTQQIA+ affiliations may vary from yours can bring a healthy array of dynamics and points of view into the therapeutic process, which could be worth considering. If the therapist's identity differs from yours, this does not mean that they do not have the professional skills required to treat you in therapy. You will have to decide to what degree these aspects matter to you, based on your preferences, needs, and issues.

If you are currently working with a trained provider who is helping you and you feel that they will continue to do so, there probably is no need to switch to a different therapist, but, again, this choice is yours. However, if you are searching for a therapist, then keep in mind that, besides training, you may want to consider these questions when selecting one:

- Do they make you feel accepted, respected, and understood?
- Do you feel that they like you?
- Are they a good listener?
- Do they give you good advice?
- Are they professional, on time, organized, and reliable?

It may take some time, but you can find a qualified therapist who is right for you. Once you do, they can become a major support and a welcome lifeline!

GRAPHICS GALORE

Splash

What do you want in a therapist? By creatively splashing words and/or short phrases, quickly attempt to express your answers randomly with as many responses as possible scattered on the paper.

GRAPHICS GALORE

Web

Why might you want to begin or continue individual therapy now?

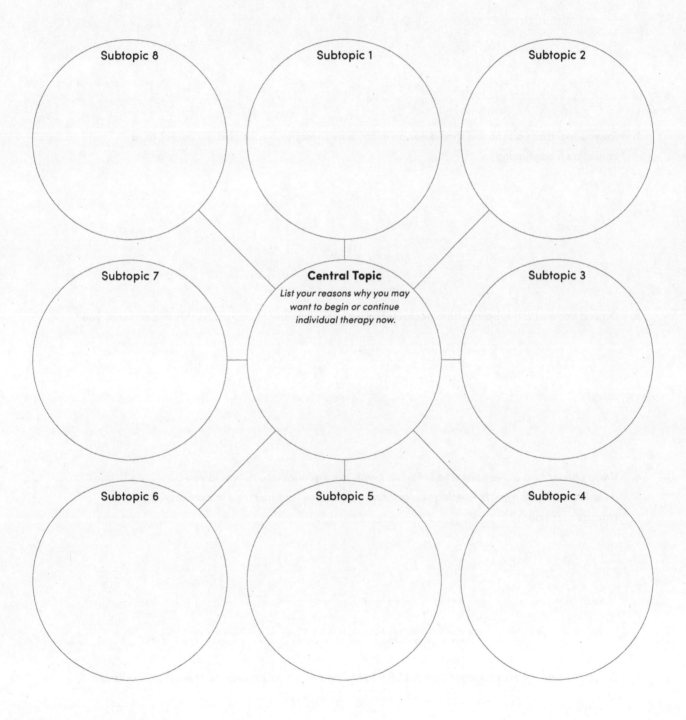

REFLECTIVE RESPONSES

1. Do you feel that you should/should not be in individual therapy as your partner begins to or considers transitioning?

....

....

....

2. Do you feel that you should/should not be in couple's therapy as your partner begins to or considers transitioning?

....

....

....

3. Do you know of a therapist who is experienced with transgender issues and is this important to you?

....

....

....

4. If you cannot find a therapist who is familiar with transgender issues, would you be willing to use a therapist who is open to helping you address your needs, but has little to no experience with transgender issues?

....

....

....

5. Do you know anyone who identifies as LGBTQQIA+ and could recommend a therapist they used?

....

....

6. Do you know anyone who is the partner of a person who has transitioned or is in the process of transitioning and could recommend a therapist they are using or have used?

....

....

....

AFFIRMATIVE ANECDOTE

We said I DO,
I don't want
To say I don't,
What DO I do?

7. Are there any support groups in your area that could recommend a therapist?

....

....

8. Are you willing to call your insurance company, if you know they will keep this inquiry confidential, to find out if and what types of therapy your insurance pays for and what percentage or portion is your responsibility?

....

....

....

9. If there is only one therapist in your area who is familiar with transgender issues, how will you and your partner decide whether this therapist will be for individual or for couple's therapy?

....

....

....

10. How will you communicate with your individual therapist if you are experiencing feelings or thoughts of needing or wanting to change to a different individual therapist?

....

....

....

11. How will you communicate with your couple's therapist if you are experiencing feelings or thoughts of needing or wanting to change to a different couple's therapist?

....

....

....

12. What do you plan to do if you see your therapist at a conference, training, support group, or any social setting outside of therapy?

....

....

....

13. Are you comfortable selecting a transgender therapist as your individual therapist?

....

....

....

14. Are you comfortable selecting a transgender therapist as your couple's therapist?

....

....

....

15. How will you address the situation if your individual or couple's therapist is focusing more on your partner's transition and not enough on your own needs or issues?

....

....

....

GRAPHICS GALORE

T-Chart

What are your thoughts about the therapist you interviewed?

What are their positive (+) aspects?	What are their negative (−) aspects?	Which aspects hold equal (=) weight?

GRAPHICS GALORE

Timeline

What did you discuss and/or discover about yourself in therapy today?

Date of service:	Response:	Do I want to share what I learned with anyone else? If so, with whom and what?
Date of service:	Response:	Do I want to share what I learned with anyone else? If so, with whom and what?
Date of service:	Response:	Do I want to share what I learned with anyone else? If so, with whom and what?
Date of service:	Response:	Do I want to share what I learned with anyone else? If so, with whom and what?
Date of service:	Response:	Do I want to share what I learned with anyone else? If so, with whom and what?
Date of service:	Response:	Do I want to share what I learned with anyone else? If so, with whom and what?

DESERVING DE-STRESS DELIGHTS

Clean and Organize

When life around me felt chaotic and out of my control during the transition, one of the things I did to de-stress and give me a sense of order and structure was to organize something. The stability of arranging my environment helped me become grounded and peaceful.

> AFFIRMATIVE ANECDOTE
>
> *I see your*
> *Joy*
> *And I can't*
> *Wait*
> *To share*
> *In it.*
> *In time,*
> *I hope*
> *To join*
> *You.*

Sometimes I sorted out papers that had piled up and other times I cleaned an overstuffed drawer or closet. On other occasions I weeded through my clothes or systemized my belongings. The act of organizing brought me comfort and was a mindless activity that was useful. Some partners have shared with me that they would rearrange the furniture in a room, wash their car, or scrub their home from top to bottom. These simple acts helped them be in control and do something that made them feel better when it was over. Other partners, who hated cleaning or physically organizing, decided to plan an event or schedule out their weekly routine on paper. Completing or structuring a task proved to be an extremely rewarding feat for numerous partners.

By organizing something, partners expressed a sentiment of achieving a tangible accomplishment and taking a visible action that felt as if they were contributing to the space around them. Many expressed that it gave them a greater sense of safety and familiarity that was obtainable and practical. So, go ahead and get organized!

Journal your reaction to this Deserving De-Stress Delight.

....

....

....

....

....

....

....

....

....

....

....

....

....

....

....

....

....

....

....

....

....

....

....

....

GRAPHICS GALORE

Box

What issues or topics do you want to discuss in either individual or couple's therapy? Suggestion: Code with "I" for Individual and "C" for Couple's therapy. (You may or may not choose to ask your trans-identified partner what they want to discuss in couple's therapy.)

1. "I" or "C"?	2. "I" or "C"?	3. "I" or "C"?	4. "I" or "C"?	5. "I" or "C"?
6. "I" or "C"?	7. "I" or "C"?	8. "I" or "C"?	9. "I" or "C"?	10. "I" or "C"?
11. "I" or "C"?	12. "I" or "C"?	13. "I" or "C"?	14. "I" or "C"?	15. "I" or "C"?
16. "I" or "C"?	17. "I" or "C"?	18. "I" or "C"?	19. "I" or "C"?	20. "I" or "C"?
21. "I" or "C"?	22. "I" or "C"?	23. "I" or "C"?	24. "I" or "C"?	25. "I" or "C"?
26. "I" or "C"?	27. "I" or "C"?	28. "I" or "C"?	29. "I" or "C"?	30. "I" or "C"?

GRAPHICS GALORE

Venn Diagram

Deciding to begin couple's therapy is an important choice and could involve much negotiation and compromise between the two of you. Finding a therapist you both agree on is critical. What are your priorities individually when searching for a couple's therapist who would fulfill your needs as a couple?

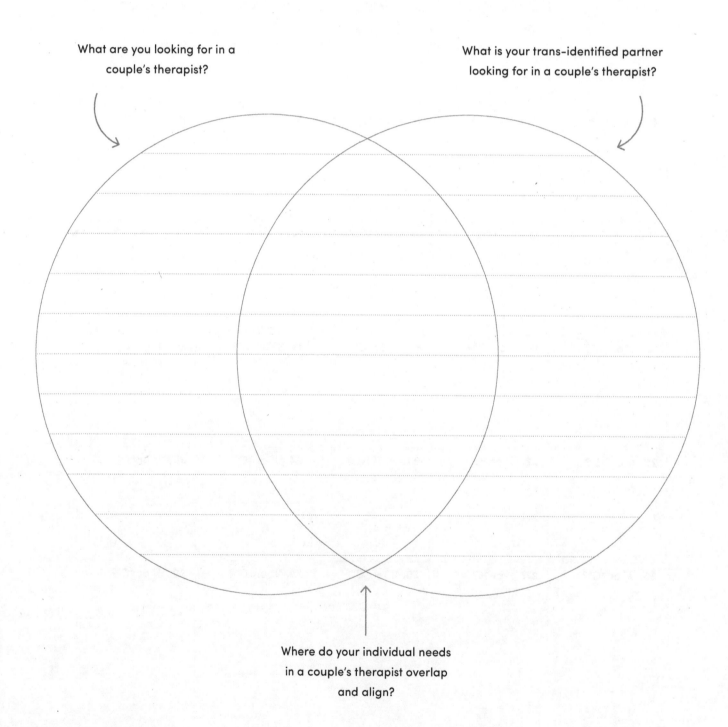

What are you looking for in a couple's therapist?

What is your trans-identified partner looking for in a couple's therapist?

Where do your individual needs in a couple's therapist overlap and align?

EMPATHY-EMBRACING EXERCISE

Understanding the need your partner has to transition is sometimes a challenge for the non-transitioning partner. Trying to view the transition through their lens may be an important step towards acceptance. Sometimes the safest and most comfortable place to discuss and sort out all of these feelings is with a therapist, a support group, by attending a conference, or from searching the Internet.

How do you think it would feel if you were asked to live your life not as your affirmed gender?

AFFIRMATIVE ANECDOTE

Storming,
Raging,
Slowly calm,
We embrace.
Let me do
No harm.

GRAPHICS GALORE

Bar Graph

To what degree do these factors matter to you when you are choosing a therapist for yourself? Based on a scale from 1 to 10, with 1 being the lowest and 10 being the highest, color or shade in your response. This visual will help you see where your greatest concerns/needs lie and can help you communicate this to your trans-identified partner, therapist, spiritual mentor, or for your own personal understanding. The bar graph results may vary as the transition progresses and your thoughts may shift.

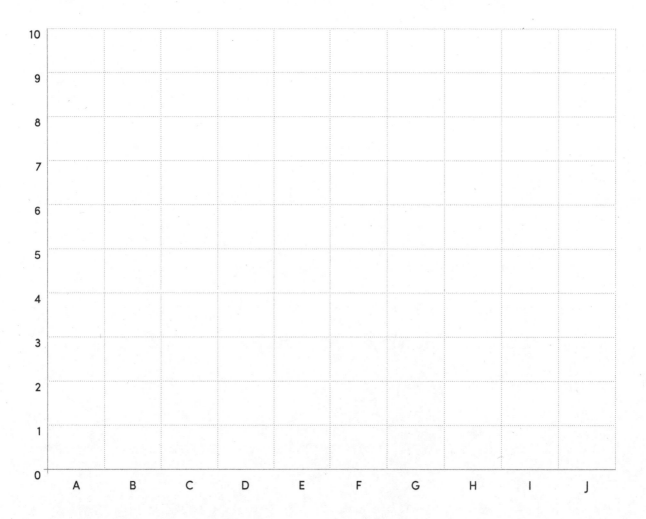

Use these ideas to fill in the bar graph or feel free to create your own!

A. The therapist identifies as part of the LGBTQQIA+ community.

B. Knowing the therapist is LGBTQQIA+ competent.

C. These aspects of the therapist's identity matter to you: age, race, religion, ethnicity, size, ability, or cultural background.

D. The therapist's gender matters to you.

E. The therapist takes your medical insurance.

F. The therapist's rate per session is affordable for you.

G. The location of the therapist's office is convenient in relation to your home/office.

H. The number of years the therapist has been in practice.

I. The areas of specialty the therapist has and any certification/s the therapist holds in relation to these areas.

J. The therapist is published on topics related to transgender issues.

GRAPHICS GALORE

Pie Graph

To what degree do these factors matter to you when you are choosing a therapist for yourself? Decide how important are these factors to you, in relation to each other, when searching for a therapist? Place the number that corresponds with a suggested topic within as many slices of the pie that conveys how each one matters to you. Only one number should be placed in each slice. You do not need to use all the topics but do fill in all the slices. Feel free to create your own topics and assign them their own number.

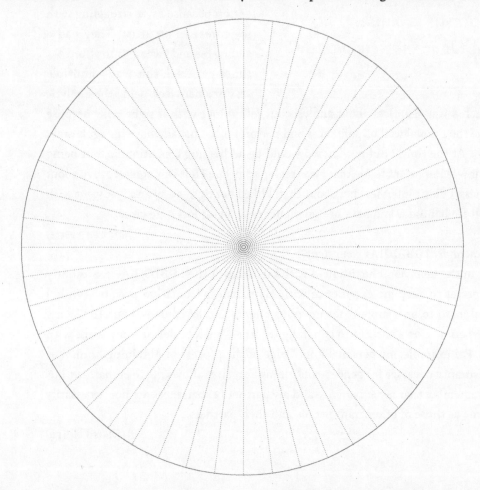

1. The therapist identifies as part of the LGBTQQIA+ community.

2. Knowing the therapist is LGBTQQIA+ competent.

3. These aspects of the therapist's identity matter to you: age, race, religion, ethnicity, size, ability, or cultural background.

4. The therapist's gender matters to you.

5. The therapist takes your medical insurance.

6. The therapist's rate per session is affordable for you.

7. The location of the therapist's office is convenient in relation to your home/office.

8. The number of years the therapist has been in practice.

9. The areas of specialty the therapist has and any certification/s the therapist holds in relation to these areas.

10. The therapist is published on topics related to transgender issues.

SAMPLER SHARE

Do you know of a therapist who is experienced with transgender issues and is this important to you?

> AFFIRMATIVE ANECDOTE
>
> *We loved the picture we drew.*
> *Now that canvas is blank,*
> *Will we both love the new picture?*

I found my therapist by inquiring at a local psychoanalytic training program that advertised that they work with artists, so it got my attention because I was struggling with my career as an artist. They had a sliding fee and I was able to afford 2–3 times per week this way—multiple sessions per week being the analytic approach. I was skeptical about analysis but fell in love with it right away because it broke the normal wall of politeness and performance I usually have in regular talk therapy. At the time, I did not know I would be addressing transitioning, but being queer, it was important to me that I was seeing someone I felt was at least savvy about queerness. I didn't interview her about that; I liked her right away and just went with it. I still see her today and have been with her now for almost nine years.

(Shared by Yvette)

Is the therapist LGBTQQIA+ competent?

I work in the behavioral health field with members of the LGBTQQIA+ community, and I prefer to keep my experience with my partner's transition private. While I do work hard to be a support for my trans clients and loved ones, I aim to use my own experience as a partner to generally inform—but not define—my work with others. For example, my personal knowledge of the process of obtaining hormones and insurance coverage for gender-confirming surgeries allows me to empathize, but I also remember that my experience and my partner's experiences are not necessarily the same as those of other trans people and their partners.

(Shared by Ivy)

COUPLE COMMUNICATION CORNER

When partners or couples speak spontaneously out of anger or fear about the unknown, without thinking it through, they can sometimes regret the way they phrased it. Rehearsing what and how partners may want to ask or discuss with their trans-identified partner, and/or others, can help partners and couples before they actually communicate their thoughts. This gives the non-transitioning partner a moment to reflect and pause before they converse about emotional topics. Partners may choose to practice asking these questions with a trusted friend, family member, spiritual mentor, or therapist first.

Explain your thoughts and feelings about these questions to each other. Do you and your trans-identified partner answer these questions in the same way or differently? Discuss your responses to understand how you view them and make time to celebrate all you learn from being willing to communicate with each other.

1.   Does it matter to you if the therapist identifies as part of the LGBTQQIA+ community?

> AFFIRMATIVE ANECDOTE
>
> *Find a quiet corner*
> *To reflect in silence.*
> *Listen to the message,*
> *There is space*
> *Enough for ME!*

The partner's thoughts: The trans persons's thoughts:

. . . .

. . . .

2.   Does it matter to you if the therapist is LGBTQQIA+ competent?

The partner's thoughts: The trans persons's thoughts:

. . . .

. . . .

. . . .

3.   Do these aspects of the therapist's identity matter to you: age, race, religion, ethnicity, size, ability, or cultural background?

The partner's thoughts: The trans persons's thoughts:

. . . .

. . . .

4. Does the therapist's gender matter to you?

    The partner's thoughts: The trans persons's thoughts:

    . . . .

    . . . .

5. Does it matter to you if the therapist takes your medical insurance?

    The partner's thoughts: The trans persons's thoughts:

    . . . .

    . . . .

6. Does it matter to you if the therapist's rate per session is affordable for you?

    The partner's thoughts: The trans persons's thoughts:

    . . . .

7. Does it matter to you if the location of the therapist's office is convenient in relation to your home/ office?

    The partner's thoughts: The trans persons's thoughts:

    . . . .

    . . . .

8. Does the number of years the therapist has been in practice matter to you?

    The partner's thoughts: The trans persons's thoughts:

    . . . .

    . . . .

9. Do the areas of specialty the therapist has and any certification/s the therapist holds in relation to these areas matter to you?

The partner's thoughts:

The trans persons's thoughts:

. . . .

. . . .

10. Does it matter to you if the therapist is published on topics related to transgender issues?

The partner's thoughts:

The trans persons's thoughts

. . . .

. . . .

Chapter 12

PARTNERS IN SEX

VITAL VIGNETTE

Genitals! There, now it is out in the open. That is what so many people often think transitioning is all about, yet it is so much more than that. Gender and sexuality are not the same thing, but they can be interrelated. Gender is how you internally experience yourself as male, female, some combination of male and female, or neither, whereas your sexuality is who you are attracted to and/or want to have sex with. The extra layer that can become complex and perhaps confusing for both the trans-identified person and their partner is when sex is added into the mix. For some trans-identified people, their attractions may remain the same as before the transition.

For many of these people, the person in transition will continue to be attracted to and desire the same form of sexual and/or intimate relationship with the same partner/s they were involved with prior to the transition. For other transgender people, their attraction to the gender or genders they desired prior to the transition may change or be extended.

If soul-searching and communication were ever important before, the topic of sex forces these skills to be loudly front and center! Partners may encounter all of the complexities involved in negotiating attraction, sexuality, desire, needs, compromise, education, trust, and honesty. For some partners, simply learning about the transition can shake the foundation of their sexual relationship. The challenge is trying to figure out where or how to begin sorting it all out. I suggest taking a close look at how your sex life was before you found out about the transition.

It requires you to take a long, hard look at your sexual history of wants, desires, needs, attractions, and so on. Once you gain a clearer awareness of what your intimacy and/or sex life was like before the transition, you can use this information to compare it with how intimacy and/or your sex life may change as your partner transitions. There may come a time when you will have to decide what is acceptable to you and what is not. Answering the questions posed in the Reflective Responses, Graphics Galore, and Couple Communication Corner may make it easier to understand your thought process, and your answers can be shared with your partner when and/or if you feel ready and comfortable doing so. It may also be critical for you to understand your own trauma history, should it be a part of your past, in relation to your partner's gender. For some partners, the transition can trigger trauma and it can affect your daily life. Should this apply to you, it may be important for you to get support and/or professional help to assist in coping with these major issues.

The decision to remain in the relationship and partake in sex is something that each person will need to determine for themselves. Over time, you may be faced with choices that you never would have even considered before the transition. Ideas and options may be discussed, which you may have never heard of prior to the transition, or which were unacceptable before but are now up for negotiation.

Many partners have shared that prior to the transition certain body parts of their trans-identified partner were off limits during sex and/or intimacy. Specific body parts may have been covered and were not to be touched or acknowledged. Yet very often, once the transition process began, these requests can become altered or lifted entirely. This change of body and identity can cause confusion for some partners, since this may affect the dynamics of the sex life the couple had in the past. Some partners expressed that they preferred not to touch or acknowledge their trans-identified partner's specific body parts. In some cases, the sexual experiences of the non-transitioning partner had encountered with their partner, prior to learning of their transition, had only focused on the genitals of the non-transitioning partner, and they both preferred sex this way.

Some people, who had been in closed, monogamous relationships prior to the transition, shared that their trans-identified partner now asked if they would consider an open and/or polyamorous relationship. Some partners were told that the person in transition wanted to explore intimate and/or sexual relationships with a wider variety of gendered people or maybe experience a particular kink they never tried before. Some even stated that their trans-identified partner told them that they were no longer attracted to their non-transitioning partner because they were no longer sexually attracted to the partner's gender. The whys and hows are very individual and something that can be discussed in therapy, with a support group, and/or with your partner in transition. There is a wide range of possibilities that can occur once the transition process begins, and for some, sex and preferences may change.

Many partners who attended my workshops discussed that their trans-identified partner requested the non-transitioning partner use their gender-affirming pronouns and name during sex and/or intimacy. Many asked for their partner to refer to their genitalia in terms of their gender-affirming body—for example, now referring to their breasts as their chest or their clitoris as their dick, and vice versa for M2F/F2F/MTF. If a person in transition elects to have surgery or take hormones, their body may change in drastic ways. The smell, feel, look, sound, and taste of the trans-identified person may change slowly or quickly, depending on levels, age, body chemistry, and procedures. There may even need to be short or longer periods of time that certain types of intimacy and/or sex will have to be put on hold as the person in transition is healing or adjusting. The non-transitioning partner may also ask not to be intimate and/or sexual for periods of time due to a desire to adjust to all this newness, simply to sort their emotions, and/or figure out their next steps. In fact, the non-transitioning partner may also require additional time to become used to any changes in the trans-identified person's body and/or the language requested to be integrated during sex and intimacy.

Another topic that participants shared in my workshops and at conferences I attended was that the trans-identified partner's transition affected not only their sex life as a couple but also the trans partner's questioning of their own gender and sexuality. A group of people discussed that their personal perspective of masculinity or femininity shifted and that they felt others perceived their masculinity or femininity differently, especially in relation to their partner in transition. This may have triggered their own desire to explore gender. Some people stated that they began altering their own way of dressing, walking, or visually expressing themselves. Others expressed that the transition granted them some type of unspoken permission to explore how they dressed or how they wore their hair. Some trans partners found the transition unleashed their own sexual desires to be with other people or to try different forms of sexual role-playing or incorporate sex toys with their partner in transition during sex and intimacy.

Furthermore, many of the partners who have participated in my workshops, or those I went to, voiced that they needed to set up dates to learn each other's body and their preferences over again. Numerous partners articulated that they felt as if they were being intimate and sexual with a post-transition body that hardly resembled the one they knew prior to the transition. Some partners had to discover whether they could be intimate and/or sexual with a gendered body that was not their preference.

In addition, several partners conveyed that they realized it was important to talk about any changes in the type or way protection was to be used by them as couples. In earnest, some partners spoke about how, when applicable, any past sexually transmitted infections (STIs) had to be addressed in connection to any varying sexual activity.

GRAPHICS GALORE

Splash

What are all the words and/or phrases that come to mind when you think about sex, intimacy, and gender? By creatively splashing words and/or short phrases, quickly attempt to express your answers randomly with as many responses as possible scattered on the paper.

GRAPHICS GALORE

Web

Have any of your sexual fantasies changed or become unleashed now that you know about the transition? (Consider sharing these with your trans-identified partner when and if you feel comfortable doing so. Perhaps you may encourage your trans-identified partner to share this information with you, too!)

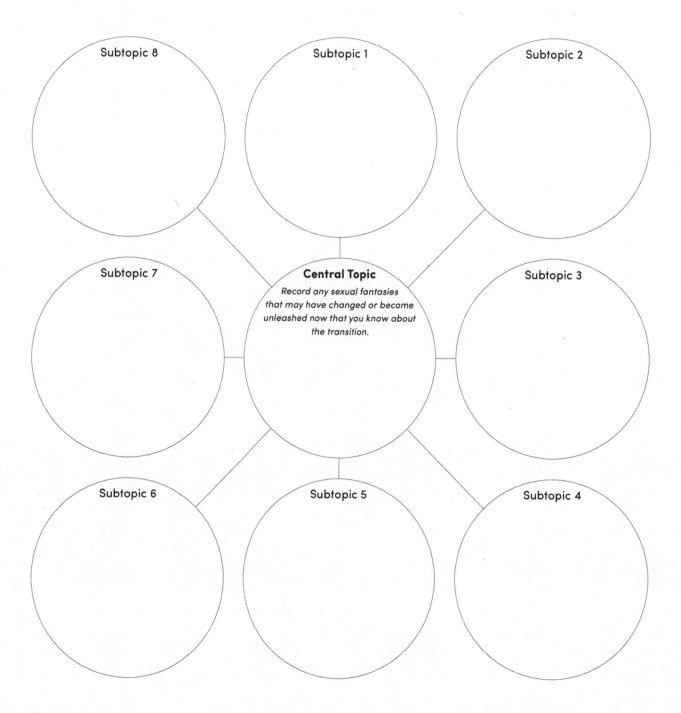

Subtopic 8

Subtopic 1

Subtopic 2

Subtopic 7

Central Topic
Record any sexual fantasies that may have changed or become unleashed now that you know about the transition.

Subtopic 3

Subtopic 6

Subtopic 5

Subtopic 4

REFLECTIVE RESPONSES

1. How would you describe your sexual and/or intimate relationship prior to, during, and after the transition?

    ....

    ....

    ....

2. Do you feel that your emotional state, in relation to the transition, has affected your sex life/intimacy?

    ....

    ....

    ....

3. Has sex and/or intimacy been the same or different throughout, compared with the way it was prior to the transition?

    ....

    ....

    ....

4. Do you miss the physical body you knew when you were initially a couple?

    ....

    ....

    ....

5. Who initiated sex before the transition and has it been the same since the transition began?

    ....

    ....

    ....

6. How do you think your partner will feel, look, smell, sound, and taste as a result of the transition, and do you anticipate wanting to have sex and be intimate with a person who fits this description?

....

....

....

7. How do you feel the transition will affect/has affected sex and intimacy?

....

....

....

8. What intimate activities can you and your trans-identified partner engage in now that promotes intimacy but may not be sexual?

....

....

....

9. What changes, if any, did you experience/are you experiencing related to your own gender identity, in regard to expressing or questioning your own gender, as a result of the transition?

....

....

....

10. What type of relationship did you or your trans-identified partner prefer prior to the transition: monogamous, polyamorous, open, or anything else? What about since the transition began? Has there been a shift? How did you/will you both communicate this decision or preference to each other?

....

....

....

11. Were there any changes in sexual functioning and/or desire for you or your trans-identified partner throughout the transition? If yes, how do you feel about these changes?

....

....

....

AFFIRMATIVE ANECDOTE

Are fear and sadness
In need of a hug?
Is being scared okay?
I'm scared,
Hold me!

12. If this is an option, do you believe you will still be attracted to your partner during sex and/or intimacy after surgeries and/or hormone treatment?

....

....

....

13. Do you believe your partner will still be attracted to you during sex and/or intimacy after surgeries and/or hormone treatment? How do you believe you would react if they are not?

....

....

....

....

14. Are there or were there any areas of your body or your partner's body that are/were off limits during sex and/or intimacy before, during, or after the transition? Is this a shift? How do or did you feel about this?

....

....

....

15. Are there or were there any activities that are/were off limits during sex and/or intimacy for you and your partner before, during, or after the transition? Is this a shift? How do or did you feel about this?

....

....

GRAPHICS GALORE

Venn Diagram

What are the sexual and intimate practices that matter the most to you and which you feel are critical for a healthy and active sexual/intimate relationship?

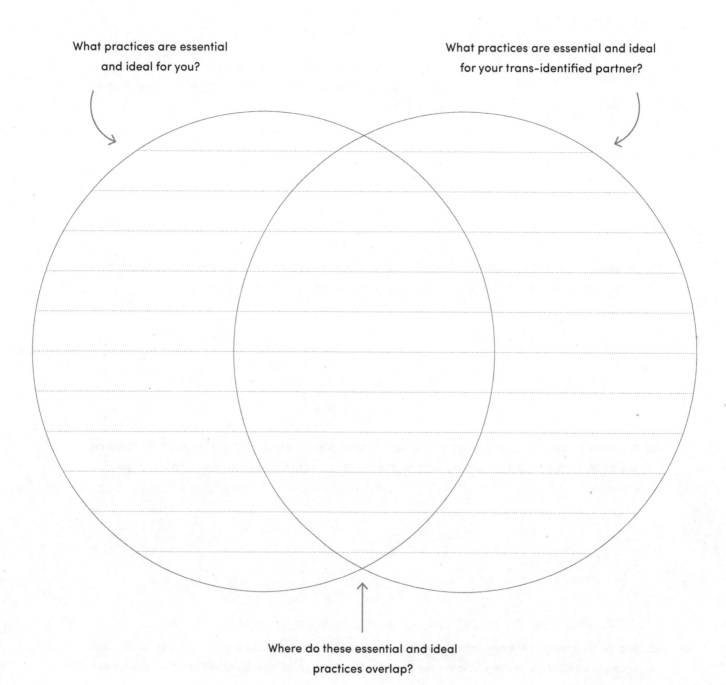

What practices are essential and ideal for you?

What practices are essential and ideal for your trans-identified partner?

Where do these essential and ideal practices overlap?

GRAPHICS GALORE

Box

List any of the possible sexual and/or intimate ways or activities you can engage with or without your trans-identified, which will help you feel closer to your partner? (These can include practices in or outside of the bedroom or location of your choosing.)

1.	2.	3.	4.
5.	6.	7.	8.
9.	10.	11.	12.
13.	14.	15.	16.
17.	18.	19.	20.

DESERVING DE-STRESS DELIGHTS

Pamper, Nurture, and Self-Care

What can be more loving than nurturing and pampering your body and soul? As a partner, I believe it was critical for my medical health and emotional sanity. Pampering can be experienced in a multitude of ways and often finances can dictate the type of things you can afford. Regardless of your budget, I think pampering yourself during the transition is essential for coping and being present for both yourself and your trans-identified partner. For me, a massage is the most calming and rejuvenating form of self-care. When I was low on funds, I offered to let my cousin, who was in massage school, practice her skills on me and no money was needed. Another time, I went to a nail salon and had an inexpensive ten-minute chair massage. Sometimes, I requested gift cards and used those funds for a luxury massage.

> AFFIRMATIVE ANECDOTE
>
> *Dysphoria robbed you, Dysphoria robbed me!*

Other ways I indulged the nurturing of my body was having my hair cut or dyed, getting my nails done, and participating in a gentle yoga class. There were days that I allowed myself to sleep longer or took an hour's nap in the middle of the day. One time I got dressed up and went out to eat in a fancy restaurant with a family member. Learning how to please yourself sexually can also be a form of relaxation that can be both liberating and empowering. I believe included in self-care is giving yourself permission to shop. Shopping, in moderation, is all part of adding fun and lightness to pampering your body. Treating yourself with a special gift that is within your budget will remind you that you have value and worth.

One partner I spoke with explained that they found being around dogs very comforting, but they did not own a dog, so they offered to dog-sit for friends free of charge. Taking care of your body by exercising can be extremely nurturing and a healthy expression of self-care. Another person enjoyed cooking. He would take the ingredients they had in their home and would challenge himself to make a meal using only the components that were free and available. Many people have shared that they found free and thrifty ways to practice self-care by going for a meditative bicycle ride in their neighborhood, using a free-pass coupon to a gym, and taking a free open yoga class on special holidays.

Caring for your own needs and focusing on your own body and soul are some of the kindest and most respectful ways a trans partner can honor themselves. As you journey through the transition process and learn how to satisfy your personal desires, lovingly pampering, nurturing, and caring for your own body must be at the top of the list!

Journal your reaction to this Deserving De-Stress Delight.

. . . .

. . . .

GRAPHICS GALORE

T-Chart

What sexual activities, familiar and unfamiliar, are currently acceptable, not acceptable, or uncertain for you, now that you know about the transition?

What is acceptable to you sexually?	What is not acceptable to you sexually?	What is something you are unsure of that you would consider trying sexually?

GRAPHICS GALORE

Timeline

What sexual practices or games, if any, have you introduced into your relationship, since your trans-identified partner told you about the transition?

What we tried?	Date we tried it:	Did I enjoy it and want to try it again?
What we tried?	Date we tried it:	Did I enjoy it and want to try it again?
What we tried?	Date we tried it:	Did I enjoy it and want to try it again?
What we tried?	Date we tried it:	Did I enjoy it and want to try it again?
What we tried?	Date we tried it:	Did I enjoy it and want to try it again?
What we tried?	Date we tried it:	Did I enjoy it and want to try it again?
What we tried?	Date we tried it:	Did I enjoy it and want to try it again?

EMPATHY-EMBRACING EXERCISE

Body dysphoria can motivate a trans person to seriously consider and eventually undergo a physical transition. It can also affect the sexual and intimate moments a couple experiences. This exercise question asks partners to examine any discomfort with their own body and reflect upon how their discomfort impacts their sexual and intimate interactions with their trans-identified partner. This question also provides an opportunity for those in the relationship to discuss how body dysphoria is impacting their sex life and intimacy. Having body parts that are off limits for touching or penetration can be a welcome reality for some and a deep sadness for others. As difficult and fragile as this topic may be, it is an essential aspect that is sometimes a silent factor. However, it must be addressed, in order to sustain a healthy sexual and/or intimate relationship.

> AFFIRMATIVE ANECDOTE
> *Let's just*
> *Laugh tonight,*
> *I can cry*
> *Again tomorrow.*

Is there any part of your body that you dislike or would prefer not to have touched by your trans-identified partner? If yes or no, why do you think you feel this way? How does this make you feel?

....

....

....

....

....

....

....

....

....

....

GRAPHICS GALORE

Bar Graph

To what degree do these intimacy- and/or sex-related topics matter to you? Based on a scale from 1 to 10, with 1 being the lowest and 10 being the highest, color or shade in your response. This visual will help you see where your greatest concerns lie and can help you communicate this to your trans-identified partner, therapist, spiritual mentor, or for your own personal understanding. The bar graph results may vary as the transition progresses and your thoughts may shift.

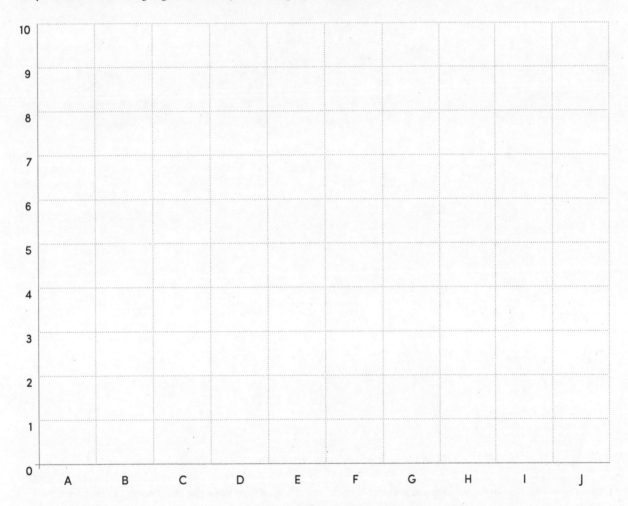

Use these ideas or thoughts to fill in the bar graph or feel free to create your own!

A. Deciding on the type of relationship you prefer to have now. (Open, polyamorous, monogamous, or any other type.)

B. Determining by whom, when, and how sex will be initiated in your relationship.

C. The use or role of toys, games, kink, and/or role-play in relation to sex and/or intimacy.

D. Deciding how the effects of attraction will play a role in your relationship.

E. Being willing to try new things sexually.

F. Time off from having sex for: healing, a break from the relationship, exploring a new partner, or refraining from sex.

G. The role sexual preference will play in the relationship in relation to sex and/or intimacy.

H. Figuring out whether you can stay in this relationship and still have a fulfilling sex life.

I. Learning the new name, pronouns, and vocabulary, and using them properly during sex and/or intimate moments.

J. Exploring each other's body and safe practices of foreplay that feel comfortable to you.

GRAPHICS GALORE

Pie Graph

To what degree do these intimacy- and/or sex-related topics matter to you? Decide how important these statements are to you in relation to each other. important are these topics to you or to you as a couple? Place the number that corresponds with a suggested topic within as many slices of the pie that conveys how each one matters to you. Only one number should be placed in each slice. You do not need to use all the topics but do fill in all the slices. Feel free to create your own topics and assign them their own number.

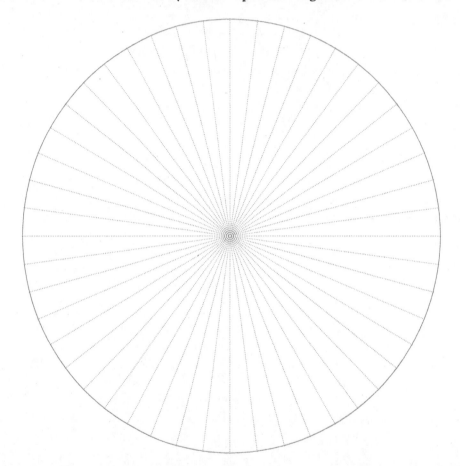

1. Deciding on the type of relationship you prefer to have now. (Open, polyamorous, monogamous, or any other type.)

2. Determining by whom, when, and how sex will be initiated in your relationship.

3. The use or role of toys, games, kink, and/or role-play in relation to sex and/or intimacy.

4. Deciding how the effects of attraction will play a role in your relationship.

5. Being willing to try new things sexually.

6. Time off from having sex for: healing, a break from the relationship, exploring a new partner, or refraining from sex.

7. The role sexual preference will play in the relationship in relation to sex and/or intimacy.

8. Figuring out whether you can stay in this relationship and still have a fulfilling sex life.

9. Learning the new name, pronouns, and vocabulary, and using them properly during sex and/or intimate moments.

10. Exploring each other's body and safe practices of foreplay that feel comfortable to you.

SAMPLER SHARE

What type of relationship did you or your trans-identified partner prefer prior to the transition: monogamous, polyamorous, open, or anything else? What about since the transition began? Was there a shift? How did you both communicate this decision or preference to each other?

When I met my partner, we met first as friends. I knew him in the early stages of his transitioning from female to male, so I was not surprised by his transition and I was comfortable with it. It was exciting and beautiful to be able to be a part of the changes he was going through. I didn't feel this would be a problem for me. What I realized later is that there is so much focus on the outward changes (which I had accepted fully and never had a problem with), but I had never really considered what would be going on internally. What went on for him? He needed to explore his sexuality as a man. We worked on having an open relationship but it did not work out because his curiosity got the best of him, and he violated the rules we set up and agreed to. I wanted very much to support him but I had to draw the line there.

(Shared by Veronica)

COUPLE COMMUNICATION CORNER

AFFIRMATIVE ANECDOTE

Show me your body,
Teach me your body,
Let me touch your body,
You love your body,
I love your body, too!

When partners or couples speak spontaneously out of anger or fear about the unknown, without thinking it through, they can sometimes regret the way they phrased it. Rehearsing what and how partners may want to ask or discuss with their trans-identified partner, and/or others, can help partners and couples before they actually communicate their thoughts. This gives the non-transitioning partner a moment to reflect and pause before they converse about emotional topics. Partners may choose to practice asking these questions with a trusted friend, family member, spiritual mentor, or therapist first.

Explain your thoughts and feelings about these questions to each other. Do you and your trans-identified partner answer these questions in the same way or differently? Discuss your responses to understand how you view them and make time to celebrate all you learn from being willing to communicate with each other.

1. What type of relationship do you prefer to have now? (Open, polyamorous, monogamous, or any other type.)

   The partner's thoughts: The trans persons's thoughts:

   ....

   ....

2. By whom, when, and how sex will be initiated in your relationship?

   The partner's thoughts: The trans persons's thoughts:

   ....

   ....

3. Will the use or role of toys, role-play, kink and/or games play any part in your sex life and/or intimacy?

   The partner's thoughts: The trans persons's thoughts:

   ....

   ....

4. How the will effects of attraction play a role in your relationship?

> AFFIRMATIVE ANECDOTE
>
> *Can we be one?*
> *Spoon and snuggle,*
> *Listen and laugh,*
> *We can become*
> *One again!*

The partner's thoughts:

The trans persons's thoughts:

. . . .

. . . .

5. Are you willing to try new things sexually?

The partner's thoughts:

The trans persons's thoughts:

. . . .

. . . .

6. Will you need to take time off from having sex for: healing, a break from the relationship, exploring a new partner, or refraining from having sex?

The partner's thoughts:

The trans persons's thoughts:

. . . .

. . . .

7. What role will sexual preference play in the relationship in relation to sex and/or intimacy?

The partner's thoughts:

The trans persons's thoughts:

. . . .

. . . .

8. Can you can stay in this relationship and still have a fulfilling sex life?

The partner's thoughts:

The trans persons's thoughts:

. . . .

. . . .

9. Is learning a new name, pronouns, and/or vocabulary, and then using them properly during sex and/or intimate moments a challenge or easy for you?

The partner's thoughts:

The trans persons's thoughts:

· ·

· ·

10. Will exploring each other's body and safe practices of foreplay feel comfortable to you?

The partner's thoughts:

The trans persons's thoughts:

· ·

· ·

Chapter 13

CELEBRATIONS COME IN DIFFERENT SIZES

VITAL VIGNETTE

There are dozens of ways to honor the transition and mark transition milestones. For some partners, the transition will be a time of celebration that will begin on day one without any hesitation, confusion, or feelings of grief. For other partners, the celebrating will evolve over time, little by little, and step by step. For a number of partners, celebrating may simply take the form of accepting or acknowledging the reality that the transition is happening or going to happen, whether they support its certainty or not. For some partners, deep down, the transition is such a loss for them that they are not genuinely able to celebrate. Furthermore, some will never celebrate and may remove themselves from the process or even leave the relationship. As has been stated many times, each partner's path is personal, based on their own needs and what feels comfortable for them.

For those partners who are able to celebrate, this can occur in an assortment of ways. There can be simple yet meaningful gestures of support or loving care in the form of hosting party-like events to commemorate the transition. Another supportive act could be joining your trans-identified partner when they are shopping for new clothes or helping them learn how to apply make-up, after which you proudly and safely stroll in the mall holding their hand as they present themselves to the world as they deserve to be seen. Attending surgeries and doctor appointments, being there when your trans-identified partner unveils their gender-affirming body, and embracing the peace your partner feels are other validating ways of celebrating the transition. Financially contributing to the fund for surgery and/or hormones, assisting in planning your trans-identified partner's binder-burning party, or being present when your partner feels nervous to share their transition with a family member who may not receive the information well—these are all ways some have shown love and support of the transition.

Besides celebrating the journey that the person who is in transition has traveled, it is critical that the partners are celebrated too, both as part of a couple and separately. This celebrating can be expressed in private with a heartfelt verbal thank-you, accompanied by a romantic dinner that is special to you. Your trans-identifying partner can show support to you by making it possible for you to pursue your own dreams. They can also celebrate the simple but powerful act when you bravely correct a person who is inaccurately gendering your partner and they cannot find the words to correct the painful error. This may seem like a simplistic act of heroism, but it can mean a lot to the partner.

It may seem ironic that this next section appears in the celebrations chapter. However, learning and understanding how to use your experiences and voice, both in solidarity with or for your trans-identified partner and as a partner, is one of the greatest ways you can celebrate your own pride and courage. I will discuss some of the challenges I have experienced, or that trans partners have shared with me, when dealing with inappropriate questions.

To this day, I am not sure if the inappropriate questions I received were due to ignorance, curiosity, or because people did not think about the insensitive manner in which they spoke. I do not believe anyone means any intentional harm, but the frequency of these inquiries can leave a partner feeling even more isolated, alone, and confused. Something that shocked me was the abundance of these unanticipated questions and statements made on a regular basis. A common but pathetically baffling theme that repeatedly occurs is that others feel it is acceptable to ask the most private and intimate questions of the partner, in lieu of offending or upsetting the person in transition. The number of inquiries or statements that partners have to endure from pure ignorance and the inconsideration of others can feel insurmountable. Frequently, questions are often fixated on how the trans-identified partner's genitals will look or function, or in what way the couple will now engage in sex, or people offer suggestions as to what they would do if their partner was in transition. Many people seem to have absolutely no ability to filter their thoughts and simply declare their curiosities to the partners. Boldly, and with some misconstrued sense of entitlement, these people comment about the person in transition's physical appearance and perceived levels or status of passing. These crude statements or intrusive questions can be asked by close and not-so-close friends, family members, co-workers, lawyers, medical professionals, and spiritual mentor; the list goes on and on.

Here are some practical suggestions I offer to assist partners when these unforeseen situations occur. It is absolutely acceptable to state that a posed question is something that you are not comfortable answering. You can also tell the person to ask your trans-identified person directly—that is often the end of that inquiry! Some partners may choose to use a stronger stance and respond by saying the inquiry is inappropriate or none of the person's business, and/or let the person know that they are being offensive. Others refer people with questions to the Internet so that they can get the information from specific credible sites, articles, books, or organizations. It must be acknowledged that there are partners and transgender people who are completely comfortable answering highly personal questions and are not insulted by insensitive statements.

One strategy that worked well for me when my partner was gendered incorrectly was to restate my partner's pronoun in the response: "Actually, *he* would prefer the vegetarian choice!" By stating it this way, there was no need to be confrontational, yet I made my point without embarrassing anyone. Other times I would ask if the person inquiring would want me to ask the same question or make the same statement about them or their significant other. When posed like that, most people apologized and explained they had never realized the implications of what they had just said or asked.

In response to my partner's transition, I had to learn a lot about the transgender experience, about language and pronouns, and how to be respectful. I recognize that I needed allowances to be made for me when I was learning, and I understand that other people also need those same allowances for errors. Most people have to be taught how to use the proper language in relation to the transition and also what questions and comments are appropriate. You will have to decide when, why, and for whom enough will be enough. This may take a while to figure out, be quite obvious to you immediately, or shift over time. The ideas discussed earlier can serve as a model of how I or others have responded to challenging moments or unexpected social situations. How you react to what people may say or ask and still retain your own dignity needs to be addressed and understood by you. I strongly suggest keeping a record of what is stated by others and decide, in consultation with your transgender partner, some responses and rebuttals that feel comfortable to use in the future.

Celebrating all you have encountered since learning about the transition may be different for every individual and couple. For some, the idea of celebrating is more aligned with acknowledging your own growth and knowing your partner is at peace with their self. Realizing that your voice matters, that you have choices, and recognizing all you have learned from every experience in relation to the transition are reasons enough to celebrate you!

GRAPHICS GALORE

Splash

What words would you use to describe how it feels to observe your partner as they are living in their affirmed gender? By creatively splashing words and/or short phrases, quickly attempt to express your answers randomly with as many responses as possible scattered on the paper.

GRAPHICS GALORE

Web

Has or did someone ask you and/or your trans-identified partner any inappropriate questions or state any inappropriate remarks? If so, record these questions and statements with the aim to help you review how you responded. Then reflect on your reply, in order to decide if there may be a better way to approach these inappropriate questions or remarks, should they ever happen again in the future.

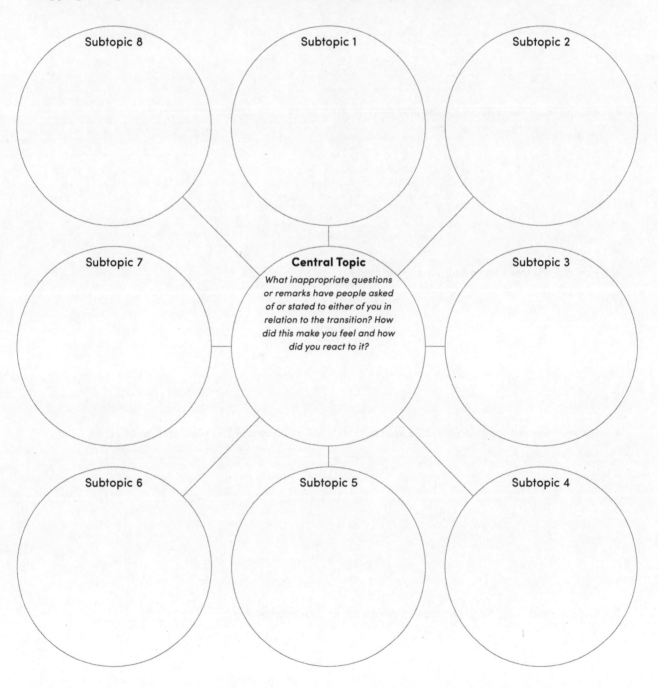

REFLECTIVE RESPONSES

1. Do you or did you demonstrate ways of celebrating or supporting your trans-identified partner throughout the transition process?

    ....

    ....

    ....

2. Did the transition affect your sex life?

    ....

    ....

    ....

3. How did the transition affect your friendships?

    ....

    ....

    ....

4. Do you think the transition affected your partner's self-confidence? Did that have an effect on your relationship?

    ....

    ....

    ....

5. Did the transition affect the communication within your relationship?

    ....

    ....

    ....

6. Did the transition affect your relationships with family members?

....

....

....

7. Do you think the transition affected your employment and/or career?

....

....

....

....

8. Do you think the transition affected your partner's employment and/or career?

....

....

....

....

9. What is the hardest change you have noticed in your relationship?

....

....

....

10. What important changes have you noticed in your relationship?

....

....

....

11. What celebrations have not occurred yet, but need to be acknowledged privately?

....

....

....

12. What celebrations have not occurred yet, but need to be acknowledged publicly?

....

....

....

13. How does it feel to express public affection, should you choose to do so? How is it different to how it was prior to the transition?

....

....

....

14. How does it feel to you when others see your partner as their affirmed gender?

....

....

....

15. How is your contribution to the transition being celebrated by you and others?

....

....

....

GRAPHICS GALORE

Venn Diagram

What are some ways the transition can be celebrated? (Consider answering this by keeping in mind that both of you deserve to be celebrated!)

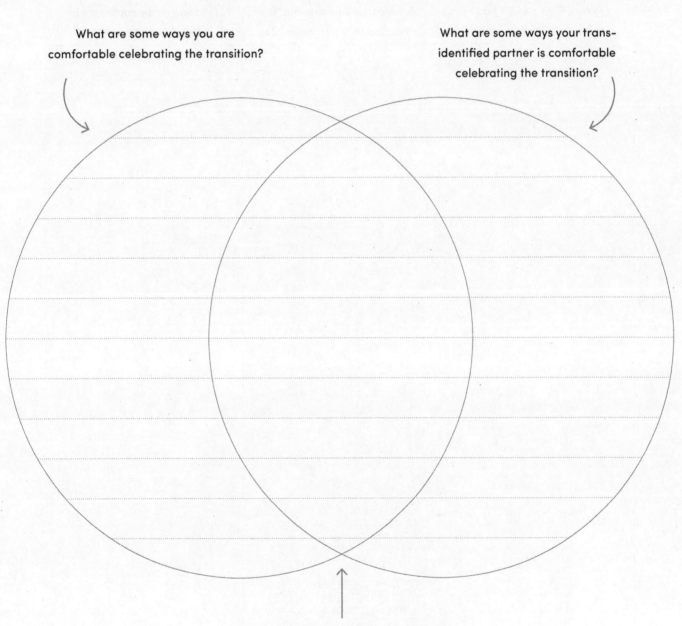

What are some ways you are comfortable celebrating the transition?

What are some ways your trans-identified partner is comfortable celebrating the transition?

What are some ways you and your trans-identified partner are both comfortable celebrating the transition?

GRAPHICS GALORE

T-Chart

How are the ways people reacted to the transition worth celebrating or not, in order to have these experiences documented and perhaps shared with others?

What were any of the positive (+) reactions people had in relation to the transition?	What were any of the negative (−) reactions people had in relation to the transition?	What were any of the neutral (=) reactions people had in relation to the transition?

DESERVING DE-STRESS DELIGHTS

Reading and Writing

There is a stillness that takes over my entire body when I pick up a warm cup of tea or coffee and snuggle up with a good book. Reading allows me to block out my worries by venturing into a land of make-believe. Some days there is no better remedy than a book or writing my thoughts in a journal. Reading or writing can bring me to a place of imagination and reflection that I find comforting. It is like being in the presence of a trusted friend who is simply there to listen and comfort me without any demands. When the transition began, reading and writing were my first course of action and, after all this time, they still do the trick and help me de-stress. If reading and/or writing are comforting for you, I suggest you cuddle up with a book based on the genre of your liking, with a beverage and/or snack of choice, in a location that feels lovely to you. Should writing be more relaxing for you, feel free to use pages in this workbook or purchase a special journal with your favorite writing utensil and begin the soothing process of writing for yourself, just for fun and without any judgment. If both reading and writing appeal to you, then indulge in both and enjoy!

> AFFIRMATIVE ANECDOTE
>
> *As sure as*
> *I am that*
> *The sun will*
> *Rise again*
> *Is as sure*
> *As I am*
> *That I will*
> *Smile again!*

Journal your reaction to this Deserving De-Stress Delight.

....

....

....

....

....

....

....

....

GRAPHICS GALORE

Box

Who would you want to celebrate for all the support that they have given you throughout the transition process? (This could be done by a simple sincere thank-you in person, by letter, or by phone.)

Friends	Family	Workplace Associates
Medical People	**Agencies**	**Others**

GRAPHICS GALORE

Timeline

Record the ways you have celebrated the transition process. This will help you keep an in-depth track of each celebration once it has occurred.

Date:	State who, what, and how you celebrated:
Date:	State who, what, and how you celebrated:
Date:	State who, what, and how you celebrated:
Date:	State who, what, and how you celebrated:
Date:	State who, what, and how you celebrated:
Date:	State who, what, and how you celebrated:
Date:	State who, what, and how you celebrated:

EMPATHY-EMBRACING EXERCISE

Whether a couple remains together or not, there will most likely be at least one aspect worth celebrating. For those who have stayed together, the celebrations will probably be abundant during the transition and even once the transition process is no longer the focus of the relationship. It is important to recognize and document these necessary changes. For those who are no longer a couple, it may take much inner strength to find the bright side of the transition, but if you take the time to reflect, most likely there will be something that you learned about yourself or your ex-partner during the transition. This exercise question asks you to ponder and celebrate the positive.

> AFFIRMATIVE ANECDOTE
>
> *Preferences come*
> *In different flavors.*
> *With experiences*
> *Our tastes may change!*

Has there been a time in your life when you did something you dreamed of or needed to do for yourself which felt worthy of celebrating but may have had a major effect or impact on another person's life? If so, what was it? How did it affect their life?

....

....

....

....

....

....

....

....

....

....

GRAPHICS GALORE

Bar Graph

To what degree does making time to celebrate the role these individuals played throughout the transition process matter to you? Based on a scale from 1 to 10, with 1 being the lowest and 10 being the highest, color or shade in your response. This visual will help you see where your greatest concerns lie and can help you to communicate this to your trans-identified partner, therapist, spiritual mentor, or for your own personal understanding. The bar graph results may vary as the transition progresses and your thoughts may shift.

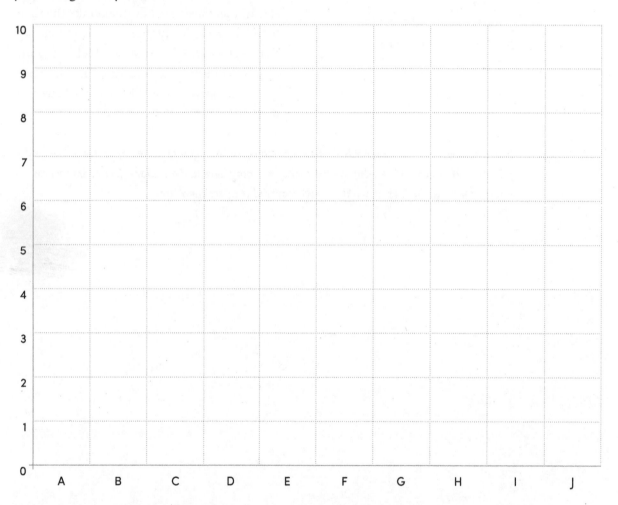

Use these ideas or thoughts to fill in the bar graph or feel free to create your own!

A. Celebrating the role you have played throughout the transition process.

B. Celebrating the role your family has played throughout the transition process.

C. Celebrating the role your friends have played throughout the transition process.

D. Celebrating the role your workplace associates have played throughout the transition process.

E. Celebrating the role your trans-identified partner has played throughout the transition process.

F. Celebrating the role your trans-identified partner's family has played throughout the transition process.

G. Celebrating the role your trans-identified partner's friends have played throughout the transition process.

H. Celebrating the role your trans-identified partner's workplace associates have played throughout the transition process.

I. Celebrating the role your children have played throughout the transition process.

J. Celebrating the role any medical professional has played throughout the transition process.

GRAPHICS GALORE

Pie Graph

To what degree does making time to celebrate the role these individuals played throughout the transition process matter to you? Decide how important these statements are to you in relation to each other. Place the number that corresponds with a suggested topic within as many slices of the pie that conveys how each one matters to you. Only one number should be placed in each slice. You do not need to use all the topics but do fill in all the slices. Feel free to create your own topics and assign them their own number.

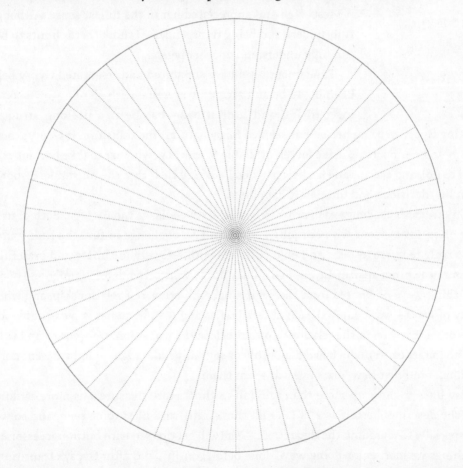

1. Celebrating the role you have played throughout the transition process.
2. Celebrating the role your family has played throughout the transition process.
3. Celebrating the role your friends have played throughout the transition process.
4. Celebrating the role your workplace associates have played throughout the transition process.
5. Celebrating the role your trans-identified partner has played throughout the transition process.
6. Celebrating the role your trans-identified partner's family has played throughout the transition process.
7. Celebrating the role your trans-identified partner's friends have played throughout the transition process.
8. Celebrating the role your trans-identified partner's workplace associates have played throughout the transition process.
9. Celebrating the role your children have played throughout the transition process.
10. Celebrating the role any medical professional has played throughout the transition process.

SAMPLER SHARE

Do you or did you demonstrate or show ways of celebrating or supporting your trans-identified partner throughout the transition process?

AFFIRMATIVE ANECDOTE

Trust is tested,
Bonds are loosened,
So love must
Hold on strong!

I learned that Gypsy was transgender a few months after we met and she transitioned after we were involved for four years, two and a half years ago. Gypsy often expressed herself as a woman before her transition. I understood from the beginning that the relationship would only work out if I respected and appreciated her in the fullest sense. Although I do not fully understand being transgender—I think there's limits to how anyone can fully understand another person.

Fundamentally, I have supported and celebrated Gypsy being herself. Learning to be and accepting myself—with all of my own contradictions, insecurities, and limitations—has been a lifelong struggle, and so supporting Gypsy in being herself has seemed fairly natural. The transition is Gypsy's journey—and while I try to be supportive, make myself available to talk (e.g. whether to take hormones, which she decided to do), and accompany her as a partner, I am very clear that she must take responsibility for her own life, decisions, and ultimately happiness.

I think we both challenge each other to be the best people we can each be. Both of us work hard and are often stressed out with our jobs, and it can be a challenge to find the time and emotional space to truly feel free to relax and enjoy life. We both feel very fortunate and grateful for all we have—our health, our apartment, enough money not to worry, friends and family, and of course each other. I think we've celebrated from the beginning: each other, our relationship, and who we are in a variety of ways—we've enjoyed each other's bodies and learning what is pleasurable to ourselves and the other. Early on in the relationship, and before the transition, we went to an LGBT(Q?) club (which no longer exists), which had a monthly or so transgender night—and we went dancing there a few times—our first New Year's Eve was spent there.

Gypsy likes to dress up more than I do (all in thrift store treasures), is more striking-looking than I (she describes herself as a TTT, a tall, thin, T-girl) and likes to be seen, and so when we go out—especially to museums, the theater, etc.—she will get dressed with outfits, accessories, etc. A lot of the things we most enjoy doing we've done before, during, and after Gypsy's transition: We both enjoy being in nature and have done a lot of outdoor activities together—hiking, swimming, cross-country skiing, and snorkeling. I realize in writing this that perhaps this is less about celebrating her transition and more about enjoying and celebrating each other—and being transgender is an important part of who she is.

(Shared by Scout)

Do you or did you celebrate or support your trans-identified partner throughout the transition process?
Whenever a picture was taken of her, pre-transition, she would generally have a close-lipped smile and a tightly held frame. Now, living as her true self, she smiles openly and broadly. Her pose is relaxed and her face radiates with joy and happiness. She is beautiful.

(Shared by Grace)

COUPLE COMMUNICATION CORNER

When partners or couples speak spontaneously out of anger or fear about the unknown, without thinking it through, they can sometimes regret the way they phrased it. Rehearsing what and how partners may want to ask or discuss with their trans-identified partner, and/or others, can help partners and couples before they actually communicate their thoughts. This gives the non-transitioning partner a moment to reflect and pause before they converse about emotional topics. Partners may choose to practice asking these questions with a trusted friend, family member, spiritual mentor, or therapist first.

Explain your thoughts and feelings about these questions to each other. Do you and your trans-identified partner answer these questions in the same way or differently? Discuss your responses to understand how you view them and make time to celebrate all you learn from being willing to communicate with each other.

> AFFIRMATIVE ANECDOTE
> *You taught me courage,*
> *I taught you*
> *Unconditional love!*

1. Do you think the transition affected your sex life?

    The partner's thoughts: The trans persons's thoughts:

    ....

    ....

    ....

2. Do you think the transition affected your relationships with family members?

    The partner's thoughts: The trans persons's thoughts:

    ....

    ....

    ....

3. Do you think the transition affected your friendships?

    The partner's thoughts: The trans persons's thoughts:

    ....

    ....

    ....

4. Do you think the transition affected your own self-confidence and in turn had an effect on your relationship?

The partner's thoughts: The trans persons's thoughts:

. . . .

. . . .

. . . .

5. Do you think the transition affected your communication with each other?

The partner's thoughts: The trans persons's thoughts:

. . . .

. . . .

. . . .

6. Do you think the transition affected your employment and/or careers?

The partner's thoughts: The trans persons's thoughts:

. . . .

. . . .

. . . .

7. What is the hardest change you have noticed in your relationship?

The partner's thoughts: The trans persons's thoughts:

. . . .

. . . .

. . . .

8. What is the most important change you have noticed in your relationship?

The partner's thoughts: The trans persons's thoughts:

....

....

....

9. What celebrations have not occurred yet, but need to be acknowledged privately?

The partner's thoughts: The trans persons's thoughts:

....

....

....

10. What celebrations have not occurred yet, but need to be acknowledged publicly?

The partner's thoughts: The trans persons's thoughts:

....

....

....

Chapter 14

WHERE ARE YOU NOW?

VITAL VIGNETTE

Welcome! This is the chapter that focuses on the future of your relationship with yourself and with your partner, while acknowledging the growth and changes of the past. It is a time to take the pulse of how your life moves from this place. All partners will get here, perhaps as part of a couple or in a poly relationship; some may have remained together as a unit as they have reached this destination, whereas others may not. So many factors could possibly have contributed to this arrival, welcome or not.

AFFIRMATIVE ANECDOTE

Ask not only
What you
Can do for
Your partner,
But also ask
What your partner
Can do for you!

Critical issues that may have contributed could have been based on sexual preferences, unexpected expectations, finances, parenthood desires, levels of communication, outside stressors and demands, and the health and/or length of the relationship prior to the knowledge of the transition. These—and/or a myriad of other factors not even recognized or completely understood—could have played a role in why some relationships remained intact and others did not. Only the individuals involved in the relationship have the right to decide the particular reasons that formed the end result—it is no one else's business. In any case, whether the relationship has continued, altered, or ended, this is a time for self-reflection and goal setting with optimism and great hope.

This is the time to take the pulse of the partner's journey by asking themselves honestly and continuously to re-evaluate their thoughts, feelings, concerns, worries, and confusions by sorting through the words scribed in their writing. The partner is now asked to embrace their future and examine how they have transitioned due to the other person's transition. For those who are single now, learning to trust again and putting yourself out there once more could be filled with fear of the future and sadness for what was not possible. I hope that the journaling and self-exploration this workbook has offered you will have resulted in you finding out what is acceptable for you and what is not. It is as important to know what you do *not* want as it is to know what you do want. Perhaps you have remained friends with the trans-identified person or may meet up again at another point in time. Sometimes life comes full circle and we are able to look at things differently after we are removed from it—and then again, maybe not.

In reality, those decisions are for you and you alone to decide. For now, you need to look inside yourself and begin, if you have not already done so, to reinvent your future by setting goals, some big and some small. Create a world that is safe and allows you to be vulnerable enough to embrace the possibilities that life has in store for you and decide if you are ready for, or even interested in, another intimate or close relationship.

For those of you who have remained as a couple or are now in a poly relationship, it is time to get reacquainted or meet each other again in different ways. Make time to explore each other romantically, physically, sexually, emotionally, and creatively. Take small, slow steps with gentle patience to navigate the path the relationship will now travel. Map it out together, with each of you expressing your individual needs and your needs as a couple. Where do you both, as individuals and as a unit, desire to go from here? Use the exercises, questions, and journaling from this workbook, and seek the advice of professionals and those who have been where you are now.

Most likely, there is an extra special bond that has developed between you, due to the experience of the transition process. Now is the moment to recognize this, by embracing and celebrating all you have been through. There may still be some rocky roads ahead, as you figure out how to move forward and make adjustments along the way. This is the journey for all long-term relationships, but through the transition you have developed a language and unique skills of communication that will help you endure what may lie ahead. Patience and honesty filled with compassion and empathy can enable a relationship more than you may know now.

Whether you are still in the relationship as a unit or not, you can choose to discuss or reassess all the things that may have been put on hold as a result of the focus on the transition. Maybe the things that took a back seat during the transition could come to fruition, such as pregnancy plans based on the educated choices you investigated as part of the transition, finally earning the college degree you can now explore, finding the job of your dreams, or buying that house you always wanted. The energy and effort that was funneled into the transition and decisions that needed to be made can now be redirected to help you feel whole again.

You may need to make additional space for outside friendships or family relationships that may have been on hold or exhausted and need tender loving care. These people will also need to be willing to see you as you are today and not as you were while navigating the transition. Important conversations may need to occur, perhaps involving your trans-identified partner, reassuring everyone that life has moved forward, past the transition, and hopefully they can respect this. Perhaps you will now be inserted into new friendships that you never had prior to the discussion of the transition. This too can be a learning curve and, again, you have a choice whether to engage in these friendships and family dynamics or not.

For all intents and purposes, the physical, emotional, and financial transition, on most levels, will be completed. It does not matter if you have entered this chapter of your life as someone who is part of a couple at this stage or not part of a couple; what does matter is your answer to the questions: What is next? Where do you go from here? For weeks, months, and years, the topic has been the transition in all its forms. Can you do this? Can they do this? How do you do this? How do they do this? The "confusing cans" and "wondering hows" are now answered. "Did you" or "did you not" is insignificant at this point. Whatever the outcome is, you are there now. There is no judgment or expectation of the choices that you found worked best for your future. The wish is that you have come out of this experience stronger and knowing yourself much better. This finish line simply celebrates a new beginning and cheers for all the possibilities of desire, dreams, and fortitude that are now lining up together, waiting for you with open arms!

GRAPHICS GALORE

Splash

What are all your favorite things to do now or that you dream of doing one day? By creatively splashing words and/or short phrases, quickly attempt to express your answers randomly with as many responses as possible scattered on the paper.

GRAPHICS GALORE

Venn Diagram

What are the things you would like to do with your partner or with someone whom you hope to meet in the future? (For those that do not overlap, perhaps you would want to try one that is only on the other one's list and open yourself up to something new. You can both try to do this for each other.)

What are all the things you would like to do with a partner?

What are all the things your partner would like to do with you? (Should you not be with a partner at the current time, feel free to fill this in at a later time, when it does apply with a different partner in the future.)

What are the things that overlap? Try them!

REFLECTIVE RESPONSES

1. How can you get to know each other again, now that the transition is not the focus of your time or life?

   . . . .

   . . . .

   . . . .

2. What can you do to get to know yourself again, now that the transition is not the focus of your time or life?

   . . . .

   . . . .

   . . . .

3. What interests do you both have in common? (Use the Venn Diagram tool above to help answer this.)

   . . . .

   . . . .

   . . . .

4. Which friends do you have in common and want to spend time with as a couple?

   . . . .

   . . . .

   . . . .

5. Will you feel comfortable becoming an advocate as a result of your own experience or would you prefer to have a low profile in the transgender community?

   . . . .

   . . . .

   . . . .

6. What do you foresee for yourselves in the future as a couple?

....

....

....

7. Are there any medical or emotional follow-ups you need to address for yourself?

....

....

....

8. Are there any medical or emotional follow-ups that need to be addressed for your transgender partner?

....

....

....

9. Are there any medical or emotional follow-ups that you need to address as a couple?

....

....

....

10. Where are you financially, individually, and as a couple?

....

....

....

11. Do you both want to remain in the same job and/or career?

....

....

....

12. Do you both want to remain in the same home?

....

....

....

13. Are there any other worries, concerns, or fears you still have and need to address?

....

....

....

14. How do you think your needs and your partner's needs will be negotiated, now that the transition is completed?

....

....

....

15. Have you found a way to balance your own personal life that embraces the changes that you have both experienced?

....

....

....

16. Is there anything you know now about yourself or others that you did not know before your partner transitioned which still upsets you now?

....

....

....

17. Is there anything you know now about yourself or others that you did not know before your partner transitioned which comforts you now?

....

....

....

18. Is there anything you know now about yourself or others that you did not know before your partner transitioned which still surprises you?

....

....

....

19. Do you feel the transition, as a part of your relationship, has made you both stronger as a couple or do you feel that you each need to move forward and not remain as a couple?

....

....

....

20. Is there any advice or suggestions you would offer someone whose partner recently told them they are considering transitioning?

....

....

21. Did you ever want to leave? Why or why not?

....

....

....

22. When did this feeling to leave or not feel the strongest?

....

....

....

23. Did you ever want to stay? Why or why not?

....

....

....

24. When did this feeling to stay or not stay feel the strongest?

....

....

....

25. Are you at peace with your decision to leave or stay in the relationship?

....

....

....

GRAPHICS GALORE

Web

What are the personal goals you have put on hold during the transition process that you would like to consider trying to achieve at this time?

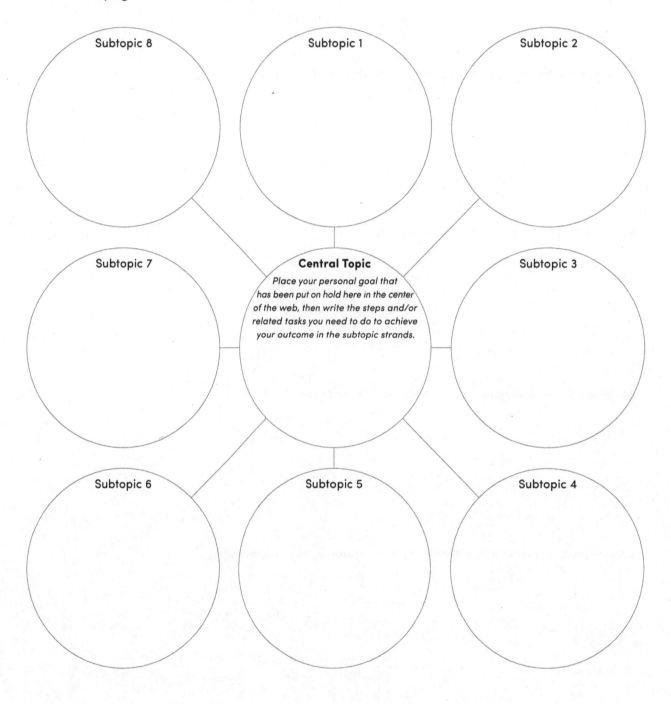

GRAPHICS GALORE

Timeline

What is the timeframe for beginning these goals?

Goal 1:	What do you need to get started?	Start date:	Completion date:

Goal 2:	What do you need to get started?	Start date:	Completion date:

Goal 3:	What do you need to get started?	Start date:	Completion date:

Goal 4:	What do you need to get started?	Start date:	Completion date:

Goal 5:	What do you need to get started?	Start date:	Completion date:

Goal 6:	What do you need to get started?	Start date:	Completion date:

Goal 7:	What do you need to get started?	Start date:	Completion date:

DESERVING DE-STRESS DELIGHTS

Volunteering

If you want to get your mind off of the transition and gain self-worth and more compassion, then volunteer somewhere. Helping others can be a very humbling experience and may allow you to see the gifts you already possess. Some partners reach a point during the transition process when they wonder if they can be a part of the journey. Others question whether they want to or can stay. Volunteering can help you understand and observe the various ways others cope with the unexpected, adversity, or things that are out of their control.

AFFIRMATIVE ANECDOTE

Change is scary,
Change never stops,
Change is hard!

These experiences can teach partners life lessons that few other circumstances can provide. Many organizations and activism groups regularly seek volunteers. Some require weekly commitments and training or a specific set of skills. If this is too much of a commitment at this point in your life, then there are other options.

Being of service to another person, outside of your home, does not always have to be a structured form of volunteering. Maybe a single parent in your area needs a free babysitter for one evening or a neighbor who uses a wheelchair wants help changing a ceiling lightbulb. Perhaps taking the time to simply volunteer to drive a recently widowed relative to a family function or offering your companionship by joining them for a movie matinee, could feel quite rewarding.

Volunteering, formally or not, may not only help another person, but might also show and teach you things about yourself and life that can prove to be invaluable at a time when you may feel in despair. Maybe working with a particular organization or person will open doors or possibilities to you that you never even considered before you volunteered. Perhaps volunteering will shed a little light on your circumstances and assist you in putting specific uncertainties into a different perspective. You may never know until you try!

Journal your reaction to this Deserving De-Stress Delight.

....

....

....

....

....

GRAPHICS GALORE

Box

Do any of these suggested ideas seem enjoyable to you? Create your own or use these! After you try the activities stated below, feel free to document your experience below.

Movies that you have been meaning to see! (With a partner or not.)	Places you hope to visit one day! (With a partner or not.)	Your favorite ways to feel pampered! (With a partner or not.)
Activities you would like to try or do again! (With a partner or not.)	Friends or family you would enjoy visiting on your own!	Concerts you would like to attend one day! (With a partner or not.)

GRAPHICS GALORE

T-Chart

What are the ways you can grow and improve your daily lifestyle? (Your trans-identified partner or new partner can be involved or included in these.)

In what ways and how can you grow academically or improve your current work status?	In what ways and how can you nurture or improve your living space and environment?	In what ways and how can you improve your social life and expand your social circle?

EMPATHY-EMBRACING EXERCISE

Understanding your next steps once the transition is no longer front and center enables the partner and relationship to move forward. This exercise grants partners the freedom to examine all the possibilities that are open for you to explore, now that most of your own energy is not focused primarily on the transition. As the partner, you can choose to decide this on your own or consult others; regardless, the choice is yours, so embrace it and soar!

AFFIRMATIVE ANECDOTE

You found you,
I lost part of me,
Let's search for us!

Now that the transition is not a focal point of your daily life, what seems to be the most important topic affecting you alone and/or your current relationship? Do you feel your trans-identified partner will support you in spending the majority of your time and energy on your own needs and dreams?

GRAPHICS GALORE

Bar Graph

To what degree do these topics or ideas matter to you at this point of the transition process? Based on a scale from 1 to 10, with 1 being the lowest and 10 being the highest, color or shade in your response. This visual will help you see where your greatest interests lie and can help you communicate it to your trans-identified partner, therapist, spiritual mentor, or for your own personal understanding. The bar graph results may vary as the transition comes to an end and your thoughts may shift.

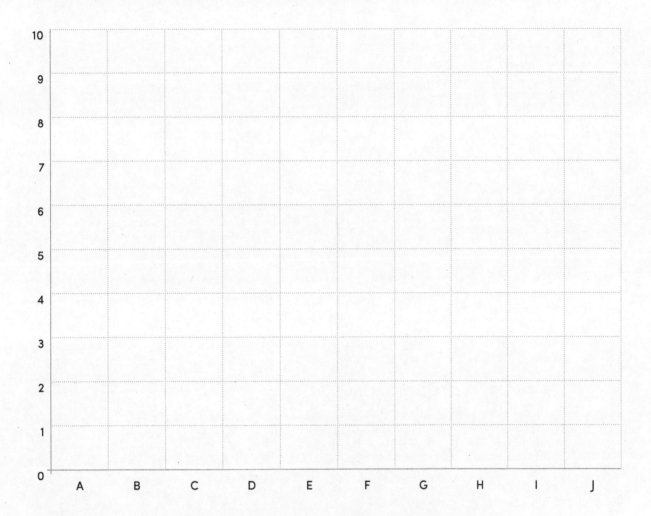

Use these ideas or thoughts to fill in the bar graph or feel free to create your own!

A. Focusing on furthering your own education and growth.

B. Focusing on your leisure and fun activities.

C. Focusing on your career, business ideas, and/or finances.

D. Focusing on your medical, emotional, and health needs.

E. Focusing on your relationships with friends and family.

F. Focusing on your home and living environment.

G. Focusing on figuring out what it is you want to focus on now but do not know yet.

H. Focusing on new parenting through available options or of children you already parent.

I. Focusing on your relationship with your partner or meeting someone else.

J. Focusing on your partner's needs in any area.

GRAPHICS GALORE

Pie Graph

To what degree do these topics or ideas matter to you at this point of the transition process? Decide how important are these topics or ideas to you, in relation to each other? Place the number that corresponds with a suggested topic within as many slices of the pie that conveys how each one matters to you. Only one number should be placed in each slice. You do not need to use all the topics but do fill in all the slices. Feel free to create your own topics and assign them their own number.

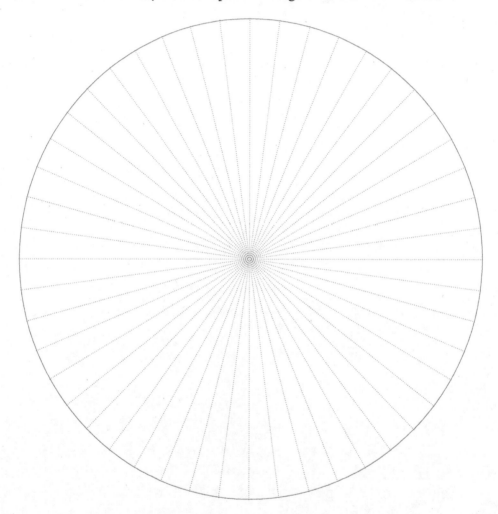

1. Focusing on furthering your own education and growth.

2. Focusing on your leisure and fun activities.

3. Focusing on your career, business ideas, and/or finances.

4. Focusing on your medical, emotional, and health needs.

5. Focusing on your relationships with friends and family.

6. Focusing on your home and living environment.

7. Focusing on figuring out what it is you want to focus on now but do not know yet.

8. Focusing on new parenting through available options or of children you already parent.

9. Focusing on your relationship with your partner or meeting someone else.

10. Focusing on your partner's needs in any area.

SAMPLER SHARE

What can you do to get to know each other again, now that the transition is not the focus of your time or life?

AFFIRMATIVE ANECDOTE

Live, craziness, live,
Cry, laugh, cry,
Love, cope, love!

It is hard to say what issues we would be dealing with whether the transition took place or not, of course, but after being together almost 20 years now, and about six years post transition, we are facing a lot of questions about staying together. It could be that the transition played a part in clarifying what it was we needed and wanted in our relationship, but whatever helped spur us to answer these questions, we are facing them now. My partner has different sexual desires than he used to, that I am not totally able to fulfill. I am seeking a new career path, and a new community in which to grow. We are not sure that community will be his community and if that will affect our ability to stay together or not. He has also been less tolerant, since his transition, of the things in me that always bothered him, and his anger about those things has been intolerable for me.

We are working very hard to reconcile who we truly are and deciding if we can each love the other in reality, not just fantasy. We have dealt so much in fantasy in so many ways, so now that things are more concrete and settled, we are looking at each other in the flesh. We have the complication of having a child together, so we are blessed that it keeps us working hard to stay together, but we are also less free because of it. We will always have to face each other, whether as lovers and co-parents, or just as co-parents, so we need to make some peace with each other no matter what. As hard and painful as it has been, and is still, I feel hopeful that I will, at the very least, grow and blossom from this process.

My advice to other partners going through a transition with their transgender partners is to find a place or way to vent away from your partner. Get as much non-judgmental support as you can build around yourself and commit to using it regularly, daily, or at least a few times a week. Don't seek advice, just look inside yourself after clearing out the painful muck of feelings that are there; you have the answer if you can honor your own needs and really listen to yourself.

(Shared by Yvette)

COUPLE COMMUNICATION CORNER

When partners or couples speak spontaneously out of anger or fear about the unknown, without thinking it through, they can sometimes regret the way they phrased it. Rehearsing what and how partners may want to ask or discuss with their trans-identified partner, and/or others, can help partners and couples before they actually communicate their thoughts. This gives the non-transitioning partner a moment to reflect and pause before they converse about emotional topics. Partners may choose to practice asking these questions with a trusted friend, family member, spiritual mentor, or therapist first.

Explain your thoughts and feelings about these questions to each other. Do you and your trans-identified partner answer these questions in the same way or differently? Discuss your responses to understand how you view them and make time to celebrate all you learn from being willing to communicate with each other.

1. As a team, what actions can you take to help you focus on furthering your education and growth?

    The partner's thoughts: The trans persons's thoughts:

    . . . .

    . . . .

2. As a team, what actions can you take to help you focus on your interests connected to leisure and fun activities?

    The partner's thoughts: The trans persons's thoughts:

    . . . .

    . . . .

3. As a team, what actions can you take to help you focus on furthering your careers, business ideas, and/or finances?

    The partner's thoughts: The trans persons's thoughts:

    . . . .

    . . . .

4. As a team, what actions can you take to help you focus on your own medical, emotional, and health needs?

The partner's thoughts: The trans persons's thoughts:

....

....

5. As a team, what actions can you take to help you focus on your relationships with friends and family?

The partner's thoughts: The trans persons's thoughts:

....

....

6. As a team, what actions can you take to help you focus on your home and living environment?

The partner's thoughts: The trans persons's thoughts:

AFFIRMATIVE ANECDOTE

Take back:
Your power,
Your self-esteem.
You are still there,
Welcome back!

....

....

7. As a team, what actions can you take to help you focus on figuring out what you both want to focus on now, but do not know yet?

The partner's thoughts: The trans persons's thoughts:

....

....

8. As a team, what actions can you take to help you focus on new parenting through available options and/or of children you already parent?

The partner's thoughts: The trans persons's thoughts:

....

....

9. As a team, what actions can you take to help you focus on your relationship with your partner, or moving on and meeting someone else?

The partner's thoughts:

. . . .

. . . .

The trans persons's thoughts:

. . . .

. . . .

10. As a team, what actions can you take to help you focus more on your partner's needs in any area?

The partner's thoughts:

. . . .

. . . .

The trans persons's thoughts:

. . . .

. . . .

Chapter 15
YOU ARE NOT ALONE (RESOURCES)

VITAL VIGNETTE

> AFFIRMATIVE ANECDOTE
> *Breathe,*
> *Research,*
> *Embrace!*

If you would like to reach out to the author to share your thoughts and questions in reference to this workbook or to learn more about her workshops, retreats, and speaking engagements, contact D. M. Maynard at: dmmaynardworkbook@gmail.com

I recognize that resources are a crucial aspect of any book, so I am providing you with ones I feel are relevant at the time of writing. Since resources and information are rapidly being updated and changed on a daily basis, some sources or recommendations listed today can be outdated within a month's time. That being said, here is the list I or others found useful.

RESOURCES/REFERENCES

Articles

Carla A. Pfeffer (2014) "'I Don't Like Passing as a Straight Woman': Queer Negotiations of Identity and Social Group Membership." *American Journal of Sociology* 120, 1, 1–44.

Jeff Schwaner (2017) "Understanding These Gender Terms Is Easy." Accessed on May 15, 2018 at www.newsleader.com/story/news/2017/09/20/understanding-these-gender-terms-easy/679663001.

Simon Van Der Weele (2017) "Mourning Moppa: Mourning without Loss in Jill Soloway's *Transparent*." *TSQ: Transgender Studies Quarterly* 4, 3–4, 608–626.

Books

Helen Boyd, *She's Not the Man I Married: My Life with a Transgender Husband* (Seal Press, 2007).
In Helen Boyd's sequel to *My Husband Betty*, Boyd candidly shares the feelings and thoughts that she experienced and pondered as her partner transitioned from being a crossdresser to living as

a woman, while exploring how gender roles and other aspects of the transition may affect being married and relationships.

Laura Erickson-Schroth (ed.) *Trans Bodies, Trans Selves: A Resource for the Transgender Community* (Oxford University Press, 2014).
This encyclopedic resource guide, written by professionals and community members who share their stories and expertise, houses major topics and current information that addresses the lives of those who are transgender or questioning individuals and others who are affected by these issues.

Jo Green, *The Trans Partner Handbook: A Guide for When Your Partner Transitions* (Jessica Kingsley Publishers, 2017).
Jo Green's guide captures the voices of partners of transgender individuals, offering a variety of views during the timeline of the transition.

Elisabeth Kübler-Ross and David Kessler, *On Grief and Grieving: Finding the Meaning of Grief Through the Five Stages of Loss* (Scribner, 2005).
Elisabeth Kübler-Ross's last book, written in collaboration with David Kessler, concludes her journey exploring the famous five stages of grief and loss. The authors discuss a vast multitude of issues affecting the varied processes of mourning and grieving.

Wenn B. Lawson and Beatrice M. Lawson, *Transitioning Together: One Couple's Journey of Gender and Identity Discovery* (Jessica Kingsley Publishers, 2017).
This highly personal narrative, co-authored by Wenn and Beatrice Lawson, offers the perspective of both the one in transition and the individual who is partnered with him throughout this process, as they each share their point of view both as an individual and as one in a relationship.

Ali Sands, *I Know Who You Are, But What Am I? A Partner's Perspective on Transgender Love* (Transgress Press, 2016).
Ali Sands' memoir discusses her personal real-life experience as the wife of a transgender man and how her identity changes as she navigates her spouse's transition.

Conferences
Fantasia Fair—Provincetown, Rhode Island, USA
http://ptownevents.com/event/fantasia-fair-provincetown
This event occurs in Provincetown, Massachusetts, every October. Throughout the week of the conference, participants are welcome to attend the workshops and social functions and "completely present" as the gender they desire, for the entire duration of time of the fair.

Gender Odyssey—Seattle, Washington, USA
https://10times.com/gender-odyssey-seattle
This conference strongly supports transgender people, their families, and allies through offering education and encouragement to be their authentic selves. Gender Odyssey Seattle also features: Expanded Professional Track, Family Track, Teen and Young Adult Tracks, etc.

Moving Trans History Forward—University of Victoria, Victoria, British Columbia, Canada
www.uvic.ca/mthf2018/index.php
Hosted on the campus of the University of Victoria, BC, Canada, on the traditional territory of the Songhees, Esquimalt, and W̱SÁNEĆ peoples, whose historical relationships with the land continue to this day, this international conference celebrates the transgender community through workshops, social events, and a wide variety of plenary panels.

Networking Empowerment Wellness Conference—Stamford, Connecticut, USA
www.eventsinusa.net/event-the-inaugural-networking-empowerment-wellness-new-conference-stamford-12304122
This conference fosters a sense of community for people from varying backgrounds and experiences, by welcoming all but especially empowering trans POC, stealth/low-disclosing people, and their allies to connect and honor their individuality while encouraging all aspects of wellness.

Philadelphia Trans Wellness Conference—Philadelphia, Pennsylvania, USA
www.mazzonicenter.org/trans-wellness/mazzoni-center-announces-dates-2018-welness-trans-wellness-conference
This Philadelphia-based conference, as part of the Mazzoni Center's mission, offers education and information for healthcare professionals and the trans community, including friends and family, by addressing a myriad of health and wellbeing issues, while promoting networking and providing an inclusive environment, which welcomes gender diversity and expression through supporting all voices.

Psychotherapy Center for Gender and Sexuality (PCGS)—New York City, New York, USA
www.icpnyc.org/pcgs
This center is a division of the Institute for Contemporary Psychotherapy, which sponsors a biannual trans clinical symposium for mental health professionals, but also welcomes educators, families of trans people, and community members.

Southern Comfort—Fort Lauderdale, Florida, USA
https://sccfla.org
This conference began in 1991 and continues in the same spirit today by creating an inclusive, relaxing, and familial environment while offering a safe place for LGBT individuals, often from the United States, to promote education and socialization with and for the trans community that it was intended to attract.

Documentaries
I saw these two documentaries at the NewFest 2018, New York's LGBT Film and Media Arts Festival, while I was writing this workbook and feel they are important films. They both include moments which focus on the point of view of those who are or were in a relationship with a transgender person:

Made-Man
2018 (USA)
1h 33m
Director: T Cooper
Writers: T Cooper and Allison Glock-Cooper
This documentary offers audiences a view into the world of transgender (transmasculine) bodybuilding, following the journeys of four contestants, while they get ready for the Trans FitCon competition in Atlanta, Georgia, USA.

TransMilitary
2018 (USA)
1h 33min
Directors: Gabriel Silverman and Fiona Dawson
Writers: Jamie Coughlin and Gabriel Silverman

This documentary exposes viewers to the lives of four transgender people who serve in the U.S. military and how they cope with the realities of being in a system that has forced them to keep their gender identity hidden, due to the U.S. military policies that could ban their service, if they came out. The film shows how these policies affect their careers, families, and their willingness to confront officers in the Pentagon as the ever-changing politics in relation to equal rights are in jeopardy for transgender people who serve in the U.S. military.

Organizations

The Jim Collins Foundation
https://jimcollinsfoundation.org
This foundation, in memory of Jim Collins, offers financial assistance towards gender-affirming surgeries.

Lambda Legal
www.lambdalegal.org
This national LGBT organization offers legal services, impact litigation, education, and public policy work.

LGBTQQIA+ Centers
There are locations, often within large cities, which house LGBTQQIA+ Centers, in the United States of America and countries worldwide. These centers can sponsor community events, meetings, and workshops for the transgender community. Occasionally, some of these meetings or workshops may even host support groups, which focus on the unique needs and challenges that partners face. If these centers do not yet have meetings or workshops geared toward supporting partners, they are often open to welcoming these programs. This can be viewed as an opportunity to create a series for partners by individuals who are knowledgeable of how transitioning affects

partners, based on the needs of the partners, and then forming a network or support program for the partners. You can search the Internet for LGBTQQIA+ Centers in your area.

World Professional Association for Transgender Health
www.wpath.org
The World Professional Association for Transgender Health (WPATH) is an interdisciplinary professional organization dedicated to transgender health. Please note: *The Standards of Care for the Health of Transsexual, Transgender, and Gender-Nonconfirming People* is available on the WPATH website. In addition, this site also offers an opportunity to search for medical and mental health providers who are members of the association.

Television Series

These series include showing, in some episodes, the point of view of those who were or are in a relationship with a transgender person:

- *This Is Life With Lisa Ling on CNN and the episode is titled: Gender Fluidity (S4 E11).*
- *Orange is the New Black* is a series on Netflix and was created by Jenji Kohan.
- *Sense8* is a series on Netflix and was created by Lana Wachowski, Lilly Wachowski, and J. Michael Straczynski.
- *Transparent* is a series on Amazon and was created by Jill Soloway.

Websites and Blogs That Focus on Partners

On the Internet you will find endless blogs that can be an incredible resource. It is important to know that each blog is usually one person's journey or experience, which may or may not help you in your time of need and/or confusion.

Crossdreamers: Resources for Partners of Transgender People
www.crossdreamers.com/2015/08/resources-for-partners-of-transgender.html
This website affords resources for partners of transgender people.

Dailystrength: Spouses of Transgender Community Group
www.dailystrength.org/group/spouses-of-transgender
This website provides an online support group for spouses of transgender people.

HealthyTrans
www.healthytrans.com
This website suggests some questions that can be asked at medical appointments, which pertain to transgender issues.

She Was the Man of My Dreams
https://shewasthemanofmydreams.wordpress.com/about
This website recommends LGBT resources, with a major focus on transgender issues.

TransGenderPartners.com: Resources for Significant Others, Friends, Family and Allies of Transgender People

www.transgenderpartners.com/resource-for-partners-2

This website offers resources for significant others, friends, family, and allies of transgender people.

Trans Partner Network

www.transpartnernetwork.com

This website is a Toronto-based program and supportive network for partners of trans, genderqueer, or gender-variant people.

EMPATHY-EMBRACING EXERCISE

Movies and theater have always been a source of information that can both educate and entertain. As the world is beginning to learn about the transgender community, more and more movie, theater, and television studios are willing to incorporate transgender characters and storylines that address the needs and realities that affect the lives of transgender individuals and their families. Although partners are not necessarily the focus of many of the plots or scripts, the movies, theater, and television shows can enlighten those in the dark. In time, the hope is that the needs and realities of partners will be portrayed in a way that brings both respect and an understanding of what their lives look like throughout the transition process on a daily basis.

> AFFIRMATIVE ANECDOTE
>
> *If I were asked to Choose again, I would still Choose you!*

The more a partner becomes aware of transgender issues, the more they often notice their relevance or lack of presence in the world around them. As you begin to observe places where transgender topics are discussed or absent, you may want to document these realities and share your experiences with others. It is important for partners or ex-partners of trans-identified people to have their journey and voice recognized in the arts, media, and literature in everyday situations. Should you find materials that honor the partner or ex-partner experience, I believe it is both critical and a responsibility to share it with others. It is equally important to state if the portrayal of the partner's experience appears accurate and realistic. When it does not, state it, and when it does, applaud it! This will be key in educating others!

Can you think of any TV show or series, movie, play, musical, book, or Internet resource that has focused on the transition through the point of view of the partner?

....

....

....

....

....

....

....

AFFIRMATIVE ANECDOTE

Seeing you happy
Makes my day brighter!

COUPLE COMMUNICATION CORNER

Which resources do you and/or your partner want to research more?

AFFIRMATIVE ANECDOTE

Let love
Fill our hearts,
Let laughter
Fill our souls,
Let happiness
Fill our days.

1. Do you know of or want to research additional references/resources which are articles?

    The partner's thoughts: The trans persons's thoughts:

    . . . .

    . . . .

2. Do you know of or want to research additional references/resources which are books?

    The partner's thoughts: The trans persons's thoughts:

    . . . .

    . . . .

3. Do you know of or want to research additional references/resources which are conferences?

    The partner's thoughts: The trans persons's thoughts:

    . . . .

    . . . .

4. Do you know of or want to research additional references/resources which are organizations?

    The partner's thoughts: The trans persons's thoughts:

    . . . .

    . . . .

5. Do you know of or want to research additional references/resources which are television series or movies?

The partner's thoughts: | The trans persons's thoughts:

· ·

· ·

6. Do you know of or want to research additional references/resources which are websites?

The partner's thoughts: | The trans persons's thoughts:

· ·

· ·

7. Do you know of or want to research additional references/resources which are blogs?

The partner's thoughts: | The trans persons's thoughts:

· ·

· ·

8. Do you know of or want to research additional references/resources which are support groups?

The partner's thoughts: | The trans persons's thoughts:

· ·

· ·

9. Do you know of or want to research additional references/resources which are LGBTQ+ Centers?

The partner's thoughts: | The trans persons's thoughts:

· ·

· ·

10. Do you know of or want to research additional references/resources which are podcasts?

The partner's thoughts: The trans persons's thoughts:

. . . .

. . . .

GLOSSARY

agender Someone who does not identify with or match any gender.

androgynous Someone who possesses both male and female characteristics.

asexual Someone who does not feel sexual attraction to other people.

bigender Someone who experiences themselves as both male and female.

bilateral mastectomy A surgical procedure that removes breast tissue from both sides of the chest and is part of the construction of a male chest for trans masculine people.

binary The belief that there are only two genders, male and female.

binding A practice of using material or clothing to constrict the breasts that enables a person to flatten their chest.

bisexual (bi) A person who is attracted to both masculine and feminine people.

bottom surgery A surgical procedure that permanently changes the genitals or internal reproductive organs.

cisgender (cis) Someone whose gender assigned at birth and gender identity are aligned.

cisgender privilege The advantages granted by society to people whose gender aligns with the gender assigned at birth.

compersion A feeling of enjoyment while knowing your partner is experiencing joy, usually when they are romantically or sexually involved with another person. Often used as a contrast to jealousy.

crossdresser (CD) A person who wears clothing and/or make-up of the gender other than the one they were assigned at birth.

drag Crossdressing for the purpose of performance and/or show.

facial feminization surgery A variety of plastic surgery procedures to create a more feminine appearance to the features of the face.

FTM (female-to-male)/F2M/MTM A person who now identifies as male gendered but was assigned a female gender at birth.

gatekeepers Mental health or medical professionals who control access to medical treatment such as hormones and surgery.

gender The aspects that culture, society, and the individual deem as feminine, masculine, and androgynous.

gender-affirming surgery (GAS) Surgeries that bring the individual's body into alignment with their gender identity.

gender dysphoria The uncomfortable and sometimes depressing feelings that occur in people when aspects of their body and behavior are not congruent with their gender identity.

gender expression The manner in which a person demonstrates their masculinity and/or femininity that can include clothing, body, behavior, speech, gestures, and other forms of appearance.

gender fluid A gender identity and expression that encompasses a variety of aspects related to femininity, masculinity, and androgyny.

gender identity One's internal sense of being masculine-identified, feminine-identified, neither, or both.

gender markers The legal designation of one's gender on official documentation or records.

gender nonconforming A phrase for people who do not meet common gender norms.

genderqueer Someone who identifies outside of the gender binary.

hir A gender-neutral pronoun sometimes used to replace "her" and "him."

intersex A group of medical conditions where someone can be born with ambiguous genitalia and internal sex organs or chromosomal differences that are not clearly male or female.

LGBTQQIA+ An all-encompassing abbreviation which stands for lesbian, gay, bisexual, transgender, queer, questioning, intersex, allies, plus others.

metoidioplasty A gender-affirming bottom surgery for trans men which releases the micro phallus and can include urethra lengthening.

misogyny A disdain, hatred, or mistrust of all people female and feminine.

monogamous A type of relationship where a person is sexually and/or romantically involved with only one person at a time.

MTF (male-to-female)/M2F/FTF A person who now identifies as female gendered but was assigned a male gender at birth.

nonbinary A gender that is not exclusively male or exclusively female.

orchiectomy The bottom surgery for trans women that involves the removal of testicles.

outing The act of disclosing someone's sexuality and/or gender identity without their knowledge and/or permission.

packing The use of prosthetics and/or other materials to enable an individual to possess the appearance and feeling of having a penis and testicles.

pan hysterectomy A type of bottom surgery that usually includes removing the uterus, ovaries, and fallopian tubes and which could involve the removal of the cervix.

pansexual Someone who is attracted to people of various genders.

partner A word used to describe a person who is in a sexual and/or romantic relationship with someone.

passing The ability for a person to be read as their affirmed gender by those who are unaware the individual's identity is transgender.

phalloplasty A type of bottom surgery that entails the construction of a penis and can include the construction of testicles and the implant of an erection device.

polyamorous A type of relationship where a person is sexually and/or romantically involved with more than one person at the same time.

...erred gender pronouns (PGP) The practice of others using or referring to a person in the way an individual desires to be addressed, when pronouns are involved.

questioning The act of a person who is attempting to figure out their own sexuality and/or gender.

queer Someone who is attracted to multiple genders and/or sexes.

scrotoplasty A surgical procedure that creates a scrotal sac and can include testicular implants.

sexuality The pattern of thoughts, feelings, and arousal that determine sexual preferences.

sie/ze A gender-neutral pronoun sometimes used to replace "she" and "he."

stealth A word used for a transgender person who chooses to keep their trans status private.

they A word that may also be used as a gender-neutral pronoun to describe a single individual.

top surgery A surgical procedure made to create a masculine-appearing chest.

tracheal shave A surgical procedure that reduces the thyroid cartilage, which makes up the Adam's apple.

transgender/trans-identified An overarching word, which can be used for people whose gender expression and/or gender identity does not align with their sex assigned at birth.

transitioning The social and medical actions a person takes to explore and/or affirm their gender identity.

transmisogyny Julia Serano, an activist for the trans community, coined this word to describe a form of misogyny that is focused towards trans women.

trans partner A person who is in a relationship with someone who identifies as transgender or gender nonconforming.

transphobia Prejudice, fear, disdain, or discrimination in respect of gender nonconforming and transgender people.

transsexual A person who identifies within the gender binary (either male or female) and may have medical procedures to bring their body in line with their identity. However, not all transgender people who have medical transitions identify as transsexual.

two-spirit An Indigenous North American identity embraced by some individuals who incorporate a variety of gender roles, identities, and expressions by embodying both masculine and feminine spirits and traits.

vaginoplasty The surgical construction of a vagina for both transgender and cisgender women.

AFFIRMATIVE ANECDOTE

If I knew then
What I know now
I would know now
I knew
Nothing then!

ANSWER KEY SECTION

Answer Key for Matching Pre-Test #1

Vocabulary Number	Definition Letter	Vocabulary Number	Definition Letter
1	D	7	L
2	G	8	B
3	A	9	F
4	K	10	I
5	H	11	J
6	E	12	C

Answer Key for Matching Pre-Test #2

Vocabulary Number	Definition Letter	Vocabulary Number	Definition Letter
1	J	7	A
2	G	8	K
3	L	9	I
4	B	10	C
5	H	11	D
6	F	12	E

Answer Key for Matching Pre-Test #3

Vocabulary Number	Definition Letter	Vocabulary Number	Definition Letter
1	A	7	J
2	G	8	D
3	B	9	E
4	I	10	L
5	F	11	C
6	K	12	H

Answer Key for Matching Pre-Test #4

Vocabulary Number	Definition Letter	Vocabulary Number	Definition Letter
1	G	7	J
2	H	8	B
3	K	9	D
4	C	10	E
5	A	11	I
6	L	12	F

Answer Key for Matching Pre-Test #5

Vocabulary Number	Definition Letter	Vocabulary Number	Definition Letter
1	F	7	D
2	A	8	B
3	G	9	J
4	K	10	L
5	C	11	H
6	I	12	E

Answer Key for Word search

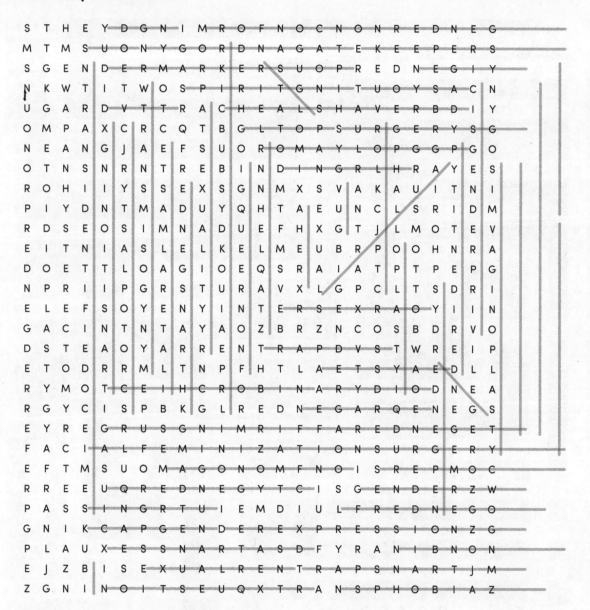

S T H E Y D G N I M R O F N O C N O N R E D N E G
M T M S U O N Y G O R D N A G A T E K E E P E R S
S G E N D E R M A R K E R S U O P R E D N E G I Y
N K W T I T W O S P I R I T G N I T U O Y S A C N
U G A R D V T T R A C H E A L S H A V E R B D I Y
O M P A X C R C Q T B G L T O P S U R G E R Y S G
N E A N G J A E F S U O R O M A Y L O P G G P G O
O T N S N R N T R E B I N D I N G R L H R A Y E S
R O H I I Y S S E X S G N M X S V A K A U I T N I
P I Y D N T M A D U Y Q H T A E U N C L S R I D M
R D S E O S I M N A D U E F H X G T J L M O T E V
E I T N I A S L E L K E L M E U B R P O O H N R A
D O E T T L O A G I O E Q S R A I A T P T P E P G
N P R I I P G R S T U R A V X L G P C L T S D R I
E L E F S O Y E N Y I N T E R S E X R A O Y I I N
G A C I N T N T A Y A O Z B R Z N C O S B D R V O
D S T E A O Y A R R E N T R A P D V S T W R E I P
E T O D R R M L T N P F H T L A E T S Y A E D L L
R Y M O T C E I H C R O B I N A R Y D I O D N E A
R G Y C I S P B K G L R E D N E G A R Q E N E G S
E Y R E G R U S G N I M R I F F A R E D N E G E T
F A C I A L F E M I N I Z A T I O N S U R G E R Y
E F T M S U O M A G O N O M F N O I S R E P M O C
R R E E U Q R E D N E G Y T C I S G E N D E R Z W
P A S S I N G R T U I E M D I U L F R E D N E G O
G N I K C A P G E N D E R E X P R E S S I O N Z G
P L A U X E S S N A R T A S D F Y R A N I B N O N
E J Z B I S E X U A L R E N T R A P S N A R T J M
Z G N I N O I T S E U Q X T R A N S P H O B I A Z

agender	gatekeeper(s)	monogamous	scrotoplasty
androgynous	gender	MTF/FTF/M2F	sexuality
asexual	gender-affirming surgery	nonbinary	sie/ze
bigender	gender dysphoria	orchiectomy	stealth
bilateral mastectomy	gender expression	outing	they
binary	gender fluid	packing	top surgery
binding	gender identity	pan hysterectomy	tracheal shave
bisexual	gender markers	pansexual	trans-identified/
bottom surgery	gender nonconforming	partner	transgender
cisgender	genderqueer	passing	transitioning
cisgender privilege	hir	phalloplasty	transmisogyny
compersion	intersex	polyamorous	trans partner
crossdresser	LGBTQ/LGBTQ+/	preferred gender	transphobia
drag	LGBTQQIA+	pronouns	transsexual
facial feminization surgery	metoidioplasty	queer	two-spirit
FTM/MTM/F2M	misogyny	questioning	vaginoplasty

333

Answer Key for Crossword

1 ACROSS: FTM
2 ACROSS: MTF
3 ACROSS: TRANSGENDER
4 ACROSS: CROSSDRESSER
4 ACROSS: GATEKEEPER
6 ACROSS: ANDROGYNOUS
7 ACROSS: NONBINARY
9 ACROSS: SEXUALITY
10 ACROSS: PANHYSTERECTOMY
13 ACROSS: GENDERMARKERS
15 ACROSS: CISGENDER
16 ACROSS: GENDER
17 ACROSS: VAGINOPLASTY
20 ACROSS: GENDERQUEER
21 ACROSS: BIGENDER
22 ACROSS: TOPSURGERY
24 ACROSS: PHALLOPLASTY
25 ACROSS: INTERSEX
26 ACROSS: TRANSMISOGYNY
28 ACROSS: ORCHIECTOMY
31 ACROSS: PREFERREDGENDERPRONOUN
33 ACROSS: TRANSITIONING
34 ACROSS: OUTING
35 ACROSS: BILATERALMASTECTOMY
36 ACROSS: GENDERDYSPHORIA
37 ACROSS: COMPERSION
39 ACROSS: LGBTQ
40 ACROSS: CISGENDERPRIVILEGE
41 ACROSS: STEALT
43 ACROSS: Z
44 ACROSS: GENDERAFFIRMINGSURGERY
45 ACROSS: BINARY

Answer Key for Crossword with Clues

ACROSS

1. **FTM** A 3-letter abbreviation that means a person who now identifies as male gendered but was assigned a female gender at birth.

2. **MTF** A 3-letter abbreviation that means a person who now identifies as female gendered but was assigned a male gender at birth.

3. **TRANSGENDER** An 11-letter overarching word which can be used for people whose gender expression and/or gender identity does not align with their sex assigned at birth.

4. **CROSSDRESSER** A 12-letter word that means a person who wears clothing and/or make-up of the gender other than the one they were assigned at birth.

5. **GATEKEEPER** A 10-letter word that means a mental health or medical professional who controls access to medical treatment such as hormones and surgery.

6. **ANDROGYNOUS** An 11-letter word that means someone who possesses both male and female characteristics.

7. **NONBINARY** A 9-letter word that means a gender that is not exclusively male or exclusively female.

9. **SEXUALITY** A 9-letter word that means the pattern of thoughts, feelings, and arousal that determine sexual preferences.

10. **PAN HYSTERECTOMY** A 15-letter phrase that means a type of bottom surgery that usually includes removing the uterus, ovaries, and fallopian tubes and which could involve the removal of the cervix.

13. **GENDER MARKERS** A 13-letter phrase that means the legal designation of one's gender on official documentation or records.

15. **CISGENDER** A 9-letter word that means someone whose gender assigned at birth and gender identity are aligned.

16. **GENDER** A 6-letter word that means the aspects that culture, society, and the individual deem as feminine, masculine, and androgynous.

17. **VAGINOPLASTY** A 12-letter word that means the surgical construction of a vagina for both transgender and cisgender women.

20. **GENDERQUEER** An 11-letter word that means someone who identifies outside of the gender binary.

21. **BIGENDER** An 8-letter word that means someone who experiences themselves as both male and female.

22. **TOP SURGERY** A 10-letter phrase that means a surgical procedure made to create a masculine-appearing chest.

24. **PHALLOPLASTY** A 12-letter word that means a type of bottom surgery that entails the construction of a penis and can include the construction of testicles and the implant of an erection device.

25. **INTERSEX** An 8-letter word that means a group of medical conditions where someone can be born with ambiguous genitalia and internal sex organs or chromosomal differences that are not clearly male or female.

26. **TRANSMISOGYNY** A 13-letter word coined by Julia Serano, an activist for the trans community, to describe a form of misogyny that is focused towards trans women.

28. **ORCHIECTOMY** An 11-letter word that means the bottom surgery for trans women that involves the removal of testicles.

31. **PREFERRED GENDER PRONOUNS** A 23-letter phrase that means the practice of others using or referring to a person in the way an individual desires to be addressed, when pronouns are involved.

33. **TRANSITIONING** A 13-letter word that means the social and medical actions a person takes to explore and/or affirm their gender identity.

34. **OUTING** A 6-letter word that means the act of disclosing someone's sexuality and/or gender identity without their knowledge and/or permission.

35. **BILATERAL MASTECTOMY** A 19-letter phrase that means a surgical procedure that removes breast tissue from both sides of the chest and is part of the construction of a male chest for trans masculine people.

37. **COMPERSION** A 10-letter word that means a feeling of enjoyment while knowing your partner is experiencing joy, usually when they are romantically or sexually involved with another person. Often used as a contrast to jealousy.

38. **GENDER DYSPHORIA** A 15-letter phrase that means the uncomfortable and sometimes depressing feelings that occur in people when aspects of their body and behavior are not congruent with their gender identity.

39. **LGBTQ** A 5-letter abbreviation which stands for lesbian, gay, bisexual, transgender, and queer.

40. **CISGENDER PRIVILEGE** An 18-letter phrase that means the advantages granted by society to people whose gender aligns with the one assigned at birth.

DOWN

1. **FACIAL FEMINIZATION SURGERY** A 25-letter phrase that means a variety of plastic surgery procedures made to create a more feminine appearance to the features of the face.

2. **MISOGYNY** An 8-letter word that means a disdain, hatred, or mistrust of all female and feminine people.

3. **TRACHEAL SHAVE** A 13-letter phrase that means a surgical procedure that reduces the thyroid cartilage, which makes up the Adam's apple.

8. **GENDER EXPRESSION** A 16-letter phrase that means the manner in which a person demonstrates their masculinity and/or femininity and which can include clothing, body, behavior, speech, gestures, and other forms of appearance.

11. **PASSING** A 7-letter word that means the ability for a person to be read as their affirmed gender by those who are unaware the individual's identity is transgender.

12. **METOIDIOPLASTY** A 14-letter word that means a gender-affirming bottom surgery for trans men which releases the micro phallus and can include lengthening of the urethra.

14. **DRAG** A 4-letter word that means crossdressing for the purpose of performance and/or show.

16. **GENDER NONCONFORMING** A 19-letter phrase that means people who do not meet common gender norms.

18. **SIE** A 3-letter gender-neutral pronoun sometimes used to replace "she" and "he."

41. **STEALTH** A 7-letter word that is used for a transgender person who chooses to keep their trans status private.

44. **GENDER-AFFIRMING SURGERY** A 22-letter phrase that means surgery that brings the individual's body into alignment with their gender identity.

45. **BINARY** A 6-letter word that means the belief that there are only two genders, male and female.

19. **THEY** A 4-letter word that may also be used as a gender-neutral pronoun to describe a single individual.

23. **PARTNER** A 7-letter word used to describe a person who is in a sexual and/or romantic relationship with someone.

27. **BINDING** A 7-letter word that means a practice of using material or clothing to constrict the breasts that enables a person to flatten their chest.

29. **MONOGAMOUS** A 10-letter word that means a type of relationship where a person is sexually and/or romantically involved with only one person at a time.

30. **POLYAMOROUS** An 11-letter word that means a type of relationship where a person is sexually and/or romantically involved with more than one person at the same time.

32. **SCROTOPLASTY** A 12-letter word that means a surgical procedure that creates a scrotal sac and can include testicular implants.

36. **PACKING** A 7-letter word that means the use of prosthetics and/or other materials to enable an individual to possess the appearance and feeling of having a penis and testicles.

42. **HIR** A 3-letter gender-neutral pronoun sometimes used to replace "her" and "him."

43. **ZE** A 2-letter gender-neutral pronoun sometimes used to replace "she" and "he."